T0348404

Cash Return on Capital Invested

With compliments

♦♦♦

To my family

To Miko

Cash Return on Capital Invested

Ten Years of Investment Analysis with the CROCI Economic Profit Model

Pascal Costantini

AMSTERDAM • BOSTON • HEIDELBERG • LONDON • NEW YORK
PARIS • SAN DIEGO • SAN FRANCISCO • SINGAPORE • SYDNEY • TOKYO
Butterworth-Heinemann is an imprint of Elsevier

Butterworth-Heinemann is an imprint of Elsevier
Linacre House, Jordan Hill, Oxford OX2 8DP, UK
30 Corporate Drive, Suite 400, Burlington, MA 01803, USA

First edition 2006
Reprinted 2007

Notice
No responsibility is assumed by the publisher for any injury and/or damage to persons
or property as a matter of products liability, negligence or otherwise, or from any use
or operation of any methods, products, instructions or ideas contained in the material
herein. Because of rapid advances in the medical sciences, in particular, independent
verification of diagnoses and drug dosages should be made

British Library Cataloguing in Publication Data
A catalogue record for this book is available from the British Library

Library of Congress Cataloging-in-Publication Data
A catalog record for this book is available from the Library of Congress

ISBN: 978-0-7506-6854-5

For information on all Butterworth-Heinemann publications
visit our website at books.elsevier.com

Transferred to Digital Printing 2010.

Working together to grow
libraries in developing countries

www.elsevier.com | www.bookaid.org | www.sabre.org

ELSEVIER   BOOK AID
            International   Sabre Foundation

Contents

Risk is a function of volatility. These things are quantifiable.
Long-Term Capital Management press spokesman

By way of introduction

A temporary confidence crisis

In the early days of September 2005, this book was starting to take the shape that I had intended. There was still a lot of work to do, but the promise to hand over a manuscript of some use to the publisher in November was not necessarily going to turn out to be a monumental lie. As I was waiting for a flight in London's City airport, I was spending my spare time at the bookshop and spotted a Peter Bernstein book that I had not read yet: *Capital Ideas: The Improbable Origins of Modern Wall Street* (John Wiley & Sons Inc., 2005). I enjoy reading Bernstein – an insightful commentator and theorist on financial markets – and I bought the book without a second thought. But I was so overwhelmed by the first page that I could scarcely get to the bottom. It started like this:

> The book could never have taken shape without the participation of the people whose work it describes: Fischer Black, Eugene Fama, William Fouse, Hayne Leland, Harry Markowitz, John Mc Quown, Robert C. Merton, Merton Miller, Franco Modigliani, Barr Rosenberg, Mark Rubinstein, Paul Samuelson, Myron Scholes, William Sharpe, James Tobin, Jack Treynor, and James Vertin.

I started to count how many Nobel Prize winners were mentioned. And it got worse:

> Each of them spent long periods of time with me in interviews, and most of them engaged in voluminous correspondence and telephone conversations as well.

It was easy to realise that P. Bernstein was friends with them all:

> All of them read drafts of the chapters in which their work is discussed and gave me important criticisms and suggestions that enrich virtually every page of the book.

And, finally, the paragraph finished with a bizarre:

> Most of them also provided their photographs.

Even the joke seemed beyond me . . .

At that point, my confidence level dropped to rock bottom. I mentally reviewed how many Nobel Prize winners in Economics I knew personally, which did not take that long ... OK, distinguished academics? Surely I could not count any of those I used to terrorise during my student years. I somehow recalled that the Head of Global Research at Deutsche Bank, incidentally my own boss, David Folkerts-Landau, used to be a Professor of Economics at Chicago. My friend and ex-colleague Jamil Baz, who kindly read the manuscript, is a Research Fellow at Oxford University, where he teaches financial economics, on top of being a proprietary trader. Of course, I was myself teaching a small postgraduate finance course at the University of Paris Dauphine. Perhaps there was a chance that some of the professors I had briefly met in the corridors there might acknowledge me, if asked. But, bar a few other acquaintances, I had to admit to myself that I was more likely to know a future Nobel Prize winner in Literature than in Economics. How, then, could I have the audacity to write something that would sit on the same shelf as the books of a guy who could call half a dozen of the very best brains in finance his friends? So I reread the manuscript, fully expecting to have to make an embarrassing call to Karen, my publisher.

Having read it again, it became obvious to me that what I had written was of a completely different breed from that which Peter Bernstein's friends, and he himself, were producing. Whilst they were in the business of producing the intellectual framework explaining the mechanics and behaviour of financial markets, I was simply giving an account of what I had found to work, and not to work, during a twenty-year career in investment analysis. To them, Black Monday, that 19 October 1987 when the market dropped by 20 per cent, meant an interesting 'six sigma event' – something that was unlikely to have happened. To me, as a young analyst, it meant the eyes of my colleagues – especially those running trading books – widened by disbelief and fright; it meant a Reuters screen not able to display enough digits to record the decline in the Dow Jones Index; and the biggest question mark of my young career on Tuesday morning: 'What do we do *now*?' To them, the craziness of the technology bubble of 2000 was yet another six sigma event. To me, then a senior market strategist, it meant the humiliation of being thrown out of a meeting in February 2000 for suggesting that a fund manager buy Utility shares – the only sector that appeared undervalued on my models. The guy in question retorted bluntly that he was 80 per cent weighted in what was then called TMT (Telecom, Media and Technology), and that he could envisage going to 100 per cent. I still meet him, occasionally, but we both pretend that this conversation never happened.

In short, I have not written a manual to cast in stone The Definitive Theory of Investment Analysis; I have no overarching theory to offer. Rather, this book is a story – an account of ten years of effort by a small group of investment analysts to find a reliable, practical and *implementable* method for valuing and selecting shares. Being investment professionals rather than academics, our research results and recommendations are tested every day in the market. 'Theory' is for us only a means to an end: investing in a way that consistently, if not continuously, minimises risk and maximises return. As a result, some of what has been written here is faithfully compliant with theory, and some of it is pure heresy. But everything has been tested, time and time again, in all market conditions, and, broadly, it works. However, this book is not a 'How to Get Rich in Ten Easy Lessons' guide. We do not predict that the Dow will go to 36 000, or 3600, because we simply don't make such predictions. We don't look at price charts either, or analyse the flow of funds. We don't do arbitrage, or design complex derivative structures; we do only hard, factual valuation analysis. We believe that markets are difficult to beat, but we don't believe that they are fully efficient either. In short, we don't belong to any chapel.

Investment analysis is about praxis, discipline and common sense set in a general framework whose basic principles were laid down quite some time ago by Adam Smith himself, and have been occasionally amended, refined and enhanced by great economic thinkers (Keynes, Tobin) and, more recently, by Peter Bernstein's talented friends. Without them, we investment professionals would be lost. But without us, what would be the point of writing up these theories? So perhaps, after all, there was some merit in this work. At least, there is something unique about it. Books on investment tend to fall into two categories; they are either written by legendary traders, investors or asset managers who tell us of their successes but don't *explain* to us how they do it, or they are written by extremely talented experts who explain to us how we *should* do it but don't show whether their method has been successful. This book attempts to avoid both pitfalls. It describes an original (if not entirely new) investment methodology, the product of ten years of investment research generically called CROCI (Cash Return on Capital Invested)*. It also shows the precise investment results of its *actual* implementation in the global equity markets since 1996. This, perhaps, is what justifies yet another book on investment analysis.

The style of this book is deliberately casual – why write about company A and B, when you can achieve the same result by telling the story of Adam and Eve in Pleasantville (see Chapter 4), or of the young foolish professional who bought the flat from the savvy old man (see Chapter 3)? Readers should not misinterpret this perhaps unusual style: we are *dead serious* about investment analysis. But we are hoping that, in the end, readers will ask themselves the question: 'is it really *that* simple?' For indeed, it is that simple, once you look at it in the right way and, most importantly, with the right numbers. It would be a bonus if we could raise a smile or two as well; investment analysis need not be dull either.

Structure of the book

The book is organised into four parts and nine chapters. In Part One I review the various issues that, as a rank-and-file professional investment strategist, I face in the conduct of this business. Why is it that most investors despise the PE ratio as a stock selection tool, but make little effort to use anything else? Are discounted cash-flow models any better? Should we think in terms of 'value' and 'growth'? The punchline is delivered early: what matters is not the model, but the numbers that go into it. Accounting numbers follow arbitrary rules, and so generate randomness for investment purposes; only economically meaningful numbers can lead to an economic definition and analysis of value creation, itself the main driver of share price performance. In Chapter 2, the Equivalence Principle, a most important

---

* CROCI is a registered trademark of Deutsche Bank AG.

economic concept, is explained in some detail. The Equivalence Principle purports that markets will try to equalise the asset multiple of a company (market value to replacement value) with the relative return, or return on assets over cost of capital. This is the 'economic version' of the actuarial principle that the value of an asset equals the net present value of expected future free cash flow discounted to infinity. Both models are interchangeable and equivalent. I argue that the economic version is better for stock selection purposes.

Part Two is dedicated to the construction of economic data, with the sole objective of calculating an economically meaningful asset multiple and relative return, the combination of which gives an 'economic' PE ratio – our main stock selection tool. This part is the engine room of the CROCI model; Chapters 3 and 4 detail which adjustments are to be made in order to transform accounting information into economic data. Chapter 5 adds a discussion on the price of growth, an oft-discussed subject in investment analysis.

Part Three is dedicated to the analysis of economic data. Once accounting data have been successfully transformed, what is an analyst supposed to do with them? Chapter 6 shows many examples of the economic characteristics of individual companies, and thence how they can be analysed and classified according to their profile of cash return and asset accumulation. Chapter 7 links these economic characteristics to valuation. How much is a rising cash return profile worth in the market? Is value creation enhanced or eroded by the fast accumulation of capital? Does the market prefer asset expansion or return expansion? Is growth always priced fairly?

Part Four deals with the implementation of an economic profit model. Most of the examples here are real examples, rather than theoretical constructs. Chapter 8 focuses on the stock-picking technique, and how to use the output of the CROCI model to identify upside potential in stocks. Chapter 9 is about investment. This is not the same as stock-picking, whose sole purpose is to seek maximum share price appreciation. Investment is about portfolio behaviour, as well as judging the attractiveness of the equity asset class. Does an economic profit model generate an identifiable style of investment? Is the model adequate for selecting sectors as well?

Those unfamiliar with economic profit models will find some detailed background information in Part One. Those who are mainly curious about the reconstruction of economic data may wish to jump directly to Chapter 3, and, finally, those who are only interested in the *results* of the implementation of an economic profit model may choose to skip the first five chapters altogether.

Acknowledgements

Mentors, peers and children

There is nothing like going away with a laptop and starting to type to bring home the realisation of quite how much one owes to so many people. They have naturally fallen into a private classification of 'mentors', from whom I have sought guidance and knowledge, 'peers', with whom I have exchanged views and ideas at arm's length, and 'children', to whom I have somehow felt compelled to pass on whatever knowledge I have accumulated over the years. Despite the strangeness of this typology, I have kept it to acknowledge and thank all the people who have influenced this book and contributed to it.

My first professional mentor was Jacques Servat, an astute fund manager at Crédit Lyonnais, now retired, who flattered my natural proclivity for scepticism. Alan Bartlett (who some will remember as one of the three musketeers of the successful Value & Momentum product of the mid-1980s, the other two being Richard Clarke and Chris Chaitow; I had the privilege of working with all three), now a part-time property developer, has to be credited for teaching me the rudiments of value analysis, as well as the fundamental distinction between value and momentum. I still remember his smug smile, having shown me a classification of stocks according to this matrix, when I said, naively, pointing at the 'bad value, good momentum' quadrant: *but these are all the stocks that I like! . . .*

I worked with Miko Giedroyc between 1993 and 1999. So many professional investors still remember Miko that it is almost unnecessary to introduce him as the former Head of Equity Research at S.G. Warburg and Deutsche Morgan Grenfell, as they were then called. Miko will not read this book, as there is nothing in here that he does not know. His interests, anyway, are now firmly focused on his many other talents, especially music. Maybe he will think that he ought to have written it himself; and I certainly think that he is likely to have done a better job at it than me. In twenty years of various involvement with analysts, economists and other financial experts, I can safely declare that I have never met anybody with a sharper financial mind, a greater ability to understand and model the economy and financial markets (and this with a *very* approximate working knowledge of a computer, although I hear that things are improving on this front . . .), and a better ability to get the information out of the most unlikely sources. Miko is my original accomplice and CROCI is our brainchild; if there is any merit in this work, half of the credit goes straight to him. It does no harm that Miko, in many, many respects, is also the most hilarious and charming person with whom to work.

By an unexpected quirk of fortune, Richard Clarke, the very same man from the Value & Momentum days, rejoined me later in his career. Richard has brought invaluable expertise in performance analysis and risk management with him, and has allowed us to venture into new avenues of research that would not have been opened without him. Thanks also to David Folkerts-Landau for having been a staunch supporter of my at times eccentric research group, and for having kindly accepted to read parts of the manuscript.

Prima inter pares is of course my wife Kerstin, whose patience with me has been (and hopefully will continue to be) infinite during the writing of this book and generally in life. Other 'peers' include a large number of colleagues, former colleagues and clients, some of whom have proofread the manuscript, and all of whom have shown continuous or sporadic support and interest in this work over the years: Katrina Abrahamson, Guy Ashton, Stephen Barrow, Jamil Baz, Christophe Bernard, Yassine Bouhara, Frederic Buzaret, Alberic de Coulange, Russell Duckworth, Hassan Elmasri, Philippe Guez, Johan Groothaert, Joe Hall, Rami Hayek, David Haysey, Serge Ledermann, Roland Lescure, William Lock, James Seddon, Steven Triantafilidis, Jacqueline Vidé, François Wat, Howard Williams ... This list is not exhaustive, and must include all of my colleagues from Deutsche Bank's Equity Research and Sales departments.

'Children' are first and foremost my own, Adrien and Emma, together with younger colleagues who have suffered (hopefully not too much *from*) my financial training. First came Diarmid Ogilvy, now a senior banker servicing hedge funds in a fast-growing prime brokerage business. Diarmid spent hours in the thankless task of co-building and testing the prototype CROCI model. Fortunately, it involved some priceless moment of hysterical hilarity as well. Despite his heavy schedule, Diarmid painstakingly dissected this manuscript and gave me invaluable suggestions for its improvement. Later, Darren Curtis, now a proprietary trader, combined his no-nonsense approach to financial modelling with his audit training to crack a number of tricky accounting and valuation issues.

Francesco Curto and Janet Lear have been my closest associates for years, and rightly deserve a very special mention, if only for allowing me to spend some time out of the office in the summer of 2005 to draft the final version of this book whilst they were looking after our practice. Together, they shaped the CROCI research from its original prototype format to the current professional valuation platform, expanded the universe to US, Japanese and Asia-Pacific companies, built up the CROCI website (http://croci.db.com), plus a million of other things of which I would not even be aware. CROCI is the result of their efforts as much as it is of Miko's or mine. Both have of course improved the manuscript. Each according to their personality, they have given me insightful and important pieces of advice, with Janet scrutinising every single number that I have quoted, and Francesco focusing on the logic of the arguments and their structure. Other senior colleagues from whom I have often sought advice include Virginie Galas, an investment analyst with more than ten years of experience in consumer stocks and an unmatched talent to understand the value of brands and intangible assets. Chris, Mauricio, Max, Sujit, Tarun and Natasha, the CROCI analysts, have all contributed to this book, explicitly by reading the manuscript, or through the CROCI research regularly published at Deutsche Bank. Some of the examples in this book have been suggested by them. Colin McKenzie has lent me his deep knowledge of the English syntax and his mathematical brain to weed out unclear explanations and arguments. Finally, thanks to Lynn Mulligan for a magnificent job on the charts.

PART • I

What is Investment Analysis?

1 Investment, investors and financial analysis

An annoying question – inquisitive colleagues

Since the very first CROCI publication on global equity valuation, more than a decade ago, I have heard the following question from colleagues and professional investors innumerable times: 'Does your "thing" work?' When this question crops up, it is referring to a valuation framework that was developed in 1995 by a group of analysts then working in the Equity Research Division of Deutsche Bank (Miko Giedroyc, Diarmid Ogilvy and myself, with later versions benefiting from the pertinent insight of Darren Curtis, Francesco Curto, Janet Lear, Colin McKenzie and Virginie Galas). For over a decade now we have been using this valuation tool, dubbed CROCI (Cash Return on Capital Invested), every time we have had to take a view on the pricing of an equity asset, be it a market, a sector or an individual share – in other words, every single working day, since it is our job to advise institutional investors on equity valuation. Although we have given it a modern name and developed it to suit many applications in investment analysis, CROCI is no more than an economic profit model.

Sceptics might have a reason to ask whether 'the thing' works, because economic profit models are not very common. It takes the thoroughness of Copeland in *Valuation* (Copeland *et al.*, 1994), the valuation bible of many investment analysts, to go into it in some detail, as an alternative to discounted cash flow models. Nevertheless, economic profit models are not exactly new, and the principles behind them have been around for a long time. Copeland traces them back at the latest to Alfred Marshall's *Principles of Economics*, published in 1890. In any case, the logic behind economic profits was well understood by the economists of the early twentieth century, who used it to analyse and explain capital formation. However, this model is still largely ignored (or at least unused) by the investment community, to the extent that we, in what has now become the CROCI Valuation and Investment Strategy Group, have to face the dreaded question time and time again.

After a while, this question becomes slightly annoying. It is the sort of question that you would ask someone who told you that you should consider eating a clove of garlic before bedtime, in order to stop smoking . . . Yet, there are no shady practices in an economic profit model. In essence, it does three things: it calculates the real amount of cash, or 'value', created by a business; it compares the market value of an asset to an approximation of its replacement value; and it assumes that the former will converge to the latter through the arbitrage of investors and capital providers. Since this is broadly the way capitalist economies operate, then these models must 'work', simply because the *economy* 'works'.

But the proof is in the pudding . . . In 2003, some colleagues from the Structured Products Group (Markus Barth, Wim Scherpereel, Benedict Peteers and Joakim Darras) had the curiosity to call me up. Since you are so sure that your model works, they said, why don't you let us construct a family of indices based on it? The idea was to create an index, an equally-weighted basket of stocks, systematically invested in companies with the most undervalued streams of economic profits. The performance of these indices would show if, and how well, CROCI 'worked' as an investment tool. They generously offered to do the back-testing work, which was easier than it sounded. Nothing is better looked after than our CROCI database, with real data (i.e. not reconstructed with the benefit of hindsight) going back ten years or more. There was another benefit: being able to measure accurately the investment performance of an economic profit model in the US, Japan, the Eurozone and Asia Pacific – something that had never been done systematically before. The results (described in Chapter 9) were compelling, and confirmed my view that there were immense rewards in the detailed analysis of 'value creation' (the modern name for economic profit) as a stock selection tool. Although value creation is in every CEO's speech, every analyst's report and every magazine article on corporate management, very few use its analysis systematically for investment. In this respect alone, it was worth the try. Furthermore, the Structured Products guys were happy, as they were able to wrap these indices into clever financial instruments that were then placed with investors. And this convinced me that it was time to tell the 'CROCI story' in a broader setting than our monthly CROCI Talk notes, which is how the idea of this book was conceived.

Emotions in motion – tea-leaf reading?

Since this book is about financial analysis and equity investment, certainly the most popular but perhaps the least understood asset class, it felt right to start by giving a synopsis, presenting the various actors and introducing the genre of the play. This is a personal assessment of the salient traits of the money management industry, what makes it great as well as what makes it bizarre. It is this hotchpotch that is at the origin of the CROCI model. From the outside, the investment process may look like a mysterious way of valuing and selecting stocks – some arcane technical analysis performed by a few in the know. From the inside, it is not much different. The demands on fund managers to perform every quarter, if not every month or even every week, are immense. I remember a meeting with a fund manager at a New York-based firm, whom I visited early one December, as part of the traditional year-end road show that analysts at investment banks do to present their views for the coming year. This senior and otherwise perfectly competent fund manager must have had a bad year, and was clearly under a lot of stress. He impatiently brushed aside my well-rehearsed pitch after a few minutes, and explained, in all seriousness, that his fund's year-end was a few days away, and that he needed something that 'worked' during the next twelve days, not twelve months . . . Had I replied that a ski-equipment company was a good idea, because it was likely to snow before year-end, he would probably have bought the shares.

The human brain, it seems, loses a lot of its rationality under pressure, and some-times prefers to hide behind bizarre metaphysical beliefs and theories. This is not an unknown phenomenon when people's health is at stake – maybe understandably so. It also seems to be quite commonly observable when their money is at stake. All sorts of charlatans can be found in financial markets, making a living out of selling magic formulae, based on the most bizarre analyses of historical patterns meant to predict the future, often superficially sprinkled with scientific-sounding names with little or no relevance to investment analysis – Fibonacci numbers or Kondratieff cycles, to name but a couple. John Allen Paulos, a Professor of Mathematics who likes to popularise his science through such books as *Mathematics and Humour* (Paulos, 1980) or *A Mathematician Reads the Newspaper* (Paulos, 1995), seems to agree with this observation. In another book, *Innumeracy – Mathematical Illiteracy and its Consequences*, Mr Paulos accuses the human brain of being 'innumerate'. He remarks that 'one rarely discussed consequence of innumeracy is its link with belief in pseudoscience ... it is especially sad that a significant portion of our adult population still believes in Tarot cards, channelling mediums and crystal power', and he lists what he calls our 'inadequacies' – 'a lack of numerical perspective, an exaggerated appreciation for meaningless coincidence, a credulous acceptance of pseudo-sciences, an inability to recognise social trade-offs, and so on.'

For too many investors, including professional ones, investment analysis and portfolio construction is a collection of recipes; a blend of fundamental analysis, tea-leaf reading and irrational statements. Take the following statement, often heard among professional investors: 'I think that these shares are a buy, but dead money for the next six months'. This observation sounds perfectly normal, but it raises an unexpectedly large amount of question marks – so many, in fact, as to make it almost meaningless. 'These shares are a buy' means that the expected return of this particular investment is high enough to warrant the risk taken over the investment horizon. The expected flows of the company (dividend or cash flow, depending on your favourite model) are discounted to their net present value already, to give the share price. The passage of time is already taken into account. If something worth 100 in the market has an expected return of 40 per cent over a given investment horizon, it does not really matter how it gets there within this timeframe – and, more importantly, it is not predictable. Could this investor possibly mean: 'I think that the true market value is 140, but I am not sure, so I prefer to wait'? But in this case, the uncertainty should already be captured in the rate used to discount this company's expected flows; the higher the uncertainty, the higher the discount rate and the lower the net present value, i.e. the target share price. Let us say that this theoretical value of 140 is achieved by discounting a cash flow of 14 to infinity with a discount rate of 10 per cent. If there is so much uncertainty about the economic value of this firm, then a higher discount rate should be used – 12 per cent would bring the theoretical value down to 116.7 – and may well mean that these shares are no longer a buy. Or perhaps our investor is sure about the future market value, but concerned about the time that it will take for others to recognise it. If these shares are ignored by other investors for a long period, it could be that they have found better returns elsewhere. In this case, our investor is again using the wrong opportunity cost (too low), and is overstating the true value of these shares. Finally, it could well be that other investors' behaviour towards these shares is irrational, and that they price them by taking random factors into consideration. Perhaps they do not like the management, the name of the company, its sector, its size, the location of its head office[1] etc. . . . In that case, the shares will move *randomly* towards their fair economic value, which suggests that the probability of their doing so in the next six months is around 50 per cent – much greater than the 0 per cent that our investor assumes by calling them 'dead money'.

This example shows that a perfectly acceptable response to uncertainty – wait and see – is in fact not that well-considered an answer in the context of an investment decision. Sadly, an initial definition of investment analysis could well be *a desperate attempt by the human brain to grapple with problems that it cannot solve*. In other words, it could be argued that we are not made to be investors in the first place. That's because there is very little room for human emotion in investment analysis. Hardly anything could be more rational, more precisely defined than the theoretical value of an operating (as opposed to artistic, for instance) asset. This value, called the enterprise or entity value, and usually abbreviated to EV, amounts *by construction* to the net present value of expected free cash flows, discounted to infinity.

The weight of emotion on our investment decisions is not simply anecdotal, and deserves the following digression. In order to investigate the role of emotions in these decisions, a group of five scientists from Stanford University, Carnegie Mellon and the University of Iowa has gone as far as to test the investment behaviour of patients with brain lesions related to emotions (Shiv *et al.*, 2005). Typically, these patients had suffered from neurological diseases which had impaired their emotional responses, but were otherwise of normal intelligence. This group, together with a test group of other participants with a similar level of IQ and another test group of patients suffering from different brain lesions that did not impair their emotions, was asked to invest $20 in twenty rounds ($1 each time) in the following manner. Either the dollar was not invested, and the participant could keep it, or the dollar was invested in a coin-tossing event. The coin-tossing could result in either a loss of the dollar, or a gain of $2.50. These parameters were set so that the rational decision was to invest every time, since the expected outcome of the toss is $1.25 (50 per cent chance of the $1 loss and 50 per cent chance of a $2.50 gain), whereas not investing would just yield $1. Investing at every round would give an 87 per cent chance of obtaining more than $20 at the end of the process. Patients with the lesions affecting emotions invested on average in 84 per cent of the rounds, and racked up an average $25.70 gain. Patients with other lesions invested in 61 per cent of the rounds, for an average gain of $20, and 'normal' participants invested in 58 per cent of the rounds, to accumulate $22.80. Strikingly, the scientists discovered that the willingness to invest decreased markedly among the emotional participants as the game progressed. They tested whether this behaviour had to do with the outcome of the previous round of investment, and discovered a significant propensity *not* to invest when the previous outcome was an investment and a loss. Less than 40 per cent, on average, decided to risk their dollar again once this had happened, against 85 per cent of the emotionally impaired group. The role of emotions in decision-making involving risk is believed by psychologists to act as a protective mechanism, by rejecting the more dangerous decisions and promoting the beneficial ones. However, as these researchers remark, 'there are circumstances in which a naturally occurring emotional response must be inhibited, so that a deliberate and potentially wiser decision can be made'. And investing is evidently one of these circumstances.

The tools of investment – a (very) brief history of financial ratios

To weed out emotions from investment analysis, *financial* analysis is supposed to use a number of objective tools to approximate 'the net present value of expected future free cash flows discounted to perpetuity', the definition of the total market value of a company (we will also often refer to a company as an 'asset' in the course of this book). The snag is that this is easier said than done. There are all sorts of issues hidden behind these innocuous words, such as the definition of cash flow, the choice of the discount rate or, incidentally, the small issue of how to deal with perpetuity. Technically, investors do know how to transform a perpetual flow into a 'stock equivalent' – in other words, to calculate the net present value equivalent to receiving this flow for ever. Indeed, this is one of the easiest financial tricks available to them. All that is required is that the expected flow is divided by a discount rate. Thus, if the flow is 10 and the discount rate is 10 per cent, it is equivalent to receiving 10 for ever, or receiving $10/10\% = 100$ today, as a lump sum. Equally, with an unchanged discount rate of 10 per cent, a lump sum of 200 received today is equivalent to receiving a flow of $200 \times 10\% = 20$ to infinity.

Although this is one of the oldest financial tricks in the book, it is so simple that it may not prove very useful on a stand-alone basis. It assumes that investors know which discount rate to use, and that a perpetual *constant* flow is a fair representation of what they are trying to value. However, we will often incorporate this calculation *within* our models. If investors want to take growth into account (most economic objects grow or fade, few remain static), and especially non-constant growth (an economic object growing forever would be difficult to value), then things soon become more complicated. So, over the years, investors have had to invent and refine various tools (and cut corners) to approximate this result – the 'net present value of expected ...' etc. And, if humans may lack rationality, they do not lack imagination. As financial markets grew and savings were channelled into equities, all sorts of ways to value them were invented. It is often lost on investment analysts that *all* valuation ratios and frameworks are an attempt to get to the *same* net present value of expected free cash flows discounted to infinity. For a given level of expectations and cost of capital, there can only be *one* fundamental or intrinsic value for an asset. Nothing is more puzzling than hearing someone talk about the valuation of a company 'on an EBITDA basis', then 'on a free cash flow basis' and finally 'on a sum of the parts basis', as if they were totally different concepts bound to yield totally different results (EBITDA is a rough measure of gross cash flow, i.e. cash flow *pre* capital spending, unlike free cash flow, which is cash flow *post* capital spending). What is even more bizarre is that some analysts seem genuinely surprised if the results are the same. The following sentence is a staple of investment reviews: 'We believe that an earnings multiple of X is justified, supporting our price target of Y. A sum of the part valuation also suggests a similar price target'. In other words, we have poured a litre of water into two glasses of fifty centilitres each, and it seems that they fill exactly half a two-litre bottle ...

Today, half a century after the emergence of the large-scale asset management industry, the world is awash with 'ways' to value assets and shares – short cuts, long cuts, narrow passages and hanging bridges – all leading (or intended to lead) to the 'net present value of expected . . .' etc. Certain investment techniques go even further, and rely on others to find out the 'net present value of expected . . .' etc. This is the case with 'momentum strategies' in general, and earnings estimates revisions in particular. In the latter case, it is assumed that analysts, who revise earnings estimates up or down, will broadly get it right. Thus, it is enough to follow their changes of estimates, and buy shares which benefit from upwards estimate revisions whilst ignoring or selling shares suffering from downgrades. This technique, like many others, has given perfectly respectable results during certain periods, and certain firms rely on it to a very large extent to formulate their investment strategy.

As a result of this flurry of investment techniques, investors often concern themselves with an abutting issue: 'What ratio should I look at to value shares?' This then leads to an almost infinite stream of metaphysical questions. Should we look at the balance sheet with or without taking goodwill into consideration? Should free cash flow be calculated after considering the full capex (capital spending) amount, or only *maintenance* capex? (Full capex includes investment made for expansion, in other words new capacity, whereas maintenance capex only measures investments made to keep existing assets in good operating condition, or to replace them.) Should returns on capital be calculated post-tax or pre-tax? What is the relevant measure of market value – the value of the shares only (i.e. the market capitalisation) or the value of the full enterprise, which includes the value of the debt and some other liabilities? There is no answer; *it all depends on what the investment analyst is trying to measure*. It depends on the final objective. Is it to get to a *fair* value of the assets? Or to understand the *current market value* of the *assets*? Or just of the *equity*? With respect to the *current* level of profitability? Or the *sustainable* level of profitability? All ratios are meaningless if they are not put in the context of what the analyst is trying to achieve.

For instance, the EV to Sales ratio, which measures how many times a company's turnover is capitalised, is useful to compare companies that are homogeneous in terms of margins, capital intensity and growth expectations, and wholly inappropriate in any other case. The EV to EBITDA ratio is particularly useless without a discussion on asset lives, capital intensity, technological progress or revenue recognition. So many people have lost so much money with this dreadful ratio that it is probably worth digressing on it for a paragraph or two. EBITDA, or any of its derivatives (EBDIT, EBITDAR, etc.), is simply a crude measure of gross cash flow. As such, it is a useful item which can find its way into a number of valuation measures, including our very own CROCI, as we will see in Chapter 4. What is far less benign is to derive all sorts of conclusions from it. The gross cash flow margin is simply a measure of the capital intensity of the business. A manufacturing business will have a significantly higher gross cash margin than, say, a retailer, because it needs to 'pay' for the capital (in an accounting sense, i.e. via the depreciation charge) of all its plant and equipment, which consumes more of it than a superstore. So Tomkins, a UK engineering conglomerate, trades on a lower EV to EBITDA multiple than does Next, a UK retailer, because the former is more capital intensive than the latter, which has a higher cash conversion ratio. It is hard to see what more that ratio can tell an investor, and it certainly does not say which shares are a buy or a sell. What matters is not gross cash flow but net (or free) cash flow, which is the amount of cash available *after* reinvestment. In the heyday of the technology bubble, the EV to EBITDA ratio was a favourite among telecom analysts. Sadly, as new entrants came into the system and pushed up the price of the UMTS licences (the third generation of mobile networks) to insane levels, the cost of replacement went sky-rocketing; expected free cash flow plummeted, and the telecom shares got more and more 'attractive' on an EBITDA basis, which could not capture any of this. Eventually, some went bankrupt, some had to undergo a debt rescheduling exercise or issue new capital, and all saw their share price collapse.[2]

The people of investment – an unfair typology

This entanglement of ratios, theories, beliefs and mantras represents the tools of investment, which tend to live a life of their own in the financial world; however, investment in the *real* world is often quite different. Witness this story that appeared in the UK press in 2004. James Murray Wells, a 21-year-old law student in Bristol, UK, needed a pair of glasses, and was faced with a bill of £150. He was staggered by the price tag, and after some research he found that the manufacturing cost of standard spectacles (frame and glasses) was less than £10. This prompted Mr Murray Wells to set up an Internet-based company to challenge what he claimed was a lack of price competition among the four major high street opticians in England. Three months into his venture, he was selling hundreds of pairs for as little as £15 to apparently delighted customers.

Let us assume that young James is right in his assertions, and examine why this story is relevant here. Economically, this means that the *replacement* value of the asset 'making spectacles and selling them' is rather low. A 21-year-old student with no expertise in the field is apparently able to replicate it from his student room, with a few thousand pounds borrowed from his father. On the other hand, the *market* value is enormous because, as previously discussed, it equals the net present value of free cash flow discounted to infinity. In other words the market value is a direct function of the economic profitability of the asset in question and, on James's numbers, with a cost of goods sold at 10 and sales at 150, it is plain that economic value added is truly staggering. Thus, 'making spectacles and selling them' has a phenomenal return on invested capital, and an equally impressive asset multiple – the ratio of market value to the replacement value of invested capital. Enter James … If he is successful in his venture, he will collapse the marginal return on capital invested of the industry by accepting a lower margin than his competitors. By investing in his Internet project, the entrepreneurial student made an arbitrage, perhaps unknowingly, between the (market) value of existing capacity and the replacement value of new capacity, which he found cheaper to create. Investors in the incumbent firms may well end up suffering a setback, if it turns out that they have paid too much for the economic value of their asset in the belief that a very high economic return on capital invested was sustainable. We will see later on in this book that investors who ignore the workings of the capital cycle, the ultimate driver of share prices, do so to their disadvantage.

'Investment' in a financial sense should just be a replication of the real-world process of arbitrage between market value and replacement value. But, of course, it would never occur to the average buyer of a BMW share to contemplate building a brand new car-manufacturing facility instead; financial investors do not have the ability to start building their own capacity and carry out the full arbitrage process. As a result, it could be said that they do not really *invest*, but *speculate*. This distinction is not new. John Burr Williams, a student and contemporary of Benjamin Graham and David Dodd, had this to say about the investor and the speculator: *the longer a buyer holds a stock or bond, the more important are the dividends or coupons while he owns it and the less important is the price when he sells it ... For this reason we shall define an investor as a buyer interested in dividends, or coupon and principal, and a speculator as a buyer interested in the resale price* (Burr Williams, 1938). Note that for these men of the 1930s this definition was a purely objective description, to which they did not attach any judgement; speculating was not 'bad'. However, it had its own logic connecting investment and speculation. Speculators could only profit as a group from selling to investors. Investors would only buy on consideration of income. Therefore, share prices are always determined, in the end, by income (dividend) considerations – i.e. on the basis of investment, not speculation.

Today, because hardly anybody buys shares for income, this subtle distinction has lost its pertinence. Instead, it could be said that the vast majority of financial investors 'speculate' – i.e. seek to benefit from a share price movement. Some investors like to look at companies' characteristics on an individual basis, and pick the best. As a group, they represent the *stock pickers*. Stock pickers (the good ones, that is) are brilliant strategy analysts. They assess the corporate strategy of companies division by division, they like to have long interviews with the Chief Executives, they love to visit factories, warehouses and logistic centres, and generally travel a lot. Their way of investing is to wrap their arms around the business case of the company that they consider. If they like the strategy, they will tend to buy the shares, speculating that there will be a broad agreement between corporate strategy and share prices. *Macro investors* love to design macro scenarios and figure out the likely outcome. What happens to consumer confidence when interest rates go up? What happens to it when they come down? This is where all their attention goes, and they invest in equities by speculating that share prices will broadly follow the general economy. To be complete, let us add that there are also some *opportunistic investors* out there. This type uses whatever 'model' is available and happens to be the flavour of the month – price momentum, earnings revision, low PE, EV-to-EBITDA, sales-to-click (a very popular ratio during the heyday of the technology bubble) – often in combination, sometimes unaware that, if not set in a multi-factor analysis, probabilities multiply and do not add (in other words, if a momentum strategy works for 58 per cent of the time and a low PE strategy works for 63 per cent of the time, their random combination will work, on average, $58 \times 63 = 36.5$ per cent of the time). They speculate that share prices will follow the general flavour of the month.

This typology of investors is, of course, slightly unfair, and should not quite be taken at face value. Nor should it be assumed that it implies some ranking of success. I know some charming and successful opportunistic investors, and some pretty snotty and unsuccessful stock pickers. Admittedly, all I know about macro investors is that they all tend to sport a vague air of superiority, which makes you feel that they can't be bothered to explain to you (who would not understand anyway) the vast economic plot that is about to unwind in front of your very eyes. Still, any of them can be enormously successful, but none use explicitly the same reasoning as Mr Murray Wells to arrive at an investment conclusion. How could they? Not even the most savvy macro investor would have the faintest idea about the replacement value of the Capital Goods sector. Any stock picker would look at you with amazement if you asked his idea of the replacement value of Microsoft. Instead, they use some sort of financial ratio, and that is where all their problems start.

In order to decide whether a particular share is worth buying according to the real-world process, investors need more than just a schematic representation of assets, liabilities or profits. They need a *real economic representation* of this potential investment, because their true economic function, as wealth owners willing to commit capital to the economy, is to arbitrage between buying an existing asset and building a new one – like the young student cited previously. Unfortunately for them, financial investors cannot easily achieve this from the tools that we have briefly reviewed. That's because the companies' financial accounts which they are using to carry out their analysis were never drawn solely, if at all, for the benefit of investment analysis. In a book that created a mini-scandal in the City in the early 1990s, *Accounting for Growth* (Smith, 1992), Terry Smith exposed enough corporate tricks for seasoned investors to be warned that they are not going to get much help from reported accounts. This is not implying that the financial information in annual reports is purposely misleading; fortunately, in most cases, it is genuine. But investors must always bear in mind that the most honest Finance Director will still use all the accounting tricks at his disposal to show his company in the best possible light, because his reputation, his stock options, the way he is considered by his peer group and at the golf club, and ultimately his job, as well as the jobs of the entire management board, are on the line. Analysts should also be mindful that the Generally Accepted Accounting Principles (GAAP) are not gospel, but just what they say they are – *generally* accepted principles. These standards are quite flexible, and provide ample opportunities for Finance Directors to make perfectly legitimate assumptions. Pension accounting, to take just one example, is clearly designed to smooth the volatility of the bottom line. The profit and loss account is impacted by an *assumed* rather than *actual* return on pension assets, which is decided pretty much at the discretion of the company's management. For most rules, there is a recommended treatment as well as an *alternative* treatment. For instance, under International Accounting Standards (IAS) rule 23, which deals with borrowed costs, Finance Directors can either expense them or capitalise them for 'qualifying assets'!

There is sometimes a temptation among investment analysts to view those producing accounting information with slight condescension, as if they are producing a useless output that somehow has to be acknowledged regardless. This is missing the point. Balance sheet, cash flow, and profit and loss information are drawn up to comply with disclosure rules, not to show an accurate economic picture. If he had been asked, Luca Pacioli, the Italian Franciscan monk who invented the modern double entry accounting system, would probably have come up with a very useful economic system (such was the genius of this typical Renaissance man that he also taught Leonardo Da Vinci proportion and geometry for seven years!). But he was only asked to write a few chapters describing an accounting system 'in order that the subjects of the most gracious Duke of Urbino may have complete instructions in the conduct of business'. In modern language, Brother Luca invented something like a highway code. There must be year-end closing entries. You must stop at the red traffic light. Debits equal credits. You must not overtake on the continuous line. These are necessary rules, but they don't teach you how to drive your car, and certainly do not tell you how much your car is worth.

In the *New Financial Order*, as Robert Shiller calls it, things are not getting any better either for the unfortunate investment analyst (Shiller, 2003). In this new world where derivative instruments allow specific risks to be shared by a great number of investors, economic agents in general and Finance Directors in particular aim at laying off as much financial burden (risk, or financial liabilities) as possible onto other agents. This means that reported balance sheets do not reflect as accurately as they should the companies' assets (capital employed) and liabilities, some of which might suddenly disappear, only to emerge later in somebody else's balance sheet. As if this were not enough of a headache in itself, once the *economic* balance sheet is reconstructed, investors must know which commitments are 'recourse' and 'non-recourse' – in other words, which ones come with the legal right to demand compensation or payment, especially if the commitment is passed on to a third party. Securitised receivables, off-balance sheet financing, share options, under-funded defined benefits schemes, warranties, vendor financing, etc., all contribute to obscure the true financial picture. Ignore them at your peril.

The economic profit framework

However, in aggregate, share prices *do* react continuously to a perpetual process of arbitrage between market value and replacement (or economic) value. It is not because accounting-based ratios are unable to capture it that this economic process does not take place. Therefore, investors need to conduct their financial analysis so that they are in a position to measure (albeit approximately) market value and replacement value, without having to build any new capacity, like James' manufacturing of cheap glasses. Thus, in the CROCI framework, or indeed in any framework resting on the logic of an economic profit model, investors have to achieve three things:

1. To calculate an accurate measure of the market value
2. To approximate in the best possible way the economic value of the asset in question
3. To calculate the economic return that this asset generates, in relation to the cost of capital.

In this framework, it is clear that financial analysis is primarily about *data reconstruction*, or the transformation of accounting data into 'economic' data. Once this economic material is in place, the choice of valuation ratio or model becomes a secondary issue. Techniques to calculate these ratios have been around for decades, sometimes centuries, and it would take a pretty poor analyst not to be able to figure out which ratio or model can apply to a particular situation. In reality, as we have seen, they all can, to various degrees of accuracy, because they all set out to approximate the 'net present value of expected . . .' etc. Inexperienced analysts may use a particular ratio or technique in the wrong context, but a few years of practice should put them on the right track. The academic world has tested all of these ratios to a high degree of accuracy, and the statistical significance of all models is scrutinised by battalions of postgraduate students. Bad investment analysis, therefore, is unlikely to be the sole result of using 'the wrong ratio'. The cardinal sin of investment analysis is to use the wrong *numbers* – that is, using unadjusted accounting data, hoping to achieve an economically meaningful valuation. The crudest investment ratio calculated with accurately adjusted financial data is more likely to lead to reliable conclusions than is a sophisticated methodology based on unadjusted financial accounts.

Based on the premise of an economic profit model it is possible to propose a unified approach to investment analysis, which adheres to a bottom-up stock selection process, without the drawbacks associated with stock-specific idiosyncrasies. Because in this model all companies are seen as a bundle of economic capital defined in the same way, producing a real return within an ambient cost of capital and growing at a certain real rate, they can be aggregated into sub-sectors, sectors or regions, or according to their economic characteristics ('cyclicals', 'defensives'), without fear of mismatch. These economic data will also ensure near-to-perfect comparability. The merits of Toyota (as an investment proposition) can be assessed against those of Volkswagen beyond the accounting differences, to produce a truly informed opinion on relative value. And, finally, once the hard work of transforming disparate accounting information into homogeneous economic data is accomplished, there will be no need for complex models. As we will see in the next chapter, valuation can be assessed with an 'economic PE' ratio. Although only a distant cousin to the accounting PE, the mechanics of this ratio are the same, and all the applications of the accounting PE ratio for stock selection are preserved. This is essential, for the PE ratio has one invaluable advantage: it is simple to implement. Bookshelves are full of impressive books on the ultimate methodology to build the perfect discounted cash flow model, with three growth rates (guessing one is hard enough), and the fifteen essential steps that you need to take to calculate the cost of capital. These models are undoubtedly superior even to an economic PE, if one has the time and the inside knowledge of the company's capex cycle, debt structure, trend growth rate etc. – which is usually not the case for a professional investor considering maybe a thousand potential investments. An economic profit model uses the simplicity of the PE mechanics in conjunction with economic corporate data to make it relevant.

The PE paradox – an introduction to behavioural finance

If accounting information is so useless, and the accounting-based ratios with it, why then is everybody using it for their investment decisions, in particular the ubiquitous accounting PE ratio? Why indeed! Although we have a name for it, *the PE paradox*, we don't really have an answer to this question. All we know is that it is likely to be linked to behavioural finance, an important aspect of financial markets' gyrations.

Behavioural finance is a relatively new field of research in the broad context of financial economics. It was brought to life in 1974 by Daniel Kahneman and

Amos Tversky, two psychologists who specialised in the analysis of irrationality in human decisions. Broadly, it purports that economic analysis cannot assume that economic agents are perfectly rational, and should assume that they are, well, human, and thus subject to all sorts of contingencies in their decision-making process (Kahneman and Tversky, 1974). To support their case the two psychologists demonstrated, through numerous experiments, the illogical ways in which people make decisions involving probabilities. This innovative work won a Nobel Prize in 2002, although Tversky could not be named or receive it, having died six years earlier. One can easily recognise an affiliation between behavioural finance and what Mr Paulos writes about the human 'innumerate' mind (Paulos, 1988). It is quite obvious to anybody who has been an observer of financial markets and investors' behaviour for long enough that there is a quasi-compulsion on the part of market participants to be comforted by a number, *any* number (in this case, 'the PE ratio'), so long as they can easily recognise it, even if this number is demonstrably misleading. This is known as 'familiarity bias' or 'preference for the familiar' in behavioural finance. Incidentally, the same holds true for macroeconomic data, which are in most cases manipulated or obscure (Fed followers may remember the story of the *hedonic deflator*[3]), only in *preliminary* form when released, often subject to hefty revisions months later as a result, mostly backward-looking, volatile to the point of uselessness, and in any case mostly irrelevant to equity returns. Yet the whole financial world stops at regular intervals a few times a month 'ahead of the figures', the release of which is followed by endless comments from 'specialists' on CNBC and in the financial press. No wonder markets appear random to outside observers!

Behaviourists would see in the PE paradox a combination of the herding instinct and 'anchoring', to use their jargon. The latter is the tendency of the human brain to moor its thoughts to the latest number registered, however unrelated this number may be to the subject of these thoughts, and then 'to adjust away from it'. (The classic illustration is the Genghis Khan's birthday test. Ask a group of people to write down the last three digits of their telephone number before asking them to guess Genghis Khan's birthday, and most of them will assume that he was born before 1000, when in fact he lived from 1162 to 1227.) As for the 'herding instinct', there is, in human psychology, a strong desire to conform and comply with the behaviour of others and their points of view. Behaviourists see this as one of the driving forces behind the way in which investors use market information. Warren Buffett merely puts it another way, when he notes that 'Failing conventionally is the route to go; as a group, lemmings may have a rotten image, but no individual lemming has ever received bad press' (Letter from the Chairman, 1984 Berkshire Hathaway Annual Report).

Some investors give a candid account of the PE paradox, namely that they know full well the accounting PE's uselessness, but want 'to look at what the market looks at'. Their argument is that adjustments are 'subjective', and since few are likely to make the same adjustments it is better to look at the raw data as delivered to the market, i.e. in their accounting format. The raw data argument seems rather weak. The 'raw data' of humans are a combination of hydrogen and oxygen, plus a few amino acids and other organic compounds, but if you stare at a bucket of water containing some fatty matter you are unlikely to become the greatest human psychologist ever seen.

What is certain is that the use of unadjusted accounting data often leads to the most abominable models. One of the most infamous of these is almost certainly the 'Fed model', so called because it is believed to be used by the US Federal Reserve to assess the valuation of US equities. In its simplest format, the Fed model says that the fair value of the S&P 500 is the earnings per share of this index divided by the bond yield. This is equivalent to saying that the inverse of the bond yield is the correct PE ratio for the market. The Fed model is not a very good model, but it appeals to investors because of its simplicity. This model applies a *nominal* discount rate, the bond yield, to a *real* claim on assets, profits. This discredits almost irrecoverably its theoretical validity. However, even if it were possible to overcome this objection, there is no attempt in this methodology to measure the real claim accurately, which is just defined as net (reported) profits. *This* is the real downfall of the model, as it is of most top-down models using *reported*, not *economic*, data. Yet the model regularly resurfaces as an asset allocation tool, especially when it sporadically *appears* to be working, during certain periods or in certain regions.

This book is not about behavioural finance – at least not explicitly – but no book about investment can ignore this major breakthrough, because the irrational behaviour of investors *in aggregate* is what makes *individual* investors money, if this paradox is not too hard to accept. And, because we are all irrational in the way we price assets, the need for using a disciplined approach to investment analysis is all the more imperative. An EP model such as the one advocated here could be seen as the response of the left side of our brain ('rationality') to the right side ('emotions'), the latter being measured by behavioural finance.

Coffee or beer? The issue of investment 'styles'

The debate about styles is another classic of investment analysis on which we need to say a few words. Years ago, if you were travelling domestically in the Netherlands on a 'City Hopper' you could be offered the rather incongruous choice above – which, said with a charming Dutch accent, would make the flight a little bit more enjoyable to mischievous foreigners. How about trying 'value or growth' for another laugh? In a remarkable achievement, the dominant index providers have managed to convince pretty much the entire world that there are only these two types of investments in equities. 'Value managers' are supposed to buy cheap shares, and 'growth managers' . . . well, growth shares. In a desperate attempt to break away from this classification some investors have come up with alternative names, especially 'core' and 'GARP' (Growth At a Reasonable Price), but 'value' and 'growth' still dominate every debate on investment style and benchmarks. Yet 'value' and 'growth' are neither complementary nor mutually exclusive, and polarising the market in this way makes as much sense as thinking about the week in terms of Easter days and Tuesdays. In most cases, the value universe is defined as the 'cheapest' 40 per cent of stocks by price-to-book or price-to-earnings multiple, whilst the growth universe comprises the 'most expensive' 40 per cent. Note the unashamed use of accounting-based valuation ratios here. Quite apart from the fact that, on this segregation, the definition of 'growth' is 'expensiveness' relative to the mean valuation . . .

No one quite knows how such a muddled view of investment strategy has managed to attain this axiomatic status. What is sure is that there are low-growth companies and high-growth companies, as well as cheaply valued shares and expensively valued shares. But *economically*, there does not seem to be any clear correlation between expensiveness and high growth rates. Figure 1.1 plots a universe of approximately 700 global stocks, with respect to their economic PE and the *trend* growth rate of their economic assets (despite not having clearly detailed any of these concepts yet, we have to use economic PE and trend economic growth here to prove our point; using accounting-based PE rations would not work for reasons which, we hope, are starting to become obvious). According to the growth versus value divide, higher PE companies should enjoy structurally higher growth rates, since they are growth stocks. As the regression line shows, there is no meaningful positive relationship between the two.

A slightly more charitable analysis is given in Figure 1.2. This time, we show the distribution of average trend growth across various economic PE levels. Very high PE companies (60× and 65× cash earnings) do have a significantly higher average trend growth in assets than the rest of the universe. But, across the whole spectrum, the regression line suggests that a change in the growth rate explains less than 20 per cent of the change in the level of the PE ratio.

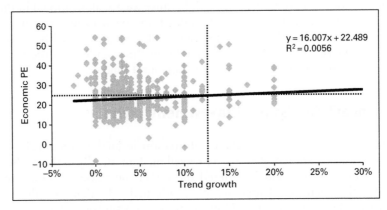

Figure 1.1 Economic PE vs trend growth rate.

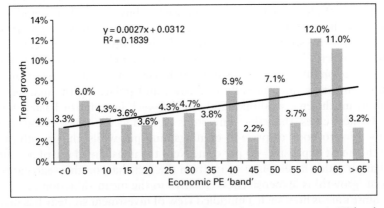

Figure 1.2 Distribution of average trend growth across economic PE levels.

In other words, in a growth index, investors will be assured of finding a number of genuine growth stocks, as well as a fair amount of simply expensive stocks. Note here that we define growth as growth in economic capital. Earnings growth, cash flow growth, sales growth *can* also stem from economic growth, as well as a whole host of other factors (inflation, margin expansion, financial degearing, replacement cost of assets etc.), as we will see in some detail in Chapter 5.

The misleading nature of this divide is starting to force the main index providers to refine their methodology. Standard and Poor's has recently reviewed its 'style indices' and has introduced a multi-factor approach to style. Value factors now include book value, cash flow and sales to price and dividend yield, whereas growth factors include five-year earnings and sales per share growth, as well as calculation of an 'internal growth rate', defined as the return on equity multiplied by the earnings retention rate. Unquestionably this offers an improvement on the splitting of the market into two halves, but all these factors are based on reported *accounting* data, which is bound to produce strange results. In fact, one does not need to go very far to find a classification at least subject to debate. It is possible to download from the very good S&P website (www.standardandpoors.com) the list of constituents for each style. The very first company which, thanks to its *accounting* characteristics, appears in the growth category is Alcoa, the US aluminium company. On *economic* data, Alcoa seems to have an inflation-adjusted trend cash return on assets of 5.6 per cent (i.e. slightly above the cost of capital) and an average growth in capital invested of 4 per cent since 1989. This is exactly what you would expect; a value-added commodity business such as aluminium should return a bit more than the cost of capital and grow like world GDP. If *this* is a growth investment, then what is an investment in Google?

Occasionally, some investors (not always purposely disparaging) enquire whether the CROCI philosophy of investing might not be '*just* a value approach'. They must wish they had not asked, because this is one of CROCI's pet subjects, and the answer can be quite lengthy. But to keep it short: *what else can it be other than a value approach?* This has to be the case for all fundamental analysis. Or, in the words of Warren Buffett 'what is "investing", if it is not the act of seeking value at least sufficient to justify the amount paid?' (Letter from the Chairman, 1992 Berkshire Hathaway Annual Report). Of course CROCI is a value approach, in the sense that it seeks to identify investment opportunities where the market value of an asset lies below its replacement value – or, in the classification of John Burr Williams, because it seeks to invest, not to speculate. But this is very different from investing indiscriminately into low price-to-book or price-to-earnings shares (on unadjusted accounting numbers), whilst systematically avoiding seemingly highly-priced shares based on the same unadjusted ratios.

We detail later in this book the results of a systematic investment in the cheapest stocks on economic PE, but to illustrate temporarily the vacuity of the value/growth divide, Table 1.1 shows the list of the five stocks that have contributed the most to the performance of these investments, by region. Each of these fifteen stocks have appeared many times in our portfolios (they were therefore, by definition, among the cheapest stocks in our universe), and have generated the very best performance whilst picked in our portfolios. They have undoubtedly been great value investments, and most of them are or were high growth stocks as well.

Table 1.1 Systematic investment in the cheapest stocks on economic PE: stocks that have contributed the most to the performance of these portfolios, by region

Top five contributors to the US CROCI portfolio	Top five contributors to the EU CROCI portfolio	Top five contributors to the Japan CROCI portfolio
Nike	Nokia	TDK
HCA	Total	Nissan Motor
Sun Microsystems	KPN	Nintendo
Occidental Petroleum	Sanofi-Aventis	Rohm
Target Corp.	BASF	Canon

'Approximately and most of the time'

Finally, no book written with the aim of presenting an investment model or philosophy, indeed no fund manager selling his services on the basis of a superb track record, can avoid touching on the issue of the efficiency of markets. The theory of market efficiency poses the simplest question of all: is it all worth it? Can this human mind which, as we have established, is ill-suited to deal with probabilities and full of unhelpful emotions, forecast the future clearly and beat the market? Or is it the case, following Nassim Taleb's argument (Taleb, 2004), that 'the hidden role of chance in the markets and in life' is behind all successful fund managers?

The premise of this theory appeared in the most unlikely source, the PhD thesis of an obscure but talented French mathematician by the name of Louis Bachelier, student of the great Henri Poincaré. This dissertation was presented in 1900. Despite being a man of his time and using Brownian motion as a model for stock exchange performance, Bachelier did not get the highest marks for his work. Finance had nothing to do with physics and mathematics in these days, and Bachelier had to spend the rest of his life in second-rate universities. Remarkably, his ideas spent the next sixty-five years in the most obscure anonymity, until Eugene Fama, now a Professor of Finance at the University of Chicago, dedicated his university career to expanding Bachelier's ideas and building a complete modern framework on the subject, by the name of Efficient Market Hypothesis (EMH). In fact, Eugene Fama was 'tipped off' by Paul Samuelson and Benoit Mandelbrot, another Frenchman who we will soon meet again: 'It was not until the work of Samuelson and Mandelbrot in 1965 and 1966 that the role of fair game expected return models in the theory of efficient markets and the relationships between these models and the theory of random walks were rigorously studied' (Fama, 1970). The rest is history. EMH changed the way we think about stock market fluctuations, so much so that, since 2003, Fama has been one of the favourites to win the Nobel Prize in Economics for his effort. So far this accolade has eluded him.

In Professor Fama's own words: 'I take the market efficiency hypothesis to be the simple statement that security prices fully reflect all available information' (Fama, 1991). More explicitly, 'competition among the many intelligent participants leads to a situation where, at any point in time, actual prices of individual securities already reflect the effects of information based both on events that have already occurred and on events which, as of now, the market expects to take place in the future'. The implications of the efficient market hypothesis for investment analysis are immense; in efficient markets, all known information (that is, facts and expectations) is reflected in the price of securities, which means that future returns are unpredictable and investment analysis worthless. Given that Professor Fama is a staunch supporter of passive investments (those funds, commonly called index trackers, that merely replicate the movements of the market without attempting to do better), there can be no doubt that he believes that equity markets are efficient. In this context, the future path of markets is often compared to the random walk of a drunken man (promptly dubbed 'the random walk theory') – a great but somewhat unfortunate image that is often erroneously understood. This does not mean that the market responds irrationally to events, as a drunken man may do. Rather, the random walk theory purports that the next step (the future movement) of the market is as unpredictable as the next step that a drunken man will take.

It goes without saying that this hypothesis, which has gained wide support in the academic world in the past twenty years, is a pretty high hurdle to clear for anybody who claims to be able to beat the market. It is estimated that a quarter of US pensions are indexed (*Pensions & Investments: The 1000 Largest Retirement Funds*, 26 January 2004) or run passively. In the UK, the figure could be as high as a third (Investment Management Association's *Asset Management Survey*, May 2004). Barclays Global Investors, the San Francisco-based world leader in passive fund management, has hundreds of billions of dollars invested in such trackers. The appeal of this theory has gone way beyond the small, dusty desks of a few university professors, and it has turned into a gigantic business. It should be noted that EMH does not suggest that investors cannot make money in the market. Given the upward trend in equity markets, even corrected for the survival bias, it would take some doing *not* to make money over a reasonably long period of time – say three years on average. What the theory disputes is the ability of the average active investor to make *more* money than the market (for instance the S&P 500 in the US), i.e. to outperform, on a sustainable basis. Any observed excess return, called 'alpha' in the jargon, is deemed random, since future movements of shares are unpredictable. There is a further complication in the fact that the record of the average active fund indeed falls short of the market return in most cases. The median fund manager of US large capitalisation funds typically underperforms over one, three or ten years.

Yet not everybody agrees with EMH. Warren Buffett does not believe any of the above, and remarked once, in his inimitable style: 'I'd be a bum in the street with a tin cup if the markets were efficient'. But the man from Omaha is hardly representative of the average mutual fund manager. His firm, Berkshire Hathaway, usually has total control over the management of the companies that it buys. Incidentally, it sometimes only makes a handful of purchases a year, and occasionally none at all. Warren Buffett is an allocator of capital – what the early twentieth century economists called a wealth owner, not a 'benchmark beater'. His opinion, as always, is interesting, but not terribly relevant in this instance. Normal fund managers have to obey strict rules of portfolio construction over controlling stakes, volatility, tracking error and so on. Furthermore, few have the luxury of being one of the richest men on earth. Some studies have pointed out that behavioural patterns are, once more, getting in the way. A money manager might find it too risky, from a personal perspective, to buy a distressed or unfavourable stock, even if the actual return distribution is no different from the stock of a financially healthy firm (Grinblatt and Titman, 1998).

The self-proclaimed maverick scientist Benoit Mandelbrot, the Frenchman of a few paragraphs ago, polymath, discoverer of fractal geometry and a keen occasional student of economics and markets, is another sceptic. Although M. Mandelbrot agrees, 'up to a point', that future prices are not predictable, and that their fluctuations follow the laws of chance, he argues that the two principles on which Bachelier built his random theory of markets – namely that price movements are independent of each other and normally distributed – are flawed. He proves, rather easily, that returns are far from normally distributed (if they were, an index swing of more than 7 per cent should come once every 300 000 years; it happened forty-eight times during the twentieth century), and believes that there is a 'long term memory' in share prices (Mandelbrot and Hudson, 2004).

John Allen Paulos, the popular mathematician we met earlier, gives an interesting critique of the EMH in his latest book (Paulos, 2003), written, apparently, after the author 'lost his shirt' by 'playing' (sic) WorldCom in the stock market. In short, Mr Paulos argues that the EMH is faced with a paradox. If the majority of market participants believe in the EMH, they will make the market inefficient by ignoring news which they will assume is already priced in. Conversely, if the majority of investors do not believe in the EMH, they will, by their constant efforts to 'beat the market', make it efficient. Admittedly this is pushing logic to its limits, but the important point made here is that the EMH is not necessarily true or false, and depends on the belief of the majority of investors or their leaders. In other words, it is behavioural. Mr Paulos' conclusion is one that we endorse entirely: 'most investors, professionals on Wall Street, and amateurs everywhere, disbelieve in it [the EMH], so for this reason I think it holds, but only approximately and only most of the time.'

Others have criticised the EMH not on principle, but over the *degree* of market efficiency. Further refinements in the EMH have led to a distinction between three levels of efficiency: weak, semi-strong and strong. The first level is associated with all past market prices and data, the second with all *publicly* available information, and the third with all information. Considering the spectacular string of corporate scandals and the ensuing share price disasters that have hit investors in the past few years (WorldCom, dear to Mr Paulos in all acceptations of the term, but also Tyco, Vivendi Universal, Enron, Global Crossing, Qwest, Arthur Andersen, Parmalat – and this list is not exhaustive), it is hard to believe that all information is quickly and efficiently reflected in share prices. The general academic view is that markets are efficient only in the semi-strong form and not in the strong form.

As we noted earlier, it is hard, if only to stick to a minimum of intellectual rigour, not to take a stance on the subject of market efficiency when writing a book on investment. But it is also a trap; be slightly too enthusiastic about EMH, and the book loses all purpose. Be in complete denial, and you are faced with a body of evidence which it is difficult to dismiss. As a starting point, let us say that twenty years of practice in modern markets will almost certainly have brought you to believe in some form of efficiency in equity markets but, to quote Paulos again, 'only approximately and most of the time'. This is because it is hard not to be equally taken by the arguments of current behaviourists such as Professor R. Thaler, also of Chicago University (Barberis and Thaler, 2003). Certainly, as we will report in detail in Chapter 9, the systematic implementation of the CROCI model has produced alpha in all markets. Alpha may be elusive, but it is not mythical.

So, in the end, what is investment? All of the above: ratios, theories, style, models, data and, hopefully, alpha. It is a difficult art – one that keeps practitioners humble, and for which no rules are ever cast in stone. It was once remarked about money managers in aggregate that it was an extraordinary thing to find so many clever people achieving such a poor result. As we have seen, the human brain has a lot to answer for. Although we will sporadically refer to behavioural finance, a framework to which we feel close, in the following chapters, we will not come back to it in great detail, and will simply take for granted that investment decisions are not really humans' *forte*. All there remains to do is to investigate whether anything can be done to improve the situation.

Notes

1. This is not anecdotal. There is a strong body of evidence which shows that investors have a preference for their own domestic equities, and even for equities where the head office is located close to them, although the latter point has to do with ease of research and local knowledge as well.
2. In June 2000, Moody's Global Credit Research published an article entitled 'Ten Critical Failings of EBITDA as the principal determinant of cash flow'. Although the market had already taken a nosedive at that point, this article probably fell on deaf ears, as it came too early in the collapse of telecom shares.
3. Simply put, a hedonic deflator adjusts the observed price increase of an item by its productivity. Economists disagree on the fairness of this deflator, which is used in the US but not in Europe. Some argue that its use is artificially boosting growth statistics in the US. Others defend it; and the whole debate is totally obscure!

References

Barberis, N. and Thaler, R. (2003). In: *A Survey of Behavioural Finance: Handbook of the Economics of Finance* (G. M. Constantinides, M. Harris and R. Stulz, eds). Elsevier Science B.V.

Burr Williams, J. (1938). *The Theory of Investment Value.* Harvard University Press.

Copeland, T., Koller, T. and Murrin, J. (1994). *Valuation: Measuring and Managing the Value of Companies.* John Wiley & Sons Inc.

Fama, E. F. (1970). Efficient capital markets: a review of theory and empirical work. *Journal of Finance*, 389.

Fama, E. F. (1991). Efficient capital markets: II. *Journal of Finance*, 46(5), 1575–1617.

Grinblatt, M. and Titman, S. (1998). *Financial Markets and Corporate Strategy.* Irwin/McGraw-Hill.

Kahneman, D. and Tversky, A. (1974). Judgement under uncertainty: heuristics and biases. *Science* **185**, 1124–1131.

Mandelbrot, B. B. and Hudson, R. L. (2004). *The (Mis)behaviour of Markets: A Fractal View of Risk, Ruin and Reward*. Basic Books.

Paulos, J. A. (1980). *Mathematics and Humour*. University of Chicago Press.

Paulos, J. A. (1988). *Innumeracy – Mathematical Illiteracy and its Consequences*. Hill and Wang.

Paulos, J. A. (1995). *A Mathematician Reads the Newspaper*. Basic Books.

Paulos, J. A. (2003). *Mathematician Plays the Market*. Basic Books.

Shiller, R. J. (2003). *The New Financial Order: Risk in the 21st Century*. Princeton University Press.

Shiv, B., Loewenstein, G., Bechera, A. *et al.* (2005). Investment behavior and the negative side of emotion. *American Psychological Society*, **16(6)**.

Smith, T. (1992). *Accounting for Growth: Stripping the Camouflage from Company Accounts*. Century Limited.

Taleb, N. N. (2004). *Fooled by Randomness: The Hidden Role of Chance in Life and in the Markets*. Texere.

2 The PE and the Equivalence principle: asset multiple and relative return

Cinderella's slipper – a misunderstanding: economic versus actuarial

This is a slightly dry subject, so let us start with a fairytale. Cinderella, the fairy-made princess with whom the Prince had fallen in love, disappeared before midnight in her pumpkin-shaped carriage. Fortunately she was eventually found again, thanks to the slipper that she had lost as she was rushing away. That slipper, as is well recorded in any children's book, was made of glass. Even by fairytale standards, glass shoes don't make much sense – and indeed they were never meant to exist. In Charles Perrault's original text, the slipper was made of *vair*, pronounced the same as *verre*, which indeed means *glass* in French. However, this ancient French word describes a squirrel's fur. Because of the mistake of one of the original editors of the book, who obviously did not have much spelling knowledge, generations of children must picture the poor princess with her grotesque shoes. (On the positive side, Cinderella can consider herself lucky that the editor did not have a Germanic accent and read *vair* as *fer* ('v' is pronounced 'f' in German). Otherwise, the poor princess would have had to walk around in iron slippers for the rest of her life . . .)

What the slipper's story illustrates is that things are not always what they are thought or meant to be; the universality of a belief has never been a guarantee of its truthfulness. In the finance world, various myths around the PE ratio have attained such universality – as has the ratio itself. It would not occur to a financial analyst not to mention this ratio in a published report, it would not occur to a fund manager not to calculate it when considering an investment, and it would not occur to the Head of an Investor Relations department not to be totally on top of this number for the company, the company's competitors, the sector, the market, etc. If it is so universally known, why then dedicate an entire chapter to it? Because of the PE paradox; what is commonly accepted about the PE ratio is not really what it is meant to be. In his thorough *Investment Fables*, Professor Damodaran has already exposed the false common beliefs in this or that ratio – what he calls 'the myths of can't miss investment strategies' (Damodaran, 2004). This chapter takes a similar approach as far as the PE ratio is concerned. Not fearing to appear contrary, we argue that those who take the PE ratio at face value (price divided by earnings) and use it in its common usage are misguided, whilst those who ignore it for its lack of sophistication are equally mistaken. The PE ratio is neither useful nor misleading *per se*; it performs a job, which is to approximate the discounting of dividends or free cash flow. It does it simply, quickly and clumsily. The results are therefore simple, quick and clumsy. It is up to the investment analyst to improve them, and this can be achieved with two prerequisites. The PE ratio needs to be calculated with *economic*, not accounting data (this vast subject will be treated in some depth in Chapters 3 and 4, and only addressed here in its generalities). But, and this is the core subject of the present chapter, it also needs to be used in its *economic* rather than actuarial logic – an argument found off the beaten track, but nevertheless crucial for the implementation of an economic profit model, of which this book is an advocate. Note that actuarial is taken here in a specialised sense, to mean the discounting of flows to determine present values, rather than the general insurance-related sense. In order to preserve the flow of the text, we have put the various derivations in the appendix at the end of this chapter.

The PE ratio and its actuarial framework

In the discounting of future expected flows to their present value (the 'actuarial framework') there are two ways to determine the value of an asset. In the *explicit* construction, cash flows are forecast by the analyst one after the other, until the horizon is so remote that the significance of the last flow is reduced to almost nothing. By way of example, the following paragraph is extracted from a research report published on a major UK company:

> We now assume that revenue growth accelerates from 2006 to 2010, to a maximum level of 5.4% ... As the business matures again, we forecast revenue growth to drop back to 3% by 2017. Peak margins under this model ... approach 25% (by 2016).

In the *perpetual* construction, one flow, which can grow or remain static, is deemed to be representative of the average flow to infinity, and is discounted to perpetuity. According to the textbooks, a professional analyst is meant to spend a large amount of time explicitly forecasting cash flows until this becomes practically impossible, and then apply a perpetuity model for the 'continuing value' of the firm.

By construction, the PE ratio belongs to the family of perpetuity models. If Company A, with a market capitalisation of 1000, is 'on a PE of 12.5×', this means that its current level of earnings (80, or 1000 divided by 12.5) is discounted by the reciprocal of that multiple, or 8 per cent,

$$12.5 = \frac{1}{0.08},$$

therefore

$$1000 = 80 \times 12.5 = \frac{80}{8\%}.$$

This connection to a perpetual (actuarial) model is often forgotten in practice, as the PE ratio is more readily assimilated to share price divided by earnings per share. Whilst undeniably true, it is not really surprising that such a definition should appear uninspiring; it is not easy to see the significance and usefulness of a multiple of earnings. Some use a magic number, like 10× or 15×, and assume that there is no value in shares trading above this multiple. The magic number usually comes from the long-term average PE ratio of the market itself. Not as simplistic as it may sound, but not entirely convincing either.

Others venture the idea of a pay-back period. Making an equity investment 'on a PE of 10' would mean that an investor has to wait ten years before recouping the original investment. This is a rough cut, because it assumes that investors receive a yearly income (dividend) equal to their share of net earnings (since they have paid ten times *earnings*, not dividends), ignoring the time value of money. This interpretation also raises more questions than it solves. Unlike bonds, which have a finite life, equities have an infinite life and are deemed perpetual, with investors assuming that their investments are 'going concerns'. Without any further information, it is not immediately clear why a perpetual annuity would require (in order to be purchased) an investment of ten times its amount in some cases, whilst in others an investment of five, fifteen or twenty times.

And so, in the end, the PE ratio hovers between universal acceptance and meaninglessness, used by everybody but trusted by no one. The real issue seems to be that the value of an investment is, theoretically, either defined by expected dividends or by expected free cash flows, but never by expected *earnings*. However, this is a false debate. The PE ratio is nothing more than a *simplification* of both a dividend discount model and, with some adjustments, a free cash-flow model. We show a numerical example for each in Box 2.1, and the full derivations in the appendix to this chapter.

It is no small feat that the PE ratio can either be described as a dividend discount model or, thanks to a few simplifications, as a FCF model, and it is no surprise that this much decried ratio has survived the tests of time. But for an investor the real value of this ratio is *not* in the actuarial approach, and here lies the misunderstanding. Although based on sound principles, the PE ratio remains a rather mediocre perpetuity model which can only approximate FCF in the manner that we have just mentioned. Its lack of pertinence is partly due to the use of *accounting* earnings, which is a very poor approximation of FCF.

Box 2.1

The PE ratio: a simplified dividend discount model and free cash-flow model

In its first guise, the PE ratio is simply another take on the Gordon Growth Model, which defines the value of equity per share as:

$$\frac{D}{CoE - g}$$

where D is the expected dividend per share, CoE is the cost of equity and g the expected perpetual growth rate of the dividend. This first definition of the PE ratio effectively discounts the payout ratio (the ratio of dividend to earnings). Consider the following profit & loss account for a firm with a cost of equity of 10 per cent and a growth rate of earnings of 4 per cent:

Profit & Loss	
Sales	100
EBIT	10
Interest	(2)
Tax	(3)
Profit	5
Payout ratio	60%
Dividend	3

On the Gordon Growth Model, the value of the firm is 50 (3 of dividend discounted by $(10\% - 4\%) = 6\%$). Calculating the PE ratio as price dividend by earnings, or 50/5 (i.e. 10×), or as payout ratio discounted by $d - g$ (where d is the relevant discount rate) or $60\%/(10 - 4)\%$, gives an equivalent answer.

There is nothing wrong with this financial construction, and the stress tests are positive. A higher-growth company would trigger a higher PE ratio, as is commonly admitted. Equally, for a given rate of growth, a higher-dividend paying company would also command a higher PE ratio, again in line with intuition and practice. But, because it is nothing more than a simplified dividend discount framework, this model appears to many as quite obsolete. Without making any adjustments, it would imply that a company not paying any dividend would have a value of zero, for instance. In this context, the market values the *probability* of paying a dividend in the future – a modification which it is possible to implement but is detrimental to the simplicity of the model. Furthermore, dividends are not the most tax efficient way to remunerate shareholders, and share buy-backs have become a more common way to hand money back to shareholders in recent years.

In a slightly more complex format (in this case, 'price' is the full economic value of the enterprise and 'earnings' are before financial charges), the logic of the PE ratio can be put to work to produce an *approximation* of the perpetual discounting of free cash flow (FCF), or

$$\frac{FCF}{d - g},$$

with d being the relevant discount rate and g the perpetual growth rate (see the appendix to this chapter for the full derivation). Consider the following assumptions:

Assumptions	
Gross after-tax cash flow	20
Investment (capital spending)	8
o.w. expansion	5
Free cash flow	12
Return on expansion investment (r)	13.5%
Operating earnings after tax	17
Discount rate (d)	11%
Growth rate (g)	4%

The value of the firm is traditionally given as 12 discounted by 7 per cent (11% minus 4%), or 170. The corresponding PE ratio is, classically, 170 divided by 17, or 10×. But it can also be calculated as $1-g/r$ discounted by $d-g$ (see appendix for the full derivation). Indeed, $1-(4\%/13.5\%)$ discounted by 7 per cent is also 10×. In this format, FCF is *approximated* by operating earnings $\times(1-g/r)$.

In addition, this one number, 10×, 14× or 22×, is also so vague that it can suggest a number of possible conclusions, without providing any analytical insight. For instance, a high PE ratio could mean that a company is expected to grow its earnings fast. This is the most common analysis of a high PE ratio, sometimes performed with the use of a PEG (price earnings divided by earnings growth) ratio. In this model, the PE ratio is supposed to approximate the earnings growth of the company, although it is hard to find a plausible theoretical explanation for why this should be the case. Based on this assumption, a company on a PEG ratio of less than one is supposed to be a good deal – but a high PE ratio could also mean that the company carries less risk than other similar investments, or that it is financially geared, or that it is at the trough of its profit cycle. There is just no way of knowing. By way of example, Table 2.1 lists six companies whose accounting PEs were around 45× in 1998 (this year being chosen to avoid the volatility of the technology bubble and its explosion).

Table 2.1 Six companies with accounting PEs of around 45× in 1998

Accounting PE in 1998	
Boston Scientific	43.8×
E.ON	44.0×
L'Oréal	44.6×
East Japan Railway	45.4×
ICI	48.1×
Microsoft	48.2×

It is hard to find a more diverse bunch. E.ON (a German utility) and East Japan Railway, both low-return and low-growth businesses, are on the same accounting PE ratio as L'Oréal (a fast-growing skincare company), Microsoft and Boston Scientific (a biotechnology company). For good measure, ICI, the venerable UK chemical company, is here as well. Can it really be the case that all these companies offer comparable investment opportunities, as their similar accounting PE ratio seems to suggest? Again, it is hard to say on the basis of this single number.

The economic construction behind the PE ratio

On the other hand the PE ratio can be construed as a more pertinent economic model, an assertion illustrated with the third, and last, rearrangement of 'price divided by earnings'. Here, the PE ratio has to be defined as *the price of a share relative to the earnings of the underlying asset.* 'Asset' means 'net asset', and is understood as the sum of all assets on the balance sheet (after depreciation for depreciable assets) minus net debt, which is total financial debt less cash and cash equivalents. In other words, it represents what a shareholder 'owns' in the books of the company, once financial debt is taken into account (or paid back). Seen from the asset side of the balance sheet this is called *net assets*, and from the liability side of the balance sheet the *book value, equity* or *shareholders' funds*.

If we now relate the level of earnings to the 'underlying asset', we can calculate the ratio of earnings to net assets, a widely used concept in investment analysis: Return on Equity (RoE). Finally, by relating this new ratio to the original definition of the PE, *share price relative to the earnings of the underlying asset*, we are able to relate the share price to the RoE via the book value, and reach the following, and third, definition of the PE ratio:

$$\frac{P/BV}{RoE}$$

where BV is book value. So, economically, the PE ratio can be expressed as price-to-book divided by return on equity. At first sight, it does not look very impressive. It is not a definition obviously superior to the two other versions of the ratio that we gave earlier, if only because the above expression is merely simplified by book value to get to the common definition of the PE ratio (i.e. price divided by earnings):

$$RoE = \frac{e}{BV}$$
$$\frac{P}{e} = \frac{P/BV}{e/BV}.$$

Therefore, *any* ratio constructed in this way would produce a PE ratio, once simplified. Price-to-debt divided by earnings-to-debt is also a PE ratio, as is price-to-sales divided by net margin, which is net profit divided by sales. But the net asset value, or book value, is not just *any* number. Economically, it represents what shareholders own, the amount of net capital that they have committed to the economy. It is also what they can dispose of if they wish, as well as the original source of earnings, the stock of capital invested to 'produce stuff', cars, cement or advertising campaigns. It is the most relevant balance sheet item for a shareholder, on which to peg the earnings multiple. And, therefore, we will progress into the economic structure of the PE ratio with this new and final definition:

$$\frac{P}{NA} \times \frac{1}{R}$$

where NA is net assets (book value in an accounting framework), P is price and R is return on net assets (RoE in an accounting framework).

The equivalence between asset multiple and relative return – the residual income model

Why is it that looking at the relationship between price-to-net assets and return on net assets is more insightful than looking at the other definitions, despite the fact that all three are rigorously the same? As we have stressed in Chapter 1, there is no absolute 'right' or 'wrong' in investment analysis, and the relevance of the tool depends largely on the question asked. The actuarial definition, which takes for granted the flows, focuses on the financial algorithm which transforms them into a capital stock. It is therefore particularly useful when investors want to compare a stock of liabilities, for instance, with a future expected flow. But it is not, as such, 'analytical'. It gives more of an answer to 'how?' (how to transform a flow into a stock, how to increase the net present value of this flow, how to reduce the risk of this flow) than to 'why?'.

The economic definition is more focused on the 'why', and it simply provides a better and more useful economic picture for investment analysis. This is partly because the PE ratio, defined as an asset multiple divided by a return on assets, carries the implicit assumption of a relationship between the price that investors are willing to pay for a given asset and the return that this asset generates. Intuitively, this makes sense; an asset or equity investment returning more than a competitor should also, logically, be priced more expensively, everything else being equal. We already have here the beginnings of a useful tool to rank comparable businesses on the basis of an *economic* characteristic: the return on assets. Say that Company A is valued on a price-to-book of 1.6× with a return on equity of 12.5 per cent, thus trading on a PE ratio of 12.8× (that's 1.6 divided by 0.125). Company B, which generates a RoE of 25 per cent, returns double the amount as does Company A to shareholders (economically, not necessarily through a dividend payment). If our intuition is correct, then Company B could logically be expected to trade at twice the price to book of Company A, i.e. 3.2×. If this is the case, then *note that the PE ratio will be the same*. As far as the stand-alone actuarial version is concerned, these two investments *are* the same; they are 'on a PE of 12.8×', and yet one business is twice as profitable as the other. There is already a lot of economic information in this knowledge. At the very least, it provides a ranking of the companies' relative economic attractiveness.

However, relative rankings do not solve the issue of absolute valuation: *what if Company A is not rightly valued in the first place?* Answering this question takes the economic logic of the PE ratio one step further, into Residual Income (RI). The concept of residual income can be seen as a derivative of the economic structure of the PE ratio, a very useful one on which we will rely heavily. It is, for that reason, also called Economic Profit (EP). Simply put, it is the amount of income left once the cost of capital (or investors' expected return in aggregate) has been accounted for. In order to perform this calculation, we need one further key variable, a common yardstick to anchor the relationship between asset multiple and return and to provide an *absolute* level of valuation. This anchor is obviously the discount rate, the very same rate with which actuarial calculations are performed. Intuitively, this absolute benchmark should be accurately approximated for all companies by the average of all returns on equity observed in the universe of investment. If an investor invests in all the shares available in a particular market, the return available to him will be the average RoE – his absolute benchmark. It seems equally certain that if a particular company wants to attract more of this investor's capital, everything else being equal, it will need to deliver a higher return than the average return. On the other hand, this investor's decision will also depend on how much he is required to pay to acquire the right to this return, i.e. the price of the shares in the market. As a result, we can safely assume that the expected return of an investor *is* the cost of capital. In Chapter 4 we will present a comprehensive way to calculate a market-derived cost of capital.

With the introduction of the discount rate into the equation it is possible to complete the presentation of the concept of residual income, probably best known through Stern and Stewart's Economic Value Added (EVA®) model. EVA® is defined as operating profit (Net Operating Profit After Tax, NOPAT according to Stern and Stewart) minus a capital 'rent', defined as capital times the cost of capital (other authors use the term NOPLAT, Net Operating Profits Less Adjusted Taxes; see appendix). This can be rearranged into the following generic formula:

$$\text{Return} - \text{cost of capital} \times \text{net assets.}$$

In the residual income framework, the value of an economic asset (E) is defined as the amount of Net Capital Invested or Net Assets (NA) plus the actuarial value of EP discounted to infinity, or

$$E = NA + \frac{(R - d) \times NA}{d}.$$

This formula is strictly equivalent to a PE ratio, and therefore strictly equivalent to a stream of constant FCF discounted to perpetuity; these demonstrations are shown in the appendix to this chapter.

Having dug further into the economic logic embedded in the PE ratio, we can now give a straightforward answer to the original question about the valuation of Companies A and B. If we assume (or observe) that the average expected return (on an equity investment), *alias* the cost of capital, is 12.5 per cent, since Company A's return on assets is also 12.5 per cent, then its residual income is clearly 0 because:

$$\frac{(R - d) \times NA}{d} = 0.$$

Thus, the value of Company A is the value of its net assets, since

$$E = NA + \frac{0}{d}.$$

In other words, the correct valuation for Company A should be 1× assets, not 1.6×, at a cost of capital of 12.5 per cent. And what about Company B, which we thought should trade at twice the level of Company A? Indeed, for 100 of capital, or net assets, Company B will generate 12.5 of economic profits, calculated as (25 per cent − 12.5 per cent) × 100. Applying the RI formula will give:

$$E = 100 + \frac{12.5}{12.5\%} = 200,$$

or an asset multiple of 2×, as predicted.

Generalising the above, if a company returns n times the cost of capital (d) at equilibrium (i.e. $R = n \times d$), then its expected RI should be:

$$EP = (nd - d) \times NA.$$

We show in the appendix to this chapter that this can be rewritten as:

$$\frac{E}{NA} = \frac{R}{d} = n.$$

It is this final identity that is at the core of the economic model embedded in the PE ratio. With this identity investors now have the beginning of a solid valuation model, with a simple but powerful relationship (we will give it some importance by calling it 'the Equivalence' from now on) between the asset multiple (market value to net assets) and the relative return (return on assets divided by the discount rate or cost of capital). The applications of the Equivalence to investment analysis are numerous and straightforward. Let us say that Company C has net earnings of 80, net assets of 500, no debt, and the discount rate is 8 per cent. In the actuarial approach, the value of the firm is 1000, given by 80 divided by 8% or multiplied by its inverse, 12.5×. There is not much more that you can say about it. In the economic version, the value of the firm (which is obviously still 1000) is given by the Equivalence between asset multiple and relative return. Analytically, this Equivalence gives out two very significant pieces of information. First, the return on net assets of the firm is 16 per cent (80 divided by 500). We already knew this from the third rearrangement of the PE ratio into price-to-book divided by RoE, but this is now framed into a coherent system. This yield can be compared to the money market rate, the bond yield or the return of another company. Second, and more importantly, it can also be observed that 16 per cent is significantly above the discount rate of 8 per cent, an indication that the firm is *creating value*; its residual income is positive. It could then be inferred, for instance, that a fade of return to the cost of capital would command a 50 per cent drop in the market value of the firm, to align the asset multiple to the relative return.

If all investors, professional and layman alike, performed this rather basic investigation as a matter of course, then perhaps they could make more sense of the PE ratio, even in its accounting version. Take Kingfisher and Next, two UK retailers, one selling goods for home improvement, the other selling clothes. At the end of the 1990s recession, in 1993, both stocks were on an accounting PE of 10×. By 1997, Next's PE had reached 20×, whilst Kingfisher's PE was still 10×. The Equivalence would have shed some light on this apparent mystery. Kingfisher's PE could be broken down into its Equivalence, a price-to-net asset ratio of about 2.1× and a relative return of 21 per cent (return on equity) divided by 10 per cent (the cost of capital). Similarly, Next's equivalence was a price-to-net asset ratio of 2.9× and a relative return of 29 per cent divided by 10 per cent. Although both companies were 'on the same PE ratio', Next was the more attractive investment for two reasons. First, its value creation (residual income) as a percentage of the market value of its assets was 6.5 per cent, i.e. (29% − 10%)/2.9, against 5.2 per cent, i.e. (21% − 10%)/2.1, for Kingfisher. Next's market value needed to go up by more than 25 per cent (to 3.65× assets) just to yield the same value-added return as Kingfisher. Second, Next was able to grow its earnings faster simply because it had a higher return on equity. Perhaps unsurprisingly, the shares of Next outperformed those of Kingfisher fourfold between 1993 and 1995.

At first sight, all of this section may run the risk of appearing as no more than financial gymnastics – trivial algebraic rearrangements which, in themselves, carry no intrinsic value. But they make an important point: *PEs, residual income and FCF formulae are strictly identical.* It is up to investors to use them wisely and in a relevant manner. If this book were written for academic purposes it would now be necessary to show the various alternatives to this model, which is very primitive – in particular because the derivations above are made *at equilibrium,* i.e. with no growth. It is quite possible to incorporate growth into these models at all stages, provided that it is *sustainable* growth – i.e. strictly lower than the discount rate. By definition, perpetual models cannot accommodate high explicit growth rates, for which only a DCF model is suited. But the purpose of this book is to show how, practically, investment professionals can use an economic profit model and the Equivalence principle for stock selection. We will therefore limit ourselves to the empirical evidence for the Equivalence being a powerful investment tool, and will deal with the integration of growth in Chapter 5. But first, let us go back to the headache of accounting numbers and economic models.

Why would you use accounting numbers to fuel the EP model?

We now have a solid principle extracted from the banal PE ratio. It is a gem, but it has only just been mined. Diamonds are found in very unpromising-looking rock straight out of the mine. Similarly, to make an EP model shine and the Equivalence principle release all of its analytical insight for stock selection, a lot more work needs to occur. This is what I sometimes feel like saying to analysts building beautiful valuation models, and then using accounting data. Take the EVA® model; its economic logic is impeccable. However, in the Stern–Stewart version it is calculated with accounting data and, as such, can only have limited impact for the purpose of selecting stocks. The irony is that the Stern–Stewart version of EP was *never* really meant to become an investor's tool. Stern Stewart & Co is not an asset management consultancy, but defines itself with a much broader brief, as a consultancy 'specialising in the management, incentive, valuation and financial applications of economic profit under the trademarked name of EVA®' (www.sternstewart.com). This did not prevent Mr Stewart's *Quest for Value* (Stewart, 1991), the first major book dedicated solely and comprehensively to the concept of economic profits, from being a huge success among asset managers in the mid-1990s. They saw in it the solution to all their problems, although it was clearly not written for them but 'for senior management, key operating people and planning and financial staff', according to the author himself (www.sternstewart.com).

The reason why investors chose to ignore this 'detail' is the same as that which prompts them to prefer the PE ratio in its actuarial guise rather than its economic one, despite the obvious shortcomings of that method. Perhaps the behavioural pattern that we identified in Chapter 1 (better *any* number than no number) also plays a role. The *main* reason, however, is that the economic profit format provides truly relevant information only when used with *corporate economic numbers*, not accounting ones. Corporate economic numbers are not available in any database, or in any annual report. They have to be painstakingly constructed, and require a deep analytical understanding of the firm for which they are being built. No statistical adjustment, no short cut, is admissible. And, as a result, only a handful of practitioners bother with them. We have already seen in the previous chapter that accounts were never designed to help investment analysis anyway. As such they also distort the actuarial version of the PE ratio, but they do much more damage to the economic construction because, in this format, investors need more data than just 'price' and 'earnings'.

The Equivalence principle for individual companies is simply a narrower version of a broader fundamental macroeconomic equivalence, the equivalence of the asset multiple and the relative return. Throughout this book we will come back in great detail to this economic equivalence, which is nothing less than the lynchpin of the capitalist system. However, there is nothing new at all here; this equivalence was clearly identified by the economists of the early twentieth century, especially Keynes, in their study of the mechanisms of capital formation. It is, put another way, a representation of the arbitrage between market value and replacement value seen in Chapter 1 – which explains why it cannot be implemented with accounting data. Economically, profitability has to be understood as the cash return on investment, not as an earnings-based measure of return. Equally, assets have to be measured at their replacement value and not at their book value. Since this is extraordinarily difficult to calculate, EP models use an approximation of the replacement value – which is good enough in most cases. Economic capital at replacement value has to be inflation-adjusted, and has to take tangible and intangible investments into consideration. Furthermore, it must be *economically* depreciated; economic depreciation is defined as the loss of cash flow through obsolescence and is not a linear decay, as accountants define it.

Plenty of great books have been published on the shortcomings of accounting information for investment purposes, most of the time written with forceful arguments. In a way this vehemence is not really necessary, because it is pretty obvious why accounting earnings are, analytically, not the right line-item to take into consideration. We will limit this discussion to two reasons. First, accounting earnings are not able to deal with the all-important question of the reinvestment rate. Unlike bonds, equities are priced as a going concern, with a perpetual life. In order for the capital to live perpetually it needs to be replaced regularly, and sometimes expanded either in order to follow the natural growth rate of the economy or to increase the company's market share. It follows that what is attributable to shareholders is the residual flow (or income) after the cost of (a) replacing obsolete capital, in current terms, and (b) expanding net capital invested. Reported earnings deal imperfectly with the first, and not at all with the second. In an earnings model the cost of replacing existing capital is taken into consideration via depreciation, which is accounted for at historical cost. Depending on the inflation rate and the rate of technological progress, the cash cost of replacing obsolete capital may vary substantially from the historical depreciation charge. As for the additional capital spending necessary to expand the business, it is simply not a profit and loss item, since the P&L, by definition, only records costs and revenues, not capital flows. It is possible to adjust for this second item by deducting a theoretical reinvestment rate from earnings, which is what the second actuarial PE formula attempts to do, but this is a very approximate adjustment that is bound to produce unpredictable results. Second, accounting is based on the accrual principle. Accruals refer to various accounting adjustments supposed to take timing into consideration. Some flows are recognised without an effective cash transaction taking place, such as when a revenue is earned but not necessarily collected. Similarly, costs are recognised when they are consumed, not necessarily when they are paid for. This creates a mismatch between what the accounts measure and the 'cash reality' of the company. In extreme cases it brings about misleading accounting practices, especially with respect to revenue recognition. In the aftermath of the technology bubble and its accounting scandals a number of painful restatements of the booking of multi-year contracts took place, especially in IT services, where such contracts are commonplace. Accounting standards produce flows which are a mixture of cash and accruals, and therefore not faithful to economic reality.

The market offers *daily* examples of the hiatus between accounting information and economic reality, both measured with a PE ratio. Table 2.2 provides an illustration taken from the 1997–1999 period (again, avoiding the bubble and post-bubble years, where it is *very* easy to find misleading accounting signals). Note how it affects all types of sectors and regions.

Empirical evidence of the Equivalence as an investment tool

We have by now completed our two prerequisites; expressed the PE ratio as the asset multiple and relative return Equivalence and derived the concept of residual income from it, as well as explained why it was necessary to implement this construction with economic (not accounting) data. We have not hidden the fact that, as such, the model remains fairly simple, especially with respect to the measure of growth expectations. Because it is a perpetual model an EP model cannot explicitly model future flows, and the model is 'at equilibrium'. Yet the information provided is still very valuable. Since very few assets (companies) are unable to grow at all, investors can use the relative return as a proxy for the minimum asset multiple on which the

Table 2.2 The hiatus between accounting information and economic reality

Company	Country	Sector	1997 Accounting PE	Economic PE	Share performance 1997–98	1997–99
Expensive on accounting PE, cheap on economic PE						
Business Objects	US	Technology	52.7×	17.6×	47%	382%
Sanofi	France	Pharmaceuticals	25.7×	17.1×	35%	86%
Deutsche Telecom	Germany	Tel. Services	30.0×	17.1×	24%	127%
KAO	Japan	Cons. Goods	36.4×	23.0×	33%	82%
Estée Lauder	US	Cons. Goods	27.7×	20.5×	40%	69%
Cheap on accounting PE, expensive on economic PE						
Alcan	US	Metal & Mining	16.8×	29.3×	−18%	9%
Citic Pacific	Hong Kong	Industrials	18.5×	64.0×	−53%	−49%
Am. El. Power	US	Utilities	13.3×	31.6×	9%	−12%
Tel. Malaysia	Malaysia	Tel. Services	17.9×	31.6×	−22%	1%
OMV	Austria	Energy	14.1×	49.6×	−6%	−21%

company should trade, at constant return. In other words, if a company returns twice as much as the cost of capital, an asset multiple of two times will imply that the company does not expand in real terms – usually too pessimistic an assumption and a good entry point for investors.

Alternatively, if the asset multiple were to drop below the relative return, this would signal that the market is removing the constant return assumption and is now expecting the future return on asset to fall below the current one. This could also be an attractive case of undervaluation, or the leading indicator of a change in the fortunes of the company's return. Either way, this would warrant an immediate investigation, especially as a shareholder.

In every day's markets the relative return exerts a powerful attractive force on the asset multiple, and we are about to see that there are many instances of this mean-reversion to the Equivalence in all markets. In the following figures, the area represents the high and low range of the yearly average asset multiple (usually between 1989 and 2005) whilst the line is the relative return, or cash return divided by the cost of capital.

The first example of mean-reversion to the Equivalence is given by Microsoft. In Figure 2.1 the Internet bubble of 1998–2002 is particularly obvious, as is the mean-reversion, which saw the share price of Microsoft shares going from approximately $60 to approximately $30. Strikingly, since 1989 the relative return has always been the bedrock of the asset multiple which, in general, has never dropped below it. This is not really surprising, since few investors would be ready to price Microsoft with no growth, or with an expected abrupt fall in return.

In the UK, the retailer Sainsbury offers another illustration of the power of the Equivalence. Figure 2.2 shows how the relative return represents, in most years, the lower boundary of the asset multiple range. In addition, the decline in the relative return (due to a steep fade in the return on assets which, it seems, retailers in the UK have routinely faced one after another) precipitates a decline in the asset multiple, at the same rate.

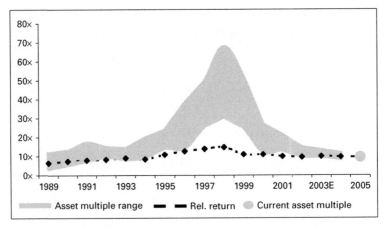

Figure 2.1 Microsoft: mean-reversion to the Equivalence.

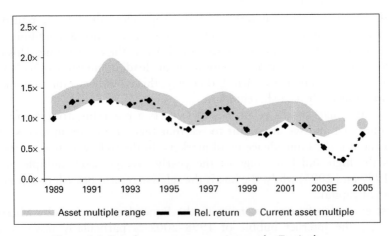

Figure 2.2 Sainsbury: mean-reversion to the Equivalence.

In Japan, Murata, the semiconductor equipment manufacturer, is another clear illustration (see Figure 2.3). Again, the spike in asset multiple represents the inflated valuations of the technology bubble of the late 1990s.

This relationship is verified at the sector level as well. Figure 2.4 shows the asset multiple and relative return for the global Consumer Staples sector, where such names as Wal-Mart, Nestlé and L'Oréal are aggregated. The magnetic force of the relative return is here to be seen, but it can be noted that, during certain periods, the asset multiple does not mean-revert fully. There is of course no need for it to do so, since a full equivalence between the two ratios implies no growth in capital invested and a constant cash return. As it happens, Consumer Staples grows on average by slightly more than 3 per cent real *per annum*, which could even justify a constant premium to the relative return.

Being able to extract such recurrent patterns is extremely valuable for investors. Consider, for instance, Figure 2.5, which shows the aggregated asset multiple and

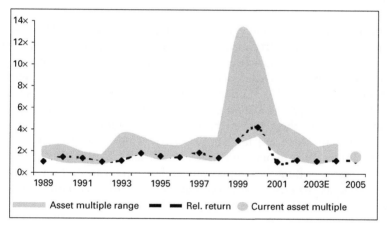

Figure 2.3 Murata: mean-reversion to the Equivalence.

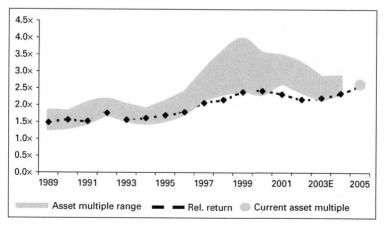

Figure 2.4 Global Consumer Staples: mean-reversion to the Equivalence.

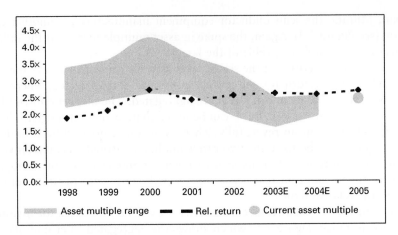

Figure 2.5 Europe and Japan Pharmaceutical and Biotechnology sector: mean-reversion to the Equivalence.

relative return of the Pharmaceutical sector in Japan and Europe. There is here a very strong message coming from investors who, by letting the asset multiple fall below the relative return, implicitly expect a drop in returns for this sector. This is in contradiction to the immediate past, which has seen stable relative returns for this sector since the year 2000. These configurations are very rare, and usually very lucrative for investors, provided that they can figure out if the market price has a predictive power over the relative return, or is just irrationally mispricing these assets. Unfortunately, there are few straws in the wind to help work out which of the two it can be, but the nature of the sector itself can also provide a hint. A stable, mature sector will tend to enjoy stable relative returns, and investors might be entitled in this case to view such a configuration (i.e. an asset multiple below the relative return) as an attractive buying opportunity.

Cost of capital and expected return

The Equivalence is made of two endogenous variables, net assets and return, and two exogenous ones, market value and cost of capital. The last deserves further study because, unlike the market value, it is not directly observable. From the Equivalence,

$$\frac{E}{NA} = \frac{R}{d} = n,$$

it is easy to observe the special case of $R = d$. In this case, $E = NA$. This corresponds to our original Company A, which returns exactly the cost of capital. Its RI is zero, and therefore the market value is simply the value of the net assets. No real economic value is created by this company, since what it returns goes straight to pay for the capital that it is using. Note that this situation does not imply, as often seen even in the most distinguished papers, 'zero growth'. In the case of a residual income model, it means that growth does not generate value, or economic profits, and can therefore be ignored. In this special case, the *growth rate does not affect the multiple* at which the assets are valued, which is always 1. However, if assets *are* growing and the marginal return on investment is exactly at the cost of capital, the market value of the enterprise will still go up by the amount of asset growth, in order to keep the asset multiple (i.e. E/NA) at 1.

With this in mind, it is possible to determine empirically a market-implied discount rate by analysing, by regression analysis, the relationship between the asset multiple and the return for a given universe of companies, as illustrated in Figure 2.6.

Here, we have randomly generated 100 returns and 100 asset multiples, paired them, and thus created 100 fictitious companies. Because returns are normally distributed, the result is a very realistic picture of any market at any period of time. For this universe, the average relationship between *any* level of asset multiple and return is described by the equation of the line, $y = 3.85x + 0.6758$ ('the PE line'). Solving the equation for $y = 1$ – in other words, when the asset multiple is 1 – gives a corresponding return of 8.4 per cent, which is the market cost of capital for this universe of stocks.

Although empiricism is probably the best form of research as far as financial markets are concerned – as Nassim Taleb argues in *Fooled by Randomness* (Taleb, 2004), there is too much randomness to pretend to anything more theoretical – it is also possible to calculate formally a cost of capital from the RI formula, the detail of which is shown in the appendix to this chapter. In essence, the cost of capital is given by the inverse of the PE ratio. This approach is usually judged quite severely by the academic world. Cleveland Patterson, in *The Cost of Capital* (Patterson, 1995), demonstrates that, for the cost of equity, a PE-based formula only works if the marginal return equals the cost of capital. Not to mention the fact that the price of the asset must be right in the first place. We also tend to be sceptical of this measure of the cost of capital, and don't use this method to calculate the discount rate for the CROCI Equivalence (see Chapter 4). However, this does not disprove the mean-reversion of returns on assets (CROCI) to the cost of capital, a well observed phenomenon. Stigler (1963) gives a good account by noting that 'under competition, the rate of return on investment tends towards equality in all industries'. So the marginal return *will* tend to the cost of capital, *but only on*

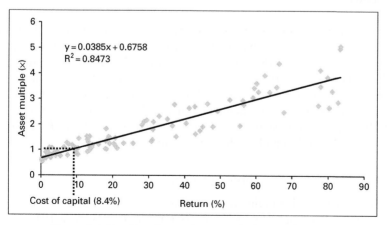

Figure 2.6 Reading the market – implied cost of capital.

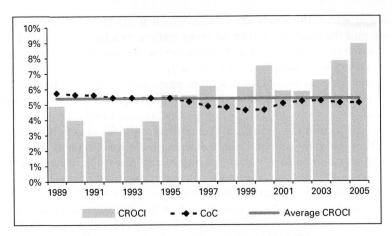

Figure 2.7 Yearly world CROCI, 1989–2005.

average. In Figure 2.7 we show the yearly CROCI for the world between 1989 and 2005, together with its average, which comes out at 5.5 per cent. The cost of capital for the market observably mean-reverts around this number. Furthermore, 5.5 per cent is bang in line with the long-term measure of the real return of the equity asset class, which most commentators put somewhere between 5.5 per cent and 6 per cent for developed markets. Thus, there is indeed a strong convergence between the *average* marginal return, the cost of capital and the long-term return of equities. But the spot CROCI was 3 per cent in 1991, and three times this level fourteen years later. This volatility, which comes from the unwinding of the business cycle, makes the calculation of the cost of capital as the inverse of the PE ratio a very hazardous venture.

Is it for real?

Rate of capitalisation, cost of capital, discount rate, expected return . . . This nomenclature is referring to one and the same thing, namely the minimum rate at which capital can be obtained from the point of view of the debtor, or the minimum return acceptable to lend capital, from the point of view of the creditor. There remains one unavoidable question: *is this rate real or nominal?* Inflation is, beyond doubt, *the* most crucial affair in investment analysis, and the most insidious, too. Rex Mottram, the unpleasant husband of Julia in Evelyn Waugh's *Brideshead Revisited*, knew as much, when talking about his parents-in-law:

> I thought they were enormously rich.

> Well, they are rich in the way people are who just let their money sit quiet. Everyone of that sort is poorer than they were in 1914, and the Flytes don't seem to realise it.

Unlike the bond yield, the 'earnings yield', as it is also sometimes called (the inverse of the PE ratio), is a real – that is, inflation-adjusted – yield. This warrants a small digression back to the Fed model, which we called 'abominable' in Chapter 1. The inflation-adjusted nature of the earnings yield explains why no credibility has ever been attached by academics to this model, which compares the earnings yield (real) to the bond yield (nominal) in an attempt to determine whether equities are overvalued or not. Confusing real and nominal returns is as close as can be to a cardinal sin for an investor, therefore the criticisms of academia and professional investors (see, for instance, Asness, 2003) may be justified. And this irrespective of the fact that the Fed model appears to be working during certain periods, which is not unreminiscent of some typical behavioural patterns already discussed.

There are various ways to explain the real (inflation-adjusted) characteristic of the earnings yield. Unlike bondholders, shareholders possess a claim on the earnings via the dividend and have ownership of the underlying assets, whose replacement value will rise and fall with the level of inflation. Furthermore, the feed-through effect of inflation in the profit and loss account has to be taken into account. Faced with rising input prices, companies will initially accept a certain amount of margin compression, but will eventually pass on this cost inflation to their customers, and all the way to the bottom line. Indeed, our research suggests that there is a 93 per cent pass-through of CPI inflation to earnings growth in the long run, as Figure 2.8 illustrates for the US, such that the yield, or the ratio of income to assets at market value, is constant, since all variables are impacted similarly by inflation. For that very reason, a change in inflation expectations does not modify the PE ratio (at constant risk premium), but only nominal earnings growth expectations.

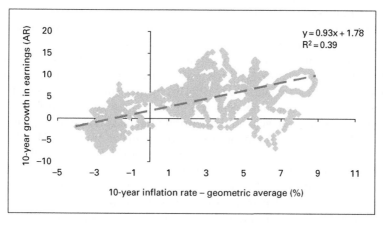

Figure 2.8 Inflation and nominal earnings growth.

Discounted cash-flow models and PE ratios – financial and investment analysis

Investors seem to face a clear choice between two evils: either they use the PE ratio in its actuarial guise, and the results will be 'quick, simple and clumsy', or they use it for its economic construction, with an analysis of residual income and equivalence between asset multiple and relative return – but in this case they cannot rely on accounting data and need to reconstruct economic data. There is a third option; the traditional discounted cash-flow model, or DCF, viewed by all professionals as the best technical instrument for valuing assets. This provides the benefit of allowing analysts to model future cash flows *explicitly*, and therefore non-constant future growth – a sophistication that is not possible with a perpetuity model. John Burr Williams, the father of the Discounted Dividend Model, had already identified in the 1930s the need to modify the rate of growth of a company's dividends through time as the business matures (Burr Williams, 1938):

> For a while ... a company grows at a constant rate, and div-
> idends increase accordingly to a compound interest law; the
> period when this happens may be called the growing period ...
> Later the rate of growth slows down, and dividends continue to
> increase, but at an ever slower rate; this second period may be
> called the maturing period.

However, investors should not overstate the power of such models for stock selection purposes. Like many tools used in equity markets, the discounted cash-flow method finds its origin in corporate finance, where it is used largely to determine an appropriate level of debt and equity funding, in the case of a flotation or a leveraged buy-out. Valuation is often an incidental issue. Furthermore, in a corporate finance department, bankers have access to confidential and private information from companies to build such models, often broken down division by division. An investment analyst at a brokers firm is not privy to such information, and will have to make general assumptions 'from the outside'. Outside views of flows are based on very general long-term assumptions with a low probability of actual realisation. Selecting stocks on the basis of such random assumptions (e.g. 'margins peak in 2016') would yield no better results than the toss of a coin.

One of the most competent and best-known advocates and defenders of DCF models, Tom Copeland, himself a McKinsey consultant, does not really aim his classic book *Valuation* (Copeland *et al.*, 1994) at investment professionals either. He does list 'investors, portfolio managers and security analysts' among his audience, but only after 'business managers' and 'corporate finance practitioners'. This is not to say that a DCF model cannot be useful for financial analysis. The discipline of a DCF approach forces the investment analyst to think through the issues of margins, growth, funding, etc. on a long-term basis. It is therefore an essential part of his investigation, which includes strategic positioning, profitability drivers, management vision, etc. But it is not one that is particularly helpful for selecting one stock over another. Furthermore, building a DCF is a subjective exercise, not standardised and quite complex to implement.

Fortunately, discounted cash-flow models are not the only ones with a good approximation of the fair value of an asset. Our favourite residual income model does just as good a job. In fact, this model has a number of advantages over DCF models. Free cash flow is a difficult and volatile measure. A company in the middle of an investment programme will have little or no free cash flow, but may invest for future riches. A residual income model does not suffer the same volatility of results, because it is based on an assessment of economic assets plus or minus value creation, which makes it a better tool to assess the company's prospects in any single year. Furthermore, because the model is derived from the great economic construction underpinning the PE ratio, a stock selection process based on residual income can be expressed in terms of 'economic PE ratios' (a PE ratio built with economic, not accounting data), which are extremely easy to use – unlike DCFs.

Ultimately, there is only one way of describing the value of an asset, famously 'the net present value of expected future free cash flows discounted to perpetuity'. Consequently, the free cash flow and economic profit approaches have to be, and indeed are, mathematically totally equivalent. Tom Copeland offers an elegant demonstration of this equivalence in Appendix A of *Valuation* (Copeland *et al.*, 1994). However, actuarial and economic versions do not form the same picture of the reality. When cloud-watching, everybody looks at the same clouds. Some see lions, others lambs and others dragons. Investment analysis is slightly less poetic. Money is at stake, and you'd better not mistake a dog for an eagle, or some other high flier. Therefore, the way in which you form your economic picture is important, and needs to be relevant to stock selection. Once the difficulty of creating good economic data is overcome, an economic profit model is a very efficient stock selection tool, equivalent in accuracy to a DCF model, and in fact superior because far easier in implementation. Regrettably, aware of it or not, almost all investors use the PE ratio in the conventional 'actuarial' way, and few for the benefits of its economic construction.

The one-man band

Despite its apparent simplicity, the foundations of the PE ratio are very solid, a remarkable economic construction indeed. It is the one-man band of the old village circuses, who used to entertain local crowds by playing numerous instruments at the same time, managing to get a recognisable melody out of it all. One minute cost of capital, the next minute expected real return on equity investment, then an abbreviated version of the equivalence between asset multiple and relative return ... We find in this toolbox all we need to value companies. However, polluted by accounting data, this does not produce the required analytical insight. At the very least, the existence of the post-market-bubble accounting scandals *à la* Enron should always make any accounting-based investment process look suspicious, if not downright unreliable, due to the inescapable limitations of accounting information. Unfortunately, in the economic version these shortcomings are made more conspicuous because of the need to calculate the replacement value of economic capital explicitly, as well as the real (inflation-adjusted) cash return on these assets. And analysts who wish to use these models must therefore at first reconstruct economic data.

Provided that it is fed with economic data, investors will need very little more than an EP model to create a comprehensive valuation platform from which systematic stock selection can be implemented. But a daunting task awaits them. The four variables of the Equivalence – namely the Economic Enterprise Value providing the market value of assets; the Net Capital Invested (NCI), or the invested value of economic capital; the CROCI (Cash Return on Capital Invested), or the real return on asset; and the market-implied cost of capital – have to be defined precisely. To do so, we have retained the logic of the Equivalence in the next two chapters. Thus, Chapter 3 will deal with the economic asset multiple, and Chapter 4 with the economic relative return.

References

Asness, C. S. (2003). Fighting the Fed model. *The Journal of Portfolio Management*, **Autumn**.

Burr Williams, J. (1938). *The Theory of Investment Value*. Harvard University Press.

Copeland, T., Koller, T. and Murrin, J. (1994). *Valuation: Measuring and Managing the Value of Companies*. John Wiley & Sons Inc.

Damodaran, A. (2004). *Investment Fables: Exposing the Myths of 'Can't Miss' Investment Strategies*. Financial Times Prentice Hall.

Patterson, C. S. (1995). *The Cost of Capital: Theory and Estimation*. Quorum Books.

Stewart, G. B. (1991). *The Quest for Value*. Harper Collins.

Stigler, G. J. (1963). *Capital and Rates of Return in Manufacturing Industries*. Prentice University Press.

Taleb, N. N. (2004). *Fooled By Randomness: The Hidden Role of Chance in Life and in the Markets*. Texere.

Appendix: The multiple guises of the PE ratio

The Gordon growth model

This model defines the value of equity per share as

$$\frac{D}{CoE - g}$$

where D is the expected dividend per share, CoE is the cost of equity and g the expected perpetual growth rate of the dividend. To turn the notation above into a PE ratio simply requires dividing it by earnings per share (EPS), such that

$$\frac{P}{EPS} = \frac{D}{CoE - g} \times \frac{1}{EPS},$$

simplified as

$$\frac{P}{e} = \frac{D/e}{CoE - g}$$

where P is the share price and e the earnings per share, and other notations as previously stated.

The perpetual discounting of FCF

In a slightly more complex format, the logic of the PE can be put to work to produce an approximation of the perpetual discounting of free cash flow (FCF), or FCF/(d − g), with d the relevant discount rate and g the perpetual growth rate.

However, there are a number of qualifications to apply to this transformation. First, it leads to a PE ratio where 'price' is the value of the entire enterprise, not just the market capitalisation, or price of the equity. Consequently, 'earnings' have to be understood pre-financing costs, as some sort of operating earnings after tax, or EBI (Earnings Before Interest), which some authors call NOPAT (Net Operating Profit After Tax) or NOPLAT (Net Operating Profit Less Adjusted Taxes). The 'adjusted' refers here to the tax-deductibility of financial charges; in an enterprise value model, the value of the company is assessed as if the company were debt-free, which means, by implication, that there are no financial charges, and therefore no tax advantage. Second, there is no straightforward bridge between FCF and earnings, and the rewriting of FCF discounted to perpetuity into a PE ratio remains the result of a number of simplifications. The first simplification is to define FCF as operating earnings minus net new capital invested. This definition assumes that the replacement cost of existing capital is equal to the depreciation charge, which is not the case. The second simplification is to assume that the return on existing capital employed is constant. But if these simplifications are acceptable, then the transformation of FCF discounted to infinity into a PE ratio is a fairly straightforward business.

Let FCF be EBI − Inv, with Inv being the net amount of additional capital (investment) this year.

Since return on asset is constant,

$$\Delta EBI = r \times Inv_{t-1}$$

where r is the return on new capital invested. The growth rate g of EBI is obtained by dividing both sides by EBI_{t-1}:

$$g = \frac{\Delta EBI}{EBI_{t-1}} = \frac{r \times Inv_{t-1}}{EBI_{t-1}},$$

simplified as

$$g = r \times \frac{Inv}{EBI}$$

and re-written as

$$Inv = EBI \times \frac{g}{r}.$$

This notation is particularly useful, because it expresses new investment as the amount necessary to grow earnings at g, given a return r. All that is left to do is to insert this formula into our original simplified definition of FCF (EBI − Inv), to arrive at

$$FCF = EBI \times \left(1 - \frac{g}{r}\right).$$

The value of the enterprise is now defined as

$$\frac{EBI \times (1 - g/r)}{d - g}.$$

Thus, by multiplying by 1/EBI, or 1/e in the traditional notation, the PE ratio can be expressed as:

$$\frac{P}{e} = \frac{1 - g/r}{d - g}$$

where P is the value of the enterprise per share, and e earnings pre-interest per share. Note that this formula only works when g < r.

PE ratio, economic profits and perpetual FCF

In the coming paragraphs, we will use the following notation: E, economic market value of the firm; NA, net assets; d, appropriate discount rate; R, return on asset; EP, economic profits; FCF, free cash flow.

The residual income formula, or

$$E = NA + \frac{EP}{d} \qquad (1)$$

can easily be re-written and expressed as a PE ratio, as follows:

$$E = NA + \frac{(R - d) \times NA}{d} \qquad (2)$$

$$\frac{E}{NA} = 1 + \frac{(R - d)}{d} \qquad (3)$$

$$\frac{E}{NA} \times \frac{1}{R} = \left[1 + \frac{(R - d)}{d}\right] \times \frac{1}{R} \qquad (4)$$

$$\frac{E}{NA} \times \frac{1}{R} = \frac{R}{d} \times \frac{1}{R} = \frac{1}{d}. \qquad (5)$$

The PE ratio is clearly recognised in $\frac{E}{NA} \times \frac{1}{R}$, or asset multiple divided by return. Furthermore, if residual income can be expressed as an enterprise value-based PE ratio, then it should similarly be equivalent to the perpetual discount of free cash flow (FCF), or:

$$E = \frac{FCF}{d}.$$

This equivalence is demonstrated as follows, from equation (2):

$$E = NA + \frac{\left(\frac{FCF}{NA} - d\right) \times NA}{d} \qquad (3.1)$$

$$E = NA + \frac{FCF}{d} - NA \qquad (4.1)$$

$$E = \frac{FCF}{d}. \qquad (5.1)$$

The substitution of return on assets by the ratio of FCF to net assets in equation (3.1) will be fully discussed in Chapter 4.

Residual income formula and Equivalence principle

If a company returns n times the cost of capital (d) at equilibrium (i.e. $R = n \times d$), then its expected residual income should be:

$$EP = (nd - d) \times NA \qquad (6)$$

$$\frac{EP}{d} = \frac{(n - 1) \times d \times NA}{d} \qquad (7)$$

$$\frac{EP}{d} = (n - 1) \times NA. \qquad (8)$$

Combining equation (8) with equation (1), then:

$$E = NA + (n-1) \times NA \qquad (9)$$

$$E = n \times NA \qquad (10)$$

$$\therefore n = \frac{NA}{E}.$$

But

$$n = \frac{R}{d}$$

$$\therefore \frac{E}{NA} = \frac{R}{d} = n. \qquad (11)$$

This last formula is the Equivalence principle, which states that an asset multiple can also be expressed as a relative return (assuming steady state, i.e. no expansion).

EP formula and the cost of capital

The EP formula can also be used to show that the PE ratio is the inverse of the expected return on equity assets, or 'cost of capital'. The PE ratio is easily recognisable in equation (14) as the ratio of an asset multiple (E/NA) and a return (R).

$$E = NA \times \left(1 + \frac{R-d}{d}\right) \qquad (12)$$

$$\frac{E}{NA} = 1 + \frac{R-d}{d} \qquad (13)$$

$$\frac{E/NA}{R} = \left(1 + \frac{R-d}{d}\right) \times \frac{1}{R} \qquad (14)$$

$$\frac{P}{E} = \frac{R}{d} + \frac{1}{R} \qquad (15)$$

$$\frac{P}{E} = \frac{1}{d}. \qquad (16)$$

However, the assumptions are onerous; no growth and constant returns. It is naturally possible to give up some of these simplifying assumptions, and include a growth factor, g. As always, the growth rate is at equilibrium, which means that $d > g$. The starting point is similar to equation (1), but we replace the discount rate d by $(d-g)$,

$$E = NA \times \left(1 + \frac{R-d}{d-g}\right) \qquad (12.1)$$

$$\frac{E}{NA} = 1 + \frac{R-d}{d-g} \qquad (13.1)$$

$$\frac{E/NA}{R} = \frac{1 + \dfrac{R - d}{d - g}}{R} \tag{14.1}$$

$$PE = \frac{1}{R} + \frac{R - d}{R \times (d - g)} \tag{15.1}$$

$$PE = \frac{R - g}{R \times (d - g)} \tag{16.1}$$

$$d = \frac{(R - g) \times \dfrac{E}{P} + Rg}{R}. \tag{17.1}$$

It is unfortunately not possible to simplify equation (17.1) further, a good deal less practical than when growth is ignored, where 'd' is simply the inverse of the PE. The benefit of this derivation is to test again the special case of $R = d$. From equation (16.1), where $R = d$,

$$PE = \frac{d - g}{d \times (d - g)} \tag{16.2}$$

which, simplified by $(d - g)$, gives $PE = 1/d$.

In the latter case, we fall back to our starting point, the situation where growth does not generate any economic profit (since $R = d$, $EP = 0$), and therefore becomes irrelevant to the multiple, itself the inverse of the cost of capital.

PART • II

Digging the Foundations: Reconstruction of Economic Data

3 Measuring the value of economic assets: the asset multiple

Tidying up a few loose ends

For the sake of simplicity, we have been so far using a number of loose definitions. First, we assumed that all companies were debt-free, such that there was only an occasional distinction between equity and enterprise value. We have been using accounting concepts, despite warning of their uselessness, such as 'book value' and 'net assets', and called the ratio of income to a 'stock of invested capital' (asset) 'return on equity', 'return on assets' or, sporadically, 'CROCI'. The message was unaffected by these simplifications: *an asset multiple, the ratio of the price of an asset to its invested value, divided by a measure of return on asset is called a PE. The PE ratio can be used in a number of ways to calculate the real expected return on equities, the cost of capital, residual income, and derives from a fundamental equivalence between asset multiple and relative return, which is, empirically as well as theoretically, the backbone of mean-reversion in equity markets.*

But, in order for the PE ratio to produce this multitude of applications, we have already made it clear that investors cannot use just *any* asset multiple or *any* return. Although they would still get a PE ratio, that PE ratio would not 'work'. Figure 3.1 provides an example of such a ratio. Here, we show the relationship between price-to-book and return on equity, thereby producing an accounting PE ratio, for a global universe of stocks.

The R-squared of the regression analysis between the two variables is 0.38. This is equivalent to saying that these two variables are dependent on one another at a lower level than the flick of a coin. This does not mean that price-to-book and return on equity are randomly associated; there is, clearly, an upward-sloping relationship between these two variables. The higher the return, the more investors are generally required to pay, in line with the findings of Chapter 2. It is the *significance* of this correlation that is not very strong, as shown by an R-squared of far less than 0.50.[1] In less technical terms, this means that an accounting PE ratio has no particular predictive power, thus does not offer a useful valuation platform – in a word, it is not an effective model. It simply reflects a loose relationship and may or may not help an investor to select stocks.

Conversely, Figure 3.2 is an example of a PE ratio that 'works'. Here, we compare an economic asset multiple to a cash return. The explanatory power is more than 0.80, meaning that a change in one of the variables is likely to explain 80 per cent of a change in the other one. This PE ratio (for it *is* also a PE ratio, given that we regress an asset multiple to a return) is an economic model on which investors can rely to pick stocks consistently. Investors need to know which PE, i.e. which asset multiple and return, to trust. And the rule is simple enough: the

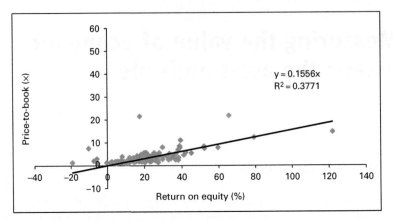

Figure 3.1 Price-to-book vs ROE.

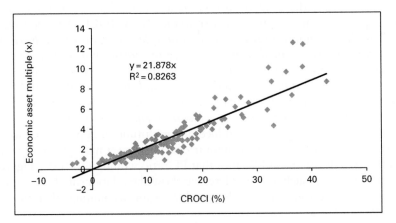

Figure 3.2 Economic asset multiple vs CROCI.

closer they get to using economic data, the more reliable their PE ratio, or their equivalence between asset multiple and relative return, will be. The purpose of this chapter is to detail the adjustments to reported accounts that will get them close enough to an economic asset multiple, the first of the two terms of the Equivalence.

The debt problem: left and right, Cain and Abel, Miller and Modigliani

Let us start with the numerator of the asset multiple, the market value of the company. On the left of the balance sheet is the invested value, in historical costs, of the assets that the company is using (in a simplified form, fixed assets and net working capital). On the right is the way in which these assets are financed (again, to simplify, shareholders' funds and debt). It is clearly the latter item that needs to be used to get to the market value of the asset side of the balance sheet, since most financial liabilities are tradable and have ... a market value. As far as the financing of assets through debt is concerned, accountants, for once, cannot be accused of making life difficult for professional financial analysts. The latter only have themselves to blame for the confusion that is sometimes entertained between the asset and the liability side of the balance sheet.

It is worth taking a detour to illustrate how a conventional accounting-based financial ratio, the return on equity (RoE), perpetuates this confusion. Recall that RoE is at the core of the accounting PE ratio, when defined as price-to-book divided by RoE. It is also often considered a standard way to measure the operating return of a business. Not only does it give the crudest idea of it, but in addition it does so at the cost of considerable confusion regarding how market value should be comprehended. Consider the following story. At the death of their father, Cain and Abel were each given exactly half of the family factory. Because Cain was the older and already in charge of a large family, their late father had specifically required that no debt should be attached to his share of the business. Abel's part, on the other hand, carried a large financial burden. Here is the profit & loss account and balance sheet of each business. See how there is no interest charge in the first case (and no interest income, since the company does not have any cash either), but a pretty hefty charge of 15.75 in the second case – the result of 150 times 10.5 per cent, the cost of bank debt for Abel's company.

Cain's Accounts

Assets			Liabilities	Sales	100
Gross assets	210	200	equity	EBDIT	35.0
Accumulated dep	105			Dep.	15.0
Net assets	105			EBIT	20.0
				Interest	0.0
NWC	95			Pre-tax	20.0
				Tax	7.0
				Profit	13.0
Total assets	200	200	Total liabilities	Cash flow	21.5

Abel's Accounts

Assets			Liabilities	Sales	100
Gross assets	210	50	equity	EBDIT	35.0
Accumulated dep	105	150	Debt	Dep.	15.0
Net assets	105			EBIT	20.0
				Interest	−15.75
NWC	95			Pre-tax	4.25
				Tax	1.5
				Profit	2.8
Total assets	200	200	Total liabilities	Cash flow	16.4

The two brothers thought that this was a fair inheritance. Cain's company had a RoE of 6.5 per cent, or 13 divided by 200, and Abel's company had a RoE of 6.7 per cent, or 2.8 divided by 50.

Six months into this new arrangement, the Central Bank having cut the level of interest rates aggressively, Abel's cost of debt has fallen from 10.5 per cent to 7 per cent. His prospective P&L looks like this:

Sales	100.0
EBDIT	35.0
Dep.	15.0
EBIT	20.0
Interest	−10.5
Pre-tax	9.5
Tax	3.3
Profit	6.2
Cash flow	18.1

Abel then runs to his brother and says:

> Brother, thanks to my hard work, I have managed to raise the RoE of my part of the business to double what it was when I inherited it. Look, the RoE is now 13.2 per cent (6.2 divided by 50), against 6.7 per cent six months ago. I believe that yours is unchanged ... I want to get out of the business to travel the world, and, since you are my brother, I am ready to sell it to you at the same value as yours, despite a much superior RoE ...

Cain embraces his brother, rejoicing at the idea of getting such a good arrangement ...

This story can be played out in all manner of ways, but here is the serious point: who is the fool? Abel, who has discovered that lower interest rates will raise the RoE of a financially geared company, and is expecting to take advantage of this? Or Cain, who thinks that he is making a good deal? In reality, both are fools, because they are attempting to value an asset based on return on equity. This ratio simply measures the profit of the firm relative to 'the part of the assets that are not financed by debt'. RoE is therefore largely a function of interest rates and financial gearing (the right-hand side of the balance sheet). In no case should this be the basis for the value of the left-hand side.

Here is a simple enough rule: if investors want to know about a company's assets for the purpose of financial analysis, they should look at the return on *assets* *(RoA)* – which means *all* assets. In the case of Cain's company, RoA is 13 divided by 200, which is 6.5 per cent. Abel's case is a bit more complicated. The asset base is, of course, 200 as well. Profits are 6.2 (with a cost of debt of 7 per cent), thus giving an apparent return of 3.1 per cent. But, in order to avoid falling into the same trap as before, we have to ignore the way in which these assets are financed – i.e. the right-hand side of the balance sheet. It could be 100 per cent equity, in which case the remuneration of capital would be a dividend clipped out of net profits, or it could be 100 per cent debt (if the bankers allowed it), in which case there would be an enormous financial charge (and a very small, or non-existent, tax charge, since interest charges are tax deductible). The assets would still be worth the same. So, the cost of the debt to net profit has to be neutralised by adding back the financial charge to it. Moreover, bearing in mind that a financially geared company will see its tax bill reduced, as mentioned above, simply adding the financial charge to net profits will inflate the latter by the amount of tax saved. It is therefore necessary to deduct the tax shield (interest charge times the marginal tax rate). For Abel's company, assuming a marginal tax rate of 35 per cent, the correct RoA is calculated as

$$[6.2 + 10.5 - (10.5 \times 35\%)]/200.$$

It will probably come as no surprise that the result is 6.5 per cent – the very same RoA as that of Cain's company – hardly a shocking conclusion, since both enterprises have exactly the same assets and the same operating P&L (i.e. before interest charges).

Clouded thinking over equity and debt, assets and liabilities, of which the heavy use of the RoE ratio is a prime example, is ubiquitous. It stems from the duality of the purpose of investment analysis in (1) determining the economic characteristics of an asset (return, growth) and its *invested* value, as well as (2) assessing its *market* value. These are related, but quite different, issues. Suppose that an investor wanted to buy a property for rental income. Surely he would wish to visit this property a few times, assess the surroundings, the amenities, the neighbours. He would make up his mind about a likely rent, the amount by which he could increase it every year, and then decide on the price that would make this investment worthwhile. Next would come haggling with the seller, and finally he would arrange financing. It would *never* occur to him to do it in any other way – especially not in the reverse of our suggested order. That is because the main objective of this property buyer is to assess the growth and return prospects of an economic object, which demands an investigation of the asset side of the balance sheet. To this end, there is no relevant information on the liability side.

On the other hand, suppose that our investor now wanted to investigate the *market value* of an economic object (of which the economic characteristics were either already known, or immaterial). The asset side is now not so useful. He will use the fact that assets equal liabilities in the balance sheet (that's always true) to derive that *market value* of assets must equal *market value* of liabilities. This relationship is very handy, because liabilities are not real but financial assets (for the *creditor*). They are therefore liquid, in most cases exchangeable, and – the key piece of information – have a readily available market price. But now the *book value* of these assets is of no interest *per se*.

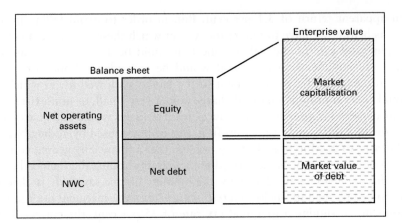

Figure 3.3 From accouting value to enterprise value.

Figure 3.3 is, of course, no more than a fairly simplistic description of the most famous Miller and Modigliani's (fondly abbreviated M&M by students in finance) axiom of 1958, which states that if the capital structure decision has no effect on the cash flows generated by a firm, the decision will also have no effect – in the absence of transaction costs – on the total value of the firm's debt and equity. The total market value of the firm is its enterprise (or entity) value, which is the same as the sum of the market values of the items on the right-hand side of the balance sheet, i.e. the combined debt and equity. This enterprise value is therefore independent of how the firm is financed. Quite why so many professional analysts insist on confusing the issue by trying to get to the value of the left by analysing parts of the right remains unexplained. In any case, to weed out any possible confusion, the original accounting PE ratio will need to suffer here its first major makeover. The relationship between the market capitalisation and the book value on the one hand, and the return on equity on the other hand, needs to be transformed into a new one. A new PE ratio, resulting from the relationship between the enterprise value and net assets on the one hand, and return on assets on the other hand, can take on this mantle.

The M&M proposition is a staple in corporate finance and research departments, and it would not occur to anybody to dispute it. But what about its *actual* implementation for stock selection purposes? If investors are going to approximate the market value of assets with the market value of liabilities, they had better have a clear idea of the definition of a liability. Financial debt, which is what is added to the market capitalisation to make up an enterprise value in 95 per cent of the cases, is easy enough to identify. But what about post-retirement benefits? Or nuclear decommissioning provisions? The stakes are high enough; missing some important liabilities will heighten the risk of underestimating the market price of the corresponding asset, which will appear cheaper than it deserves to an investor. Inevitably, this brings about another issue; assuming that all liabilities can be identified to give the full market value of the enterprise, is it still appropriate to compare it with the same old book value of net assets?

Liable: legally bound, under an obligation – beware of hidden liabilities

Consider another story, which illustrates the concept of hidden liabilities. It is the story of a young professional who has just found the flat of his dreams – prime location, close to all amenities, *piano nobile*, south-facing, original wood flooring, and what seems to be an undemanding old person living in there. As for the price, it is a good 20 per cent cheaper than comparable properties. The young professional does not think twice and is ready to move in within four weeks, the removal truck double-parked early on that Saturday morning to avoid creating too much congestion in the leafy avenue. What this hasty young man does not realise is the type of contract that he has signed, and he will therefore be very surprised to see the old gentleman opening the door as he is trying to get in 'his' flat with his newly packed boxes of books at his feet. In certain countries, property owners can sell their asset forward, by agreeing a lower than market price against the right to remain in the property until they die, plus a small amount of income. Lured by the apparent cheapness of the market price, investors usually underestimate the real cost of acquiring these assets, because they do not correctly assess the hidden liabilities attached to their property.

Hidden liabilities are only hidden for the careless, and are certainly evident for the counterparty: one person's liability is always another's asset. In the mind of the buyer above, his balance sheet looked identical to the one below (note that we assume that his flat is purchased on a debt-free basis, but the introduction of debt would not change a thing):

Assets		Liabilities	
Flat	1000	1000	Equity

In reality, there were two liabilities attached to this asset. The first one was the cost of hiring a similar flat for the new owner, during the remaining life of the original owner. Assuming that latter has a life expectancy of ten years, that residential property has a yield of 5 per cent and that inflation is 2 per cent, the liability will amount to 419, calculated in the following manner:

Years	1	2	3	4	5	6	7	8	9	10
Cost of renting	50	51.0	52.0	53.1	54.1	55.2	56.3	57.4	58.6	59.8
Net present value	47.6	46.3	44.9	43.7	42.4	41.2	40.0	38.9	37.8	36.7
Total liability	419									

Furthermore, the buyer was liable for a payment of, say, 15 during the same period. Assuming that this is a constant payment, the net liability would amount to 116, calculated in the following manner:

Years	1	2	3	4	5	6	7	8	9	10
Yearly allowance	15	15	15	15	15	15	15	15	15	15
Net present value	14.3	13.6	13.0	12.3	11.8	11.2	10.7	10.2	9.7	9.2
Total liability	116									

The balance sheet should have looked like this:

Assets		Liabilities	
Flat	1535	1000	Equity
		419	First liability
		116	Second liability
Total	1535	1535	Total

Beware of concluding too hastily that, since assets *must* equal liabilities, the true value of the flat is 1535, and that it is a happy day for the buyer who bought it for 1000. The value of the flat is indeed 1535 (hence the apparent bargain price at 1000, 'a good 20 per cent cheaper than comparable properties'), but this is the price that he will end up paying. The buyer has simply 'decided' to finance it with some equity, plus a commitment to pay certain future liabilities in the next ten years, for which he will incur some debt. Here is the balance sheet again, this time with headings closer to the reality of corporate balance sheets:

Assets		Liabilities	
Fixed assets	1535	1000	Equity
		419	Pension provisions
		116	Health-care benefits
Total	1535	1535	Total

As we have seen, since assets always equal liabilities, market value of assets must equal market value of liabilities. *All* liabilities. Declared, and hidden. So a share 'clearly' looking 20 per cent cheaper than its peers may not be such a bargain after all. The problem is that liabilities are a bit of a mess for the outside observer. Depending on the accounting standard and the tax system, investors can find, beyond shareholders' funds and retained earnings, restructuring provisions, unspecified 'other operating provisions', pension fund provisions, post-retirement benefits, nuclear decommissioning provisions, warranties, other long-term provisions, deferred tax liabilities, long-term debt, short-term debt, etc. In addition, some are off balance-sheet, such as leasing liabilities, or parts of on-balance sheet pension funds, not to mention the murky areas of vendor financing, securitisation of receivables etc. This obscure state of affairs stems from the fact that 'liabilities' is a generic term covering (1) money that needs to be reimbursed (bank debt, for instance) and (2) money that needs to be paid later (e.g. deferred tax liabilities). In short, a liability is any claim on future cash flow. Because the market is a discounting mechanism of cash flows, it rightly sees no distinction between the two categories above. *Hidden liabilities can do some serious damage to the capital of a careless investor*, and as such need to be systematically investigated. We can only provide an approximate guide, because generic solutions are rare in financial analysis, and stock-specific situations are bound to appear.

The quoted market value will apply, obviously, to all categories of shares, convertible debt and other quoted debt. In some cases, it is probably good practice to apply the price of quoted debt to unquoted debt – i.e. bank debt. This is a standard practice among investors concerned with credit risk, for instance those dealing with corporate bonds or Credit Default Swaps (CDS) (see, for example, Davydenko, 2005). These investors will apply the yield spread between high-yield and risk-free bonds to bank debt. Note that in the case of a distressed company, this will *reduce* its market value. Some due diligence will need to be carried out on the cash flow before concluding that this particular company is a bargain. Other liabilities have to be taken at book value, because they do not trade. These liabilities can be classified into four categories: finance, employees, operations and tax.

Financial liabilities

Other than bank and bond debt, financial liabilities concern off balance-sheet funding, mainly operating leases. The technique for capitalising leases is fairly straightforward. Companies have to disclose their lease commitments in the notes of the Annual Report (with varying levels of detail, unfortunately). The capital part of the lease commitment is then capitalised over the estimated life of the lease, at a discount rate which can either be standard (for instance the average credit yield) or company-specific. The net present value of this commitment is then added to other financial debt and to net assets. The yearly payment, now effectively a depreciation charge for this capital, needs to be added to the cash flow. In practice, only non-cancellable lease commitments of some size should be taken into consideration. Three sectors in particular are avid users of operating leases: hotels, air transport and retail. Coincidentally or not, companies in these sectors (especially the last two) have an annoying tendency to go bankrupt, which makes the adjustments on the debt side particularly important. It is possible to find retailers with capitalised lease commitments representing half of the enterprise value. There is nothing wrong *per se* with this, except that the company is effectively geared 100 per cent, and therefore very sensitive to a change in top line growth.

Employee-bound liabilities

Employees also generate large liabilities, mainly in the form of pension and health-care commitments. In most cases pensions are *funded* by segregated financial assets but, with the 40 per cent collapse in equity markets during the explosion of the technology bubble (2000–2002), most pension schemes are now *underfunded*, which means that pension fund assets cover less than 100 per cent of liabilities. This shortfall is, effectively, a corporate liability that needs to be included in the enterprise value. In a small number of cases, notably in Germany, pension commitments are unfunded, and recognised as a provision on the balance sheet. In the case of relatively young companies the charge is largely a non-cash item (it represents the building up of the provision), but in the case of older companies, where the number of retired employees is higher than the number of active ones, the charge is a very real cash charge, representing the pensions paid out of the company's own cash flow (this is the case for ThyssenKrupp, a German steelmaker, for instance). The balance sheet provision, therefore, has to be treated as a liability and added to the enterprise value in all cases. Health-care and post-retirement benefits other than pension payments are usually not asset-backed, i.e. unfunded. They represent colossal future liabilities, especially for US companies where the security system is largely private. We are of the view that these liabilities should also be integrated into the market value of the enterprise.

Other operational liabilities

These liabilities have to be dealt with on a case by case basis, but need to be well identified. As a rule we are not in favour of treating unspecified operating provisions as debt-like liabilities, but we do so for specific ones – which can cover a vast array of different situations. Litigation liabilities such as asbestos can represent a very large percentage of the enterprise value, and need to be taken into account. Contingent liabilities of all sorts can also creep up and need to be investigated carefully. In areas of high research and development content, for instance, it is possible to see acquisitions made with the commitment of further payments contingent upon the success of the products acquired. Warranties are a staple of car manufacturers; General Motors has more than $6bn of such liabilities (net of deferred tax assets relating to these warranties) on its balance sheet. These warranties can be analysed as commitments to repair cars free of charge, which is obviously a net cost to shareholders – unless they hedge themselves by buying a fleet of cars from the worst manufacturers! Because these costs are determined statistically (i.e. from the observed percentage of the park of vehicles which have actually broken down whilst under warranty), it is a definite liability. Companies are also held liable for the environmental damage that their industrial activity has caused. This represents huge liabilities for utilities running nuclear plants in particular, dressed under various headings on the balance sheet – from the explicit 'dismantling of nuclear facilities' to the good corporate citizen 'social cost payable' and the discreet 'decommissioning provisions'. Land reconstruction provisions for mining companies are taken for the same purpose.

Tax liabilities

To simplify, tax liabilities arise from the mismatch between accounting and fiscal treatments of depreciation (in most cases). The profit & loss account reports the accounting tax charge, and the cash flow statement the amount of tax actually paid. The difference is capitalised as a liability, but some other mismatches (mainly related to pension accounting) come from an early use of funds for the firm, and end up on the asset side of the balance sheet. As a general rule, deferred tax assets and liabilities can be netted off and the net result added to the enterprise value as a liability (as in most cases, deferred tax assets will be smaller). However, this is not a universal rule, and analysts faced with large amounts on both sides of the balance sheet have to investigate further, as these assets and liabilities may not come from the same source of mismatch and cannot, in some cases, be amalgamated. For instance, a tax loss carry-forward, which is an asset, can only be used when the company makes a loss, and so could be a permanent 'investment', if the company never loses money again.

The final calculation of the economic enterprise value

In most cases the previous steps will capture all relevant associated economic liabilities, and will get the financial analyst to an acceptable proxy of the economic market value of net assets. But some fine-tuning is needed with respect to certain assets which are not operational in nature, and should really be considered as cash. The most common are financial assets, mainly equity-accounted holdings. Their cash-equivalent value will of course be their market value, which the analyst needs to estimate. This is fairly easy when the shares of these companies are quoted – famous examples include the stake that Nestlé has in L'Oréal, for instance. If this is not the case, a good proxy will be obtained by applying to the book value of this stake (which is reported) a price-to-book ratio of the same sector or, failing this, the price-to-book of the market or of the company under analysis. It is advisable to cross-check this cash value by applying a PE ratio to the *income* of these associates, if the information is available. Other non-operating assets can include other financial holdings (bonds, for instance), or deferred tax assets (when they cannot be directly netted off against deferred tax liabilities). All these items come as a deduction of the enterprise value, just as cash would.

Similarly, an adjustment must be made to minority interests, to avoid a mismatch between cash flow and assets. Minority interests appear in the book value and at the very end of the P&L, as a reminder that some dividend or some earnings stream does not belong to the group. Anything above the bottom line, such as cash flow, will always be fully consolidated. However, the book value, or net assets, of the group will exclude them. Without any adjustments, the return on assets would therefore be falsely inflated. Since it is usually impossible to consolidate proportionally those subsidiaries where there are minority interests, the best practice is to consider a fictitious purchase, again at market value. The multiple of the company under study can be used as a good proxy to determine the market value in the absence of better information, done again for the balance sheet (with a price-to-book) and for the P&L (with a PE ratio) data, to ensure some cross-checking. Once the analyst is satisfied with his estimate of the market value of minority interests, this amount is

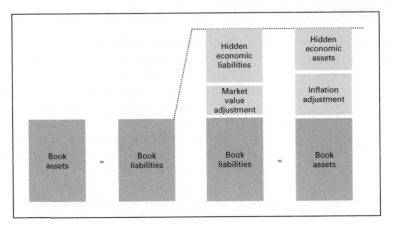

Figure 3.4 Economic data include *all* liabilities and *all* assets.

treated as debt (the debt that the company would need to contract to actually buy the minorities out) and added to the enterprise value.

If investors need to expend such efforts to determine the market value of liabilities as a proxy for the market value of assets, then they simply cannot relate it back to the *book value* of net assets to calculate the asset multiple. At the very least, there now seems to be a mismatch between an economic Enterprise Value (EV) at market value, by definition expressed in real terms, and a book value of assets, accounted for in *historical* costs. In addition, if it is the case that there are such things as hidden liabilities, can we be so sure that there are no such things as hidden assets?

To reiterate, economic data include *all* liabilities and *all* assets (Figure 3.4).

The following sections detail the adjustments needed on the asset side of the balance sheet to obtain an *invested* value of assets directly compatible with the EV, or *market* value of assets, to complete an economic asset multiple.

Inflation: apples and oranges, age and half-life, PPP

Let us reiterate that ignoring inflation is a cardinal sin in finance. This is true when assessing market performance (inflation has been by far the single biggest contributor to the nominal performance of equities, historically) as well as when assessing a stock of assets, i.e. a balance sheet. The reason for which inflation adjustment is necessary is pretty simple: apples and oranges cannot be compared.

Let us say that an analyst wishes to compare Arcelor, the European steel company, with its Korean competitor, Posco. Arcelor is the amalgamation of layers of the European steel industry, mainly in France, Germany and Belgium. Some of these layers are quite old, going back to the golden age of European growth, somewhere between the mid-1950s and mid-1960s. Let us say that a steel mill was built in Belgium in 1962, with an asset life of fifty years. Some extensive renovation work will have been done to the ovens, and the equipment will have been modernised two or three times, but the shell of the mill and the structure of the ovens date back to that year of 1962. Say that exactly the same mill was built by Posco in

1992, with the same asset life. At the onset of the projects, both have exactly the same internal rate of return (IRR) of 6.2 per cent real, based on an investment of 100 and a projected *constant* gross cash flow (i.e. pre re-investment) of 6.5 per annum. Let us say that the inflation rate is 2 per cent in Belgium and 3 per cent in Korea. At year 12 for the Korean company, the nominal cash flow is 9; at year 42 for the Belgium company it is 14.6. If the value of the asset is taken straight from the Annual Report, and a return is calculated (for the sake of simplification) as the ratio of gross cash flow over the gross value of assets, the calculation will be the following for the Belgian company:

$$\text{Gross cash flow}_{2004}/\text{Gross assets}_{1962}$$

and for the Korean company:

$$\text{Gross cash flow}_{2004}/\text{Gross assets}_{1992}.$$

This ratio makes no sense for each individual company, as the numerator and denominator are not expressed in the same base-currency. Furthermore, these two wrong ratios do not make a right, and their comparison is also meaningless. The older company will always enjoy the higher return (and therefore would always appear as the more attractive investment . . .?), since its denominator is more deflated than that of the younger company, relative to the cash flow. The return would be 14.6 per cent for the Belgian company, and 9 per cent for the Korean company. Note that an earnings model would make things *much* worse; assuming no tax and 100 per cent equity financing, earnings are cash flow (6.5) minus 2, the constant depreciation charge of the original asset worth 100. The RoE of the Korean company in year 12 is 9.2 per cent, close enough, but the RoE of the Belgian company is 79 per cent . . . (this is compounding the inflation error with the book value error, which is debated in Chapter 4).

This simple example shows that numerator and denominator (cash flow and assets) have to be expressed in the same current cost terms. This is achieved by adjusting net assets, which are booked in the accounts at historical costs, for inflation. In order to perform this adjustment, the analyst needs to work out the assets' average age, and apply the compounded GDP deflator associated with the reporting currency to their net value. The average age of assets can be broadly approximated by calculating the ratio of accumulated depreciation to the depreciation charge, always found in the Annual Report. Analysts with an in-depth knowledge of a company can always refine this approach, if, for instance, they have the knowledge of the age of each plant or major manufacturing site. Alternatively, it can be borne in mind that most companies tend to invest mainly to replace assets, unless they are significantly outpacing GDP growth. This means that for most companies, say those growing at between 1 per cent and 4 per cent real per annum, the average age will be equal to or very close to half-life. The half-life trick offers a good cross-check on other estimates of age. Capex is also a useful tool. If the analyst can identify at least one year where the age of assets is reasonably easy to estimate (maybe because clues were given during an analyst meeting, or in the speech of the Chief Executive on future investments), then the replacement rate given by capex will offer a lead into how much younger or older the stock of assets become. Say that it is reasonable to assume that the assets of a company are ten years old on average. Depreciation is 1000, and the average deflator is 2 per cent. The current cost-accounted depreciation charge is 1000 times 1.02^{10}, or 1219. If capex is 1500, assets will have a tendency to get younger. Ultimately, the age of a company is a function of its growth rate.

A conscientious analyst may be tempted to try to inflation-adjust a company's assets according to the inflation rate of the sector where it operates. In practice, we think that this is not as good an idea as it initially seems. First, the data are not available. Second, it is not because a company is selling a product with a 10 per cent inflation rate that the cost of building a new plant to manufacture this product will incur the same inflation rate. In most cases, asset inflation will be closely linked to the inflation rate belonging to the cost of adding new capacity, itself likely to be linked to a mixture of construction and capital goods inflation, which tends to follow the GDP deflator.

In the case of foreign subsidiaries, using the GDP deflator of the reporting currency assumes that the theory of Purchasing Power Parity (PPP) works on average. This theory argues that, in the long run, a difference in the inflation rate between two countries will be reflected in their real exchange rate. Or, more precisely, that the exchange rate between one currency and another is in equilibrium when their domestic purchasing powers at that rate of exchange are equivalent. The basis for PPP is the 'law of one price'. Goods should cost the same in, say, the UK and France (in the absence of transportation costs, barriers to trade and other transaction costs) once you take the exchange rate into account. PPPs (calculated jointly by the OECD and Eurostat) are the rates of currency conversion that equalise the purchasing power of different currencies by eliminating the difference in price levels between countries. Whilst there are as many supporters as detractors of PPP, it is a fact that countries which tolerate high inflation rates will tend to be forced to devalue their currencies, which would support the choice of a unique deflator. As we mentioned earlier, the inflation adjustment is a steady contributor to performance in the CROCI selection process, and the benefits in its implementation far outweigh the noise that it might create in some specific cases. However, there are two specific issues to watch.

In the case of certain hyperinflation situations, the currency never falls in line with the difference in inflation, and this could lead to an over- or understatement of the asset value of the foreign operations situated in these high inflation areas. The following example is of a group with one foreign and one domestic operation, according to the data in the following table:

	Asset value 5 years ago	Annual inflation	Asset value inflation adj. today
Foreign	100	10%	161.1
Domestic	100	2%	110.4

The inflation rate in the foreign operation has outstripped that of the domestic operation by 8 per cent per annum, leading to an inflation of the foreign subsidiary's asset over the domestic operation of $(1.08^5 - 1)$, or 47 per cent. In order for the GDP deflator of the domestic operation to be applicable to all of the company's assets, the currency needs to fall by 31.5 per cent, or $1 - (110.4/161.1)$. Large investments in Turkey or Latin America by US or European groups provide good live examples of this issue. In the 2002 Annual Report of Carrefour (p. 60), the management report for Latin America states that 'sales revenues declined 36.2% from 2001 to 2002, under the impact of the devaluation of the Argentine currency and the sharp drop in the Brazilian currency'. That year, the average peso/euro exchange rate had fallen by 68 per cent, and the average real/euro exchange rate by 25 per cent. Assuming that Carrefour was equally exposed to these two currencies, then the currency impact would have been 46.5 per cent on unchanged sales. Sales were in fact up 7.8 per cent at constant currency; 46.5 minus 7.8 is 38.7 per cent, close enough to the 36.2 per cent reported by the company (which would not have been equally exposed to these two currencies anyway, and might have put some hedging in place). However, the Argentine GDP deflator was only 30.6 per cent for 2002, and 10.2 per cent for Brazil. Quite clearly, the currencies fell much more than the inflation rate rose that year. Interestingly, two years out the gap had narrowed considerably. The average cumulative inflation rate was 46.7 per cent, and the average cumulative drop in the currency 58.6 per cent. So the technique can be imperfect in these high inflation areas. However, it remains that the principle is right. In the case of Carrefour in 2002, the impact on its net assets was a \$1billion write-down. Since the cash flow was also impacted by the currency change (through the sales decline in euros), it would be incorrect to inflate the Latin-American asset base by the local deflator.

Another limitation of the inflation adjustment by the GDP deflator is the case of reserve assets, i.e. oil or mining companies, or land-banks for real estate companies, where asset inflation has nothing to do with the GDP deflator. In these cases, we suggest inflation-adjusting all the assets directly related to the reserves (including equipment) by the inflation rate of the underlying commodity. There is evidence that commodity producers increase the number of projects as the selling price of the commodity rises. Not only do they get more cash flow out of their operations, but also their hurdle rate decreases. An oil price at \$45 will allow certain projects to take place which would not be viable with an oil price at \$25. Suppliers of equipment on new projects then find tightness in the market and can raise prices, thus increasing the replacement cost of new projects. During the commodity boom of 2003–2005, mining companies were reporting that some spare parts on very special mining equipment, such as the Caterpillar gigantic trucks, diggers and excavators, had a waiting list of more than a year.

As we explained in the introduction, we don't make adjustments for the sake of it, but only if they demonstrably enhance an investor's ability to select stocks. Adjusting for inflation is controversial. On the basis of certain research reports, there does not seem to be much enhancement of investment returns from it. John O'Hanlon and Ken Peasnell, from the University of Lancaster, UK, report for instance in a paper dated January 2003 that they find 'no theoretical basis for the argument that residual income valuation needs to be carried out on the basis of inflation-adjusted residual incomes' (O'Hanlon and Peasnell, 2003). Our own tests are less definitive. Over an eight-and-a-half year period, from January 1996 to June 2004, we find that such an inflation adjustment adds 6.7 per cent of performance to a basket of the forty cheapest US stocks, selected monthly on economic PE. Inflation adjustment impacts the economic PE because it is defined as the ratio of EV to inflation-adjusted net economic assets, divided by the inflation-adjusted return on economic capital. That's an additional average annual alpha of 75 basis points – not an insignificant improvement.

Invisibility and unaccountability: get a life, a non-smoker's dream, the asset test

'One sees clearly only with the heart; the essential is invisible to the eyes', wrote Antoine de St-Exupéry in his philosophical novel *The Little Prince*. Bizarrely, the second part of this quotation can be applied to today's financial analysis (as for the first part, it is a well known fact that financial analysts have no heart). The emergence of the service industry as the largest contributor to GDP in developed economies, the progressive migration of the production of goods from Japan, the US and Western Europe to Asia and Eastern Europe, and, most importantly, the legal protection of intellectual property, have all had a similar effect on the way capital has been allocated in the developed economies in the past fifty years. Investment in tangible fixed assets has been de-emphasised, and new investments in research and development, marketing, advertising, branding and training have emerged. In the mind of a Chief Executive, as well as *economically*, there is no difference between building a new factory, drilling a new well or launching a new global marketing campaign; all three have an *invested* value, which is the initial cost of setting up the investment, as well as a *market* value, which is the net present value of future expected free cash flows. But in the hands of accountants, modern balance sheets are drained of their substance because *only* tangible fixed assets are recorded. Note that this is a different type of issue from that we saw earlier, where some financial hocus-pocus makes certain liabilities disappear, *possibly* with the indirect intention of moderating the market value of assets, *possibly* with the indirect intention of boosting the share price beyond its economic value . . . In the accounting framework, there is no need for such suspicion; intangible 'spending' is not an asset, end of debate. The introduction of IFRS will modify this slightly, but the definition of what can be capitalised remains very narrow. In their comprehensive *Company Valuation under IFRS*, Nick Antill and Kenneth Lee (2005: 156) admit that 'a purchased intangible has a much better chance of recognition than [when] internally developed'. Incidentally, this leads to exactly the reverse effect, namely reducing the invested value of the assets relative to their market value – in other words, making them look more expensive.

This is probably where accounting is furthest away from the economic reality, and at its most distorting for an investor. Invisibility does not mean unaccountability. On the basis of our CROCI work, we estimate, for instance, that at least 12 per cent of all net *economic* assets in the US are invested in R&D, brands and similar assets. Only a fraction of this is recorded on balance sheets. The investment analyst has no choice but to find a way to take into account the vast sums invested in intangible assets. Fortunately, the accounting rules are crystal clear about the attributions and characteristics of an asset; why accountants do not follow their own by-laws is what remains opaque.

Take the photocopier: the cash cost of the ink appears in the P&L, but the cash cost of buying the machine does not; one is not an asset, the other is, because one has no economic life and the other does. The ink does not live, economically of course, more than a few days or months, depending on your eagerness to press the green button. It is consumed in the economic process, is transformed by the Economic Value Added machinery of the firm into something more valuable. It is a cost that does not produce anything beyond the twelve-month horizon of the P&L. And, if investment stops (in this case buying new ink), everything stops. At the other end of the 'social' accounting spectrum are assets, which belong to the aristocracy of the financial statements. Unlike costs, assets have an economic *life* (in the case of the photocopier, probably three, possibly four, years). During its life, an asset will produce whatever it is meant to produce and generate (or participate in generating) some cash flow, *even if no new additional capital is committed to it*. Thus, the definition of an asset is an object that produces cash flow (or contributes to the production process) for a certain number of years (its economic life), even in the absence of new investment in this object. This example warrants a digression. If you work in an office, you have surely noticed that a photocopying machine spends most of its life jammed, in need of bizarre substances and of trays to be closed – preferably the one you can't find – but above all, in need of the attention of the Man from Xerox. The tender love from the Man in the Grey Overalls is called *maintenance*, and is a cost, not an investment. A new investment in the photocopier would be, for instance, a new, faster sorter, which is not a necessary expense for the machine to produce the promised number of copies during its life.

Now that we know what constitutes an asset and what does not, according to the very definition of accountants, let us examine the case of some imaginary brave government (maybe inspired by Mr Ahern, the Prime Minister of Ireland, who banned smoking in all public places), which decides to curb public smoking by preventing the brand with the highest market share from promoting any of its smoking products – TV spots, radio commercials, glossy magazine advertising, sponsoring; *any* form of publicity is forbidden. After two years a public study is conducted, and the government observes with some surprise that no material decline in sales growth is noticeable for this leading brand; the majority of this brand's customers have simply kept on buying it. If this generic example is not explicit enough, try the same story with the following names: Coca-Cola, McDonald's, Danone, Nescafé, Microsoft, Gucci, Louis Vuitton, Hermès, Smith Haut-Laffitte, L'Oréal, Nivea, Prozac, Viagra, Porsche, Rolls-Royce, Harley Davidson, Dunhill, Arsenal Football Club. For those of us who already consume these products and are satisfied with them, how long will it take to drop them solely because we are not constantly reminded that they exist? The economic value of advertising depends on the answer to this question.

Beyond the intrinsic qualities of the products that they name, these random brands have achieved worldwide recognition because of two factors, sometimes in isolation, most of the time combined: advertising, and research & development. The latter achieves excellence and innovation, and is often ring-fenced by a patent which protects the original idea from copies for a certain number of years. The former creates uniqueness, belonging and 'brand recognition'. It is quite clear, though only intu-itively so and thus impossible to prove, that none of these products would witness any short-term or medium-term change in their fortunes if R&D and advertising stopped overnight. In other words, these expenses are able to generate some cash flow for a certain number of years without demanding a continuous investment – nothing less than the exact definition of an asset.

Accountants have their reasons for expensing advertising and research & devel-opment in the P&L; their intangible nature makes them more difficult to assess, and their uniqueness means that only a handful of buyers would consider paying for these items separately, if the company were to be broken up. Remember that the prime objective of accounting is to design prudential rules to protect creditors in case the company goes bankrupt (*ergo*, the prime objective is not to help investors). But there can be no doubt that, economically speaking, keeping these items out of the balance sheet makes very little sense. Take a pharmaceutical company of some size; it is hardly contentious that its biggest asset is its pipeline of compounds, molecules, processes and patented drugs. There can be many arguments about the potential value of each of them, and how this differs from phase one to phase two to phase three, but there can be *no* argument that the most incorrect invested value to ascribe to this asset is zero, as if it did not exist, which is what expensing R&D amounts to. For an *economic* analysis, R&D and advertising should be capitalised on the balance sheet and amortised through the P&L.

The practice of capitalising rather than expensing R&D and advertising spend usually sparks numerous debates with investors and management of companies. Its logic can be explained further by the following clarifications. First, the capitalisation of intangibles does not aim at getting to the *market value* of R&D or brands; this can only be provided by the market, which, in the CROCI approach, comes from the Enterprise Value. Rather, the exercise tries to approximate the *invested value* of intangibles, in the same way as the net asset value of tangible fixed assets is an approximation of their invested value, after depreciation. Second, all the R&D effort should be capitalised, not just the expenses leading to a successful compound in the pharmaceutical industry, or a productive well in the exploration industry. To draw a comparison with the world of tangible assets, buildings are capitalised *including* the cost of the foundations. Third, if a company finds itself in the fortunate situation of benefiting from an intangible asset *without* any initial investment, nothing should be capitalised. Again, there are similar examples in the world of tangible assets. Utilities, especially when they are privatised, are sometimes given state assets, usually quite old, against the charge of maintaining and upgrading them. Alternatively, they can be given very long-term concessions. Fashion can sometimes gift a company with such riches. Hermès, the well-known luxury goods company producing its famous silk scarves and ties, in fact started as a leather goods manufacturer for horse equipment, back in the nineteenth century. What was originally a small diversification, the silk products, became a huge money spinner thanks to the whims of fashion, but for years the company hardly spent any money on advertising. The invested value of the brand was, correspondingly, small, even if the market value was enormous. Fourth, people businesses have few or no assets. There can be little doubt left of this after applying the asset test to a business made of people, like investment bankers, consultants or . . . accountants.

Stop investing, i.e. paying them, and they will stop 'producing' at once – a situation as remote as can be from our previous list of brand name/assets, which could carry on producing cash flows for years to come, even without a single additional marketing campaign. The overnight demise of Arthur Andersen or Barings, admittedly under special circumstances, may be a good illustration of the ephemeral nature of people businesses.

In practice, we have found that only R&D and advertising spend constitute intangible assets worth capitalising. Most companies like to mention somewhere in their annual report the amount of R&D for the year. This is usually a very stable amount as a percentage of sales, and the only difficulty is to calculate it from the relevant sales number. For instance, most health-care companies spend a fifth of their pure pharmaceutical sales in R&D, but most also have small over-the-counter businesses (vitamins, drinks, even chemicals) which do not require any, and applying 20 per cent to total sales would overstate R&D spending. Advertising requires a bit more digging, as consumer goods companies are less forthcoming with these numbers. It is usually possible to obtain a good approximation of A&P (Advertising and Promotion) spending, from which promotions, which are really a rebate, need to be deducted. We have never encountered insurmountable difficulties in obtaining these figures, and even the most opaque cases will only require a good deal of cross-checking with other companies in similar businesses, the patient siege of the Finance Director's office, some vicious questioning in public meetings, the thorough reading of professional reviews and journals of advertising and, in the end, a small degree of guesswork.

As we have already pointed out, assets have a life. In the case of a tangible asset, the physical decay will give a good idea of its economic life. Intangible assets do not offer such a luxury. The economic life of an intangible asset can be estimated by answering the following question: *with no new investment, how long will it take for the last euro of R&D or advertising spend to become uneconomic, that is, not to generate incremental sales?* It goes without saying that the answer can only be approximate. This seems to bother some investors, who think that attempting to answer this question is 'too subjective'. At the same time, none of them seem to think that the answer is 'less than twelve months' for every single company, which is effectively what *not* capitalising intangible assets implies. We are equally wary of the approach that ascribes, in all the sectors where they can be identified, a constant number, usually five years, to the economic life of R&D and advertising spend. The idea is that the market does not care beyond this timeframe anyway. There is something deeply unsatisfactory in assuming that one dollar of R&D at Microsoft contributes to the same competitive advantage (which in this case is just another name for 'economic life') as does one dollar of advertising at Colgate or one euro at BMW.

We prefer to argue that there is a link between economic life of intangibles, competitive advantage and the lifecycle of products. The benefit of such an approach is that these are quite well-researched concepts. An extensive literature has followed in the wake of Michael Porter (1980, 1985) and deals with product lifecycles, product innovation, competitive advantage periods etc. Everybody knows what the lifecycle of a Mercedes car is. It is obvious to all that Microsoft brings a major marketing or technical innovation to the market roughly every three years. It is equally obvious that the rate of innovation at McDonald's is much lower. In the end, it is possible to come up with a classification of sectors according to their rate of technical or marketing innovation, or product lifecycle. Note that for the purpose of capitalising intangibles, both have to be considered. Whilst the technical innovation in the production of a disposable razor can be assumed to be quite low, the marketing innovation is quite high. Incidentally, this would be disputed quite vigorously by the manufacturers, since part of their advertising is to make the public believe in their ability to bring in new technical innovations.

What links the product lifecycle with the economic life of intangible assets is the idea that, in the absence of new R&D or advertising, a company will struggle to build a new cycle of products, and its competitive advantage will be sharply reduced, unless it enjoys a monopolistic situation. A product line with an average lifecycle of three years, say in consumer electronics, will force companies to innovate at that frequency, if not in its main brand, certainly in R&D.

Once the investment analyst is satisfied with an estimate of yearly R&D or advertising spend and its economic life, these assets can be accumulated and depreciated on the balance sheet in the same way as tangible fixed assets are. This manipulation needs meticulous modelling but is extremely simple in principle, and only three fairly obvious points need to be kept in mind. First, for the sake of consistency, intangible assets need to be inflation-adjusted in the same way as other assets are. This can be done by applying the same deflator, or by creating the stock of intangible assets directly in real terms – for instance by considering real, not nominal sales, if sales are the basis from which intangible assets are estimated (i.e. if they are expressed as a percentage of sales). Second, this accumulation of assets is *pre*-depreciation. A depreciation charge needs to be calculated, based on the economic life used to build up the assets in the first place. Third, the yearly cash charge for R&D or advertising needs to be removed from the P&L, as it is now an asset and not a cost. Only the depreciation should now appear below the EBDIT line.

Let us assume that a pharmaceutical company spends 20 per cent of annual sales in R&D with an economic life of fifteen years. At any time, there will be a stock of fifteen layers of R&D spend to be capitalised: the expense of fourteen years ago, in its last year of economic usefulness; plus the expense of thirteen years ago, with two years to go before becoming obsolete; the expense of twelve years ago, and so on until the latest expense, that of the current year, which will carry on having an economic value for the firm for another fourteen years. If the analyst has access to historical data, it will be possible to recreate the stream of fifteen years of R&D spend, by taking a fifth of sales every year. This stream will be in historical costs, and will need to be inflation-adjusted by a deflator, with the general formula

$$R\&D \times (1+d)^a,$$

where d is the deflator, and a is the age of the expense (from zero to fourteen). Alternatively, if no historical data are available, the analyst will need to create a stream of historical sales based on an estimate of real growth, with the general formula

$$S_{y-n} = \frac{S_y}{(1+g)^n},$$

where S is sales and g the real growth rate in sales. Note that in this case, the historical sales stream is real, and there is no need to inflation-adjust the R&D spend derived from it. Piling up the fifteen layers of R&D spend will give the equivalent of gross assets, i.e. pre-depreciation. With $g = 0$ the stock of R&D will constantly be at half-life, which in our example means 7.5 years. In this case, net assets will be half of gross assets exactly. As the growth rate (of R&D) increases, the stock of assets becomes younger, and net assets will represent more than 50 per cent of gross assets.

Is it all worth the trouble? Again, economic adjustments are only valid for an asset manager if they can be proved to enhance investment returns. As with inflation adjustment, we have tested the impact of the capitalisation of intangibles on stock selection. Over an eight-and-a-half year period from January 1996 to June 2004, we find that the recognition of intangible assets, which of course greatly modifies the PE ratio (by increasing the asset base, capitalised intangible assets will lower the level of cash return and the economic asset multiple), can add significant performance to an investment strategy. In the US market, a portfolio made up of forty stock selected monthly on the basis of economic PE performs 10.6 per cent better over that period, if intangible assets are capitalised and added to the asset base in the way that we have just described. That's an average 119 basis points of additional annual performance – a very substantial enhancement.

A certain Nobel Prize winner – not much for half a million – physical assets

Hitherto, we have advocated the reconstruction of the *market* value of an asset via the market value of the liabilities which finance it, and the reconstruction of the real (inflation-adjusted) *invested* value of this asset by a number of economic adjustments, mainly inflation and invisible capital. We call the ratio of the two 'the economic asset multiple'. However, it has a more prestigious name. In the late 1960s, a Professor of Economics from the University of Yale by the name of James Tobin introduced a new economic concept, the 'q' ratio. This is how he later described it in his 1977 article 'Asset markets and the cost of capital' (Tobin and Brainard, 1977):

> The numerator is the market valuation: the going price in the market for exchanging existing assets. The other, the denominator, is the replacement or reproduction cost: the price in the market for newly produced commodities. We believe that this ratio has considerable macroeconomic significance and usefulness, as the nexus between financial markets and markets for goods and services.

James Tobin, who was a great admirer of Keynes, must have found the premises of his idea of the 'q' ratio in the following paragraph of *General Theory* (Keynes, 1936):

> The daily revaluations of the Stock Exchange, though they are primarily made to facilitate transfers of old investments between one individual and another, inevitably exert a decisive influence on the rate of current investment. For there is no sense in building up a new enterprise at a cost greater than that at which a similar existing enterprise can be purchased; whilst there is an inducement to spend on a new project what may seem an extravagant sum, if it can be floated on the Stock Exchange at an immediate profit.

The enterprise value of the economic asset multiple corresponds exactly to the numerator of Tobin's 'q' ratio. As for the denominator, we believe that its CROCI version both falls short of some of Tobin's requirements, and also offers a significant enhancement on some of its later implementations. The replacement or reproduction cost obviously needs to take inflation into consideration. What cost 100 ten years ago costs $100 \times (1+n)^{10}$ today, where n is the rate of increase of prices for this particular good. In this respect, the CROCI inflation adjustment is in line with the spirit of Tobin's 'q' ratio. But replacement cost is a more complex notion than inflation-adjusted cost, as the following example shows.

Between 1943 and 1945, the US Army paid \$486 804.22 to the University of Pennsylvania to develop ENIAC, the first computer – a mastodon that barely fitted in a warehouse, and had the same power and functionality as a bottom-of-the-range calculator bought today in any supermarket for far less than \$5. Assuming a conservative 2 per cent inflation rate for sixty years would give an inflation-adjusted value of this original investment of approximately \$1.6 m, in 2004 money. And yet, the replacement cost of ENIAC is less than \$5 ... An accurate replacement cost must take into account technological progress as well as inflation. The former can be approximated by productivity for the general economy, but would be of little use in this form, as technological progress varies greatly from one sector to the next. We don't believe that it is possible to come up with a useful number at the firm or the sector level. As a result, the inflation-adjusted value of net assets will always overstate the replacement value of net assets, and the discrepancy will be larger for high-productivity industries. However, this is not as bad as it sounds, because these sectors also tend to have quite short economic lives. For instance, we estimate that the average asset live of the global technology sector is ten years, against sixteen for the entire market/economy. As a result, the replacement cycle is faster, and productivity can 'sink in' equally rapidly into economic capital, reducing the need to make an adjustment for technological progress.

The 'q' ratio is a small part of Tobin's economic legacy, but financial markets enthusiastically adopted it as their new mantra in the 1980s, only to dismiss it in the 1990s in their usual fickle way. By that time, the 'q' ratio was starting to suggest that the US stock market was overvalued – a cardinal sin in the eyes of Wall Street in any case, but especially so with hindsight, considering that in the second part of the 1990s US shares were about to enter the last and most spectacular leg of the great bull market of 1983–2000. Of course, Tobin was a macroeconomist who never intended to research the daily gyrations of the stock market. Incidentally, investors sometimes get impatient and have difficulty in accepting that equities are a very long-term asset class. Equities can be approximated as a perpetual bond, in which case their duration is the inverse of their coupon; a dividend yield of 2.5 per cent would correspond to a duration of forty years. With this in mind, a warning by, say, 1996, that the stock market was overvalued, which proved right four years later, was a reasonably accurate prediction.

However, the reason that Tobin's 'q' ratio did not 'work' when applied to financial markets was more than just a timing issue. The market strategists who applied the 'q' ratio to investment analysis saw it as a glorified price-to-book ratio, and calculated it accordingly. Ironically, Tobin himself may have been at the origin of this rough cut. In his 1977 article, he called 'q' 'the ratio between two valuations of the same *physical* asset' (our emphasis on physical) – in other words, the market value over the replacement value. But a few pages later, in the same article, Tobin adds an important qualification, contradicting his general description: '"replacement costs" must be interpreted to cover *not only physical assets* but other items on the firm's balance sheet' (again, our emphasis). Either the early implementers did not bother to read on after the first pages, or they did not know what Tobin meant (admittedly, it was not very clear). What is indubitable is that the market *will* value all assets when it can reasonably ascertain that they exist and have a resale value. This must include intangible as well as physical assets, and booked as well as 'omitted' assets. Tobin's own intuition and belief was that his 'q' ratio had 'considerable *macro economic* significance'. In this case, 'q' must concern itself with the replacement value of *economic* assets, not just accounting (book) tangible assets. We believe that the CROCI version of Tobin's 'q', which includes, as we have seen in this chapter, a thorough process of capitalisation of intangible assets, offers a significant enhancement on earlier implementations of the ratio, and is closer in spirit to Tobin's original idea. What's more, it seems to 'work' as the great economist predicted.

Figure 3.5 shows the economic asset multiple for the world, Europe, the US and Japan over a seventeen-year period, from 1989 to 2005. The numerator is the enterprise value, as described earlier, and the denominator is the inflation-adjusted *economic* net asset value (net capital invested, in CROCI speak), made up of tangible *and* intangible assets.

There is in Figure 3.5 a strong support for the mean-reversion of the 'q' ratio. Japan was the first region of the world to be hit by a substantial wave of equity speculation in the past quarter of a century. By 1987 Japan-mania was in full swing, and it lasted for a few more years after that. In 1989, the first year for which we can calculate a CROCI asset multiple, the Tobin 'q' approximated by EV/NCI was 1.65×, and it took four years to take this ratio down to a mere 0.85, although this mean-reversion was precipitated by a collapse of cash return (as per the rule of the Equivalence) from 5.7 per cent in 1989 to a microscopic 1.1 per cent in 1993. At the end of 2005 the Japanese market was trading on a Tobin's 'q' of 1× exactly, with a cash return of 5.3 per cent, very close, if not exactly at, the cost of capital.

Even more spectacular was the mean-reversion following the US technology bubble. The market's average 'q' ratio peaked at an incredible 3.3× in 2000, but the

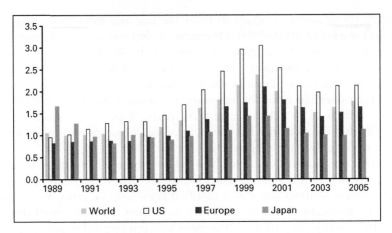

Figure 3.5 Regional asset multiple: a good proxy for Tobin's 'q'.

high-water mark was reached in March of 2000, with an unbelievable 4.4× 'q'
ratio, which, in the following four years, halved to reach 2.3× at the end of 2004.
Thanks to the recovery of 2003, a 50 per cent devaluation of the dollar against the
euro, a very aggressive delocalisation of capital in cheaper areas (mainly Asia) and
a quasi-freeze of investments, US firms managed to produce a remarkably muted
cash-flow cycle during the period; cash returns hit their trough in 2000 at 6.8 per
cent, and recovered swiftly to more than 9 per cent in 2004. It is this recovery
in returns that has prevented a complete mean-reversion of the 'q' ratio to 1, as
9 per cent is materially above the cost of capital.

We have by now inflicted a major makeover on the confusing price-to-book
value ratio. An economic asset multiple, made of an enterprise value and net economic capital, or net capital invested, has now replaced it. Apart from being able
to approximate the 'q' ratio, this ratio forms the first term of the Equivalence,
seen in Chapter 2. In the same way that the computation of economic assets was
instrumental in achieving a relevant measure of the asset multiple, it will serve
for the calculation of an economic return, the Cash Return On Capital Invested.
CROCI divided by the cost of capital will then get us to an accurate measure of
the relative return, the second term of the Equivalence, and the subject of the next
chapter.

Note

1. Looking at this chart, there might be a temptation to take away a few outliers to
   improve the statistical significance of the relationship. Indeed, genuine outliers are the
   most interesting observations for investment purposes, because they are either the very
   expensive or the very cheap companies. Provided, of course, that the data is economically
   meaningful.

References

Antill, N. and Lee, K. (2005). *Company Valuation Under IFRS*. Harriman House Publishing.

Davydenko, S. A. (2005). *When Do Firms Default?* London Business School.

Keynes, J. M. (1936). *The General Theory of Employment, Interest and Money*. Harcourt Brace.

Modigliani, F. and Miller, M. (1958). The cost of capital, corporation finance and the theory of investment. *American Economic Review*, **48**(3), 261–297.

O'Hanlon, J. and Peasnell, K. (2003). *Residual Income Valuation: Are Inflation Adjustments Necessary?* Management School Lancaster University.

Porter, M. E. (1980). *Competitive Strategy: Techniques for Analyzing Industries and Competitors*. Free Press.

Porter, M. E. (1985). *Competitive Advantage: Creating and Sustaining Superior Performance*. Free Press (reprinted 1998).

Tobin, J. and Brainard, W. C. (1977). Chapter 11: Asset markets and the cost of capital. *Cowles Foundation Paper 440*, reprinted from *Private Values and Public Policy, Essays in Honor of William Fellner*. North-Holland.

4 The relative return

Keynes the speculator, Tobin the investor; jinxed in Pleasantville

We saw in the previous chapters how the ratio of market value to replacement value, the economic asset multiple, is the result of an arbitrage on the part of the 'wealth owners', according to Keynes. If similar assets are more expensive to buy than to build, then capitalists will obviously build. In doing so, they will create more capacity, until the point when excess supply drives the price of the entire stock of comparable assets down to their replacement value. But, paradoxically, Keynes presents such an arbitrage almost as if it was the result of pure speculation. Wealth owners would only accept to build a new asset 'if it can be floated off on the Stock Exchange at an immediate profit' (Keynes, 1936: 151). Although Keynes seems to believe that physical investment and financial capital are perfect substitutes, he does not appear to take this assumption to its full conclusion, which is that the marginal efficiency of capital, in his words, or CROCI here, should equal the cost of capital at all times. In fact, the first chapter of Book IV of the *General Theory*, entitled precisely 'The marginal efficiency of capital', gives enough evidence of independent variations of the marginal return on capital and the rate of interest. This means that investment cannot only be related to this arbitrage in a vacuum, and has to be related to discrepancies between 'marginal efficiency' and cost of interest, or the ratio of the two, which we call the relative return. Keynes seems to have spent relatively little time in addressing this issue. However, Tobin, who dedicated a large part of his career to expanding the subject, saw very clearly the link between the asset multiple, 'q', and the relative return. 'Under special conditions', he writes, 'q could be equivalently defined as the ratio of the marginal efficiency of capital R to the interest rate r_k used to discount future earnings streams' (Tobin and Brainard, 1977). With this sentence, we have nothing but the description of the Equivalence of Chapter 2. Furthermore, we already know that the special condition mentioned by Tobin is the assumption of no growth, which we will discuss in more detail in Chapter 5.

For a macroeconomist, the study of the ratio of market value to replacement value brings about enough information in itself. We know, after James Tobin, that it should converge to one. However, it should not be forgotten that there is a hidden assumption which had better not be ignored when looking at the equity market, a much narrower aggregate than Gross Domestic Product, or indeed individual shares. This assumption is that the market value of an asset converges to its replacement value *because, and only if*, the marginal return on investment converges to the cost of capital. This last point was almost a secondary consideration for Keynes, and even

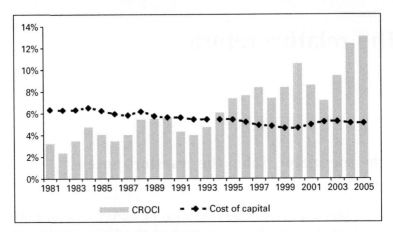

Figure 4.1 US CROCI since 1981 – sample of large companies.

Tobin, because their prime objective was to understand the mechanics of capital formation. Book IV of the *General Theory* is entitled *The Inducement to Invest*. For that purpose, it was enough to observe and analyse the arbitrage between market value and replacement value. Furthermore, at the level of an economy, it is a given that the aggregated real return converges to the cost of capital – in fact it mean-reverts around it. This is what constitutes the business cycle. In Figure 4.1, which aggregates the cash return of a sample of large US companies since 1981, it can be seen that the first decade, structurally below the cost of capital, is followed by another decade of structural *excess* return, or cash return above the cost of capital. This does not bode well for corporate profitability in the coming decade, but this is another story.

However, investment analysis does not just deal with aggregates, and needs to drill down to individual sectors, and stocks, which do not all follow the same business cycle and are not placed in the same spot on the lifecycle curve. Figure 4.2 shows

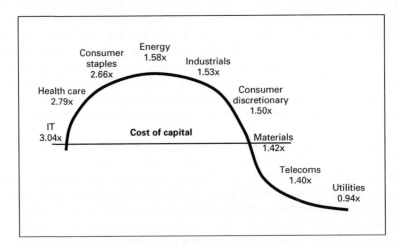

Figure 4.2 A schematic sector lifecycle.

the positioning of nine economic sectors according to their asset multiple in 2005. If we arrange the sectors from the highest to the lowest asset multiple from left to right along a standardised lifecycle, we obtain a very plausible hierarchy, starting with new and high-growing sectors (such as Technology or Health Care) and ending with old and recessive sectors (such as Utilities). Furthermore, the overlap with the level of cash return, or CROCI, is perfect; sectors to the left (i.e. with the highest asset multiple) also have the highest cash return, and sectors to the right the lowest.

At the *microeconomic* level the asset multiple has to be analysed with its twin, the relative return; where the first one goes, the second must follow. There is only a handful of exceptional cases where this is not quite the case. Here is the story of Adam and Eve, as such an example. The father of Adam and Eve was a forward-looking man, who wanted his inheritance to be shared fairly between his two children. For that purpose he bought a piece of land on the outskirts of Pleasantville and, as the small city expanded, built exactly the same house on each side of what had now become Sunny Street, at exactly the same cost. At his death, he thought, both children would inherit one of the houses. Given that he had spent scrupulously the same amount of money on each house, he could leave this world with the certainty that his wealth was fairly split among his heirs. Sadly, ten years after his death, sister and brother had had numerous arguments and had finally fallen out completely when Eve was able to sell her house at a considerably higher price than her brother had achieved just a few weeks beforehand. Why did it all go horribly wrong?

Sunny Street runs West/East in Pleasantville, which means that Adam's house was north-facing, whilst his sister's house, on the other side of the road, was south-facing. As Sunny Street became more upmarket with the development of the city, renters became more choosy and accepted paying a higher rent for the south-facing house. In figures, the free cash flow (FCF), which we can define as the rent minus maintenance and repair costs, that Eve was able to extract from her house was much higher than that which Adam was receiving. Since the market value of an asset is the net present value of future FCF, the market value of the south-facing house became higher than that of the north-facing one, despite the fact that the replacement value (i.e. the cost of building the house) was the same. Let us say that Eve received 10 in FCF, and Adam only 7. Discounted at 10 per cent, Eve's house was worth 100, and Adam's only 70. If the cost of building the house was 50, then Eve's economic return was 20 per cent (10 of FCF over 50 of replacement value, ignoring depreciation, which is very slow for buildings), and Adam's return was 14 per cent (7 of FCF over 50 of replacement value). Logically, the ratio of market value to replacement value is $2\times$ for Eve (100 over 50), as is its relative return, 20 per cent over 10 per cent. For Adam, the asset multiple is $1.4\times$ (70 over 50), as is his relative return, 14 per cent over 10 per cent. Because the rent difference between a south-facing house and a north-facing house should never narrow, if everything else remains constant, the asset multiple of Eve's house will never converge to that of her brother, let alone to $1\times$, because there is no reason to expect that the return of her asset will converge to that of her brother's, nor indeed to the cost of capital.

Here is a rare situation where the mean-reversion of return, under bouts of competitive pressure, does not seem to occur, because the location of a house is a unique 'business proposition' to which it is usually not feasible to add capacity.

But in fact, if we push the level of sophistication of this example up by one notch, it is possible to show that the mechanics of convergence between asset multiple and relative return remain, albeit not quite as expected. Although the replacement value of the house is identical for both offspring, the replacement value of the land won't be. A south-facing plot of land is worth more now in Sunny Street than a north-facing one. The sequence of convergence is not, as is conventional, new additional capacity collapsing return and dragging down the market value, but, rather, the price of existing capacity (land) going up, augmenting the theoretical 'replacement' value, and driving both return and asset multiple down to a point of convergence. Let us modify the example by assuming that the initial cost is still 50, made of 20 for the land and 30 for the house (in real terms). As Pleasantville develops, a sunny plot of land might be worth 40 at 'replacement' cost, such that the replacement value of Eve's asset is now 70. Her cash return has collapsed to 10 over 70, or 14.3 per cent, almost like her brother's. The asset multiple is 100 over 70, or 1.4×, as is, of course, the relative return, or 14.3 per cent over 10 per cent.

These are unusual circumstances because the laws of supply and demand cannot apply to a unique situation – here, a sunny plot of land. Everywhere else, it is very difficult for asset multiple and relative return *not* to converge and, ultimately, *not* to converge to 1×. The laws of competition will ensure that the cash return converges to the cost of capital, and the asset multiple will follow. At the aggregated level, asset multiples, or Tobin's 'q' in economic jargon, offer a powerful tool for analysing stimulations and impediments to capital formation. Applied to investment analysis, however, investors must always confront it with the relative return, which is the subject of the present chapter. The same principles as in earlier chapters will hold. The return on invested capital will need to be an *economic* return, which implies the calculation of cash return on economic capital. Yet an asset multiple deals with a stock of assets and liabilities, which are static measures. A return is a slightly more dynamic concept, dealing with flows expected to occur in the future. Some adjustment is required to take into consideration the time value of money. And there can be no one better than Harold Hotelling to deal with these actuarial issues.

Hotelling; a Stephen Hawking definition of assets – straight line's not so straight

In December 1924, Harold Hotelling, a mathematician from the Food Research Institute, Stanford University, presented before the American Mathematical Society a paper called *A General Mathematical Theory of Depreciation*. Although a virtually unknown figure in the investment world, Hotelling was a well-regarded statistician who wrote on such diverse subjects as competition, game theory, resource exhaustion (he is held in high esteem by the supporters of the Hubbert peak of oil production theory) and … depreciation. This paper (Hotelling, 1925) is probably the least remembered, but it is this that will, indirectly, be of some interest to investors.

In this paper, Hotelling defined economic depreciation as the difference between the value of an asset at two different points in time. Since depreciation is usually taken as a yearly charge, economic depreciation will therefore be the difference in the value of an asset between two years. 'Asset value' is understood here as 'economic value of an asset' – in other words, as the net present value of future cash flows discounted over the economic life of an asset (we are using modern language here; Hotelling speaks of the 'net present value of the remaining services provided by the asset . . .'). Presented as such, depreciation is nothing but the loss of a cash flow brought about by the ageing of the asset.

Suppose that an asset worth 100 has an economic life of ten years, during which it produces ten cash flows of 18 annually. 'Economic life' is the time during which the asset is able to produce cash, and 'cash flow' is *gross* cash flow, i.e. before depreciation (naturally) or investment. Graphically, this can be schematised as in Figure 4.3.

The internal rate of return of this asset is 12.4 per cent, assuming that the initial investment is done in year 0. Net asset values are taken at the beginning of the period. In other words, and by construction, the value of this asset (100 at the beginning of the period) is the net present value of ten cash flows of 18 each discounted at 12.4 per cent for one, two, three . . ., and ten years, respectively (Table 4.1). In year 2, and following the same principle, the value of this asset becomes the net present value of *nine* cash flows of 18 each discounted at 12.4 per cent, or 94.4. In year 10, the value of this asset becomes the present value of one cash flow received in a year's time, or 16.01. Thus, each asset can be thought of as made of a number of cash flows released through time. A good, if maybe unexpected, way to think about the equivalence of cash flows and asset values is to compare it to the law of conservation of energy, the First Law of Thermodynamics. It states that there can be no loss or creation of energy in a closed system. Likewise, in the smaller universe of finance, the sum of all energy (cash flows) released has to be precisely equivalent to the amount of energy (value) contained in the asset.

Since the economic definition of an asset is the net present value of *remaining* cash flows, it follows that the difference between the value of the asset in year y and in year y + 1 is the *loss* of one cash flow. Thus, economic depreciation reflects a loss of cash flow. To illustrate this, we can use some more of our DIY physics and picture an asset as the water inside a clepsydra. The flow of water from one part to the other as time passes by is cash flow, *and also depreciation*. When time is up and the upper part is empty, which for us means that the asset has become economically obsolete and cannot produce any more cash flow, there is an exact mirror image (same volume of water) in the bottom part, ready to replace the extinct

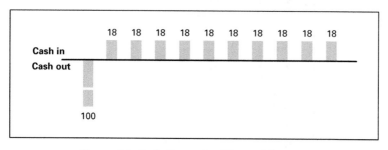

Figure 4.3 Cash flows of a 10-year life asset.

Table 4.1 Calculation of economic net asset value

Years	1	2	3	4	5	6	7	8	9	10	Net asset value
Cash flows	18	18	18	18	18	18	18	18	18	18	

IRR on 100 of investment: 12.4%

NPV of Cash Flows:

	1	2	3	4	5	6	7	8	9	10	Net asset value
	16.01 +	14.24 +	12.67 +	11.27 +	10.03 +	8.92 +	7.93 +	7.06 +	6.28 +	5.59	= 100.0
		16.01 +	14.24 +	12.67 +	11.27 +	10.03 +	8.92 +	7.93 +	7.06 +	6.28	= 94.4
			16.01 +	14.24 +	12.67 +	11.27 +	10.03 +	8.92 +	7.93 +	7.06	= 88.1
				16.01 +	14.24 +	12.67 +	11.27 +	10.03 +	8.92 +	7.93	= 81.1
					16.01 +	14.24 +	12.67 +	11.27 +	10.03 +	8.92	= 73.1
						16.01 +	14.24 +	12.67 +	11.27 +	10.03	= 64.2
							16.01 +	14.24 +	12.67 +	11.27	= 54.2
								16.01 +	14.24 +	12.67	= 42.9
									16.01 +	14.24	= 30.3
										16.01	= 16.0

asset. In practice, depreciation is simply a non-cash charge which builds up a virtual 'sinking fund' which, at the end of the life of the asset, can buy a replacement for it.

It follows from the above that straight-line depreciation is not a very good way of depreciating an asset economically. Straight-line depreciation decreases the value of an asset by a constant amount, calculated as its gross value divided by an approximation of its life. In the previous example, the initial capital cost of 100 depreciated in a straight line would decrease by 10 per year during ten years. With *economic* depreciation, the time value of money is taken into consideration (hence its name). As a result, the money that needs to be set aside in year one, after the loss of the first cash flow, to contribute to the replenishment of the asset back to 100, in year 10, is considerably less than the money needed to be set aside in year 9 for the same purpose. In our original example, in order to get back the 18 of the first cash flow at the end of the ten-year period, the company only needs to set aside 5.59, because $5.59 \times (1 + 12.4\%)^{10} = 18$. Similarly, at year 5, in order to get back the 18 of the fifth cash flow in year 10, when the asset will have collapsed and will need to be rebuilt or repurchased, the company will need to set aside 10.03, because $10.03 \times (1 + 12.4\%)^{5} = 18$. Note that the discount rate used is the IRR of the project or asset (12.4 per cent), not an exogenous cost of capital.

The Hotelling model of economic depreciation primarily applies to single assets – a piece of equipment, a plant or a machine. This model, by and large, does not deal explicitly with growth considerations. Unlike an entire company, single assets have a finite life and cannot 'grow'; they are simply replaced at the end of their economic life. But the model still carries important consequences for the EP framework and the valuation of companies in general. The first consequence is that the accounting book value, depreciated in a straight line, underestimates the residual economic value of an asset – providing yet another reason not to use accounting data. In Figure 4.4, we show the residual values of 100 depreciated linearly and economically over ten years. Straight-line depreciation decays the value of the asset far too quickly. Some of this accelerated depreciation may account for technological progress; the latter does not benefit an existing asset, as capital is 'sunk' for the duration of the asset life, but benefits competing younger assets, thereby diminishing the residual value of

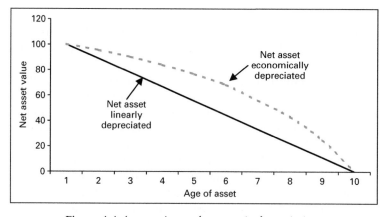

Figure 4.4 Accounting and economic depreciation.

older assets. It is easy to grasp the concept of technological progress and the fall of residual values by applying it to a computer or a car and imagining what happens to their value just before the release of the next model, which will incorporate a higher content of technology. In the case of high technological progress, accountants go even further and purposely accelerate the depreciation of assets faster than straight-line depreciation, using the declining-balance method.

However, technological progress may not always account for the whole gap in residual values between economically and linearly depreciated assets. This gap could just be a bias introduced by accounting, and may explain the existence of goodwill in some acquisitions, alongside the necessity of valuing intangible assets never booked on balance sheet (as seen in Chapter 3). Economic depreciation is the third major adjustment to assets after inflation and the capitalisation of intangibles, and in that respect belongs to the previous chapter; however, because it is a by-product of the return calculation according to Hotelling, we preferred to present it in the context of this chapter.

The second point emerging from the Hotelling demonstration is even more funda-mental to the understanding of asset valuation. It is tautology to say that economic depreciation is the difference between gross cash flow and net cash flow (we are using the term 'net cash flow' here rather than 'free cash flow', which is cash flow after maintenance *and* expansion). This can be written as the following equivalence:

$$D = CF - rV$$

where D is depreciation, CF is gross cash flow, and rV is net cash flow, expressed as the residual value of net assets (V) times the return on asset (r). The fact that net cash flow is the result of the economic return on net assets is also fairly obvious. The above can be rearranged in the following manner:

$$D = CF - rV$$
$$V = \frac{CF - D}{r}$$
$$r = \frac{CF - D}{V}.$$

The second of these equations shows that there is in fact a link between a finite life depreciation model and a perpetuity, since this definition is very close to a perpetuity stream of free cash flow. As for the third rearrangement, it brings about a little revolution. By definition, in an economic depreciation model, *the ratio of net cash flow to net assets is a constant, which is equal to the rate of return of the original project.* This is important for two reasons. First, this ratio provides an accurate calculation of the internal rate of return (IRR) of the investment (the asset) at any point in its life. In an *accounting depreciation model*, the ratio of cash flow (or earnings, or any measure of profits) to book value is never constant. Using our original example and depreciating capital linearly, that ratio looks like Figure 4.5.

The asset seems to get more profitable as it gets older, and therefore, presumably, more valuable. Following this logic, a second before the asset ultimately collapses its return will be infinite, and maybe also its value? We have already seen with Cain

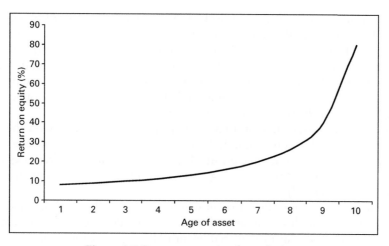

Figure 4.5 Return on equity through time.

and Abel how unsuitable RoE was for valuation analysis; in their case, the level of the ratio was a function of interest rates. Here, we see that it gives ten possible answers to the question of knowing which is the economic return on this asset. In an *economic depreciation model*, the ratio of cash flow to net assets (as defined above) is constant, and equal to the IRR of the project, calculated earlier at 12.4 per cent, or the rate of return of ten cash flows of 18 each produced by an original investment of 100.

Figure 4.6 provides an illustration based on the same asset as earlier, 100 producing ten cash flows of 18 each. The calculations might be more obvious with the help of Table 4.1. In year 2, net cash flow will be 11.72, or 18 of gross cash flow minus 6.28 of economic depreciation. This last number is calculated as $18/1.124^9$, or how much needs to be set aside in year 2 to produce 18 again in year 11 (i.e. nine years

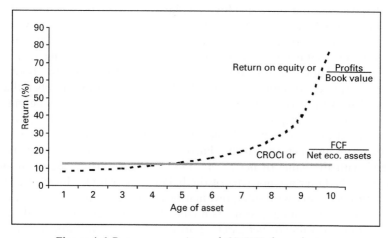

Figure 4.6 Return on equity and CROCI through time.

hence), when the asset has become obsolete. Net economic asset will be 94.41, or the original investment, 100, minus 5.59. This last number is the economic depreciation in year 1, defined as the amount necessary to reproduce the *first* cash flow, now consumed, in ten years time, or $18/1.124^{10}$. The ratio of 11.72 and 94.41 is 12.4 per cent, the IRR of this steam of ten cash flows. In year 7, the same principle will give 6.73 in net cash flow (18 minus 11.27) and 54.20 in net economic assets. *Their ratio still gives the same number, 12.4 per cent.*

Incidentally, this closes the loop that we left open in Chapter 2, with the proof that the enterprise value could equally be defined as free cash flow discounted to infinity, or net assets plus economic profits discounted to infinity in a zero expansion model. This proof required transforming CROCI into FCF/NA, a manipulation that we had yet to explain fully.

The second, equally compelling reason why Harold Hotelling did the investment world a favour is that his economic depreciation model proves a mathematical equivalence between a return calculated as an IRR of *gross* capital and *gross* cash flows over a *finite* economic life, and a return calculated as a ratio of *net* cash flow to *net* assets (economically depreciated, of course). In the latter case, life is, in practice, infinite, because assets are constantly renewed (but, as already mentioned, not *expanded*) by a capital allowance, which is the difference between gross and net cash flow – also called . . . economic depreciation! This is quite practical for the economic profit approach, which does not look for complexity with modelling (and is therefore quite content with the model's inherent simplifications), but rather seeks as accurate as possible an economic picture of a firm. Hotelling allows a company to be represented as a single asset producing (gross) cash flows over an economic life, and this is going to prove a very valuable representation.

Dealing with infinity – cash return on capital invested

The reason is that it is very much preferable to calculate a cash return on capital invested with a finite life model – that is, with the IRR model. This is solely for the sake of convenience and clarity, since gross or net and finite or infinite models will theoretically give the same answer. However, investment analysts will greatly limit misjudgements if the focus is on gross assets, gross cash flow and asset lives.

The first practical reason is that analysts have to *transform* accounting information into economic data; therefore, the more reliable the accounting item is, the easier and more reliable the transformation process will be. And the book value of gross assets (pre-depreciation) is a much cleaner accounting number than net book assets. This is the case because the accounting *net* asset value, by definition, is polluted by straight-line depreciation, write-downs, accelerated depreciation etc. – precisely the kind of noise that will take the analysis away from a fair representation of the *economic* net asset value. Furthermore, companies are more inclined to 'interfere' with the value of net assets only and leave gross assets untouched, simply because the latter are not part of the balance sheet total. 'Interference' may include impairment, asset write-offs, revaluations – all perfectly legal, if not always legitimate, adjustments, but adjustments nonetheless that may indirectly distort the underlying economic value of net assets. Fortunately, these adjustments are rarely reflected at the gross level.

The combination of free cash flow and infinity is equally tricky to handle. Perpetuity means quite a lot of cash flows, and if the rate of reinvestment (the economic depreciation), which is only supposed to keep the assets in steady state in a Hotelling model, is otherwise miscalculated, the compounding effect of the assumed growth (positive or negative) will send the results wildly off-course. It is almost worse if the analyst attempts to take growth into consideration explicitly, as growth to infinity is not a very practical concept. The only practical way out is to assume that growth stops after a certain period, but there is no way of knowing the duration, and the fade, of the asset's competitive advantage (the period during which it produces an excess return), so it ends up being a pure 'educated' – the polite form of 'random' – guess.

In a finite model, cash flow is gross cash flow, a number that is going to be reasonably well approximated by Earnings Before Interest, Tax, Depreciation and Amortisation, although EBITDA will need to be adjusted for capitalised costs and other economic adjustments (leasing costs, for instance), as well as non-cash costs. Practically, there are just fewer ways of getting it wrong. Of course, there is no such thing as a free lunch, and the issue of depreciation still needs to be addressed, but in this model it is expressed in terms of asset life (in the accounting world, linear depreciation is simply the inverse of the life of asset) since the return is calculated as an IRR of gross assets and gross cash flow over n periods. Thinking of an asset (in practice a company) in terms of its asset life is a very therapeutic and beneficial exercise to investment analysis, because it is the language of the management of a firm. A Chief Executive Officer does not think of a plant in terms of its depreciation rate; he thinks of it as an asset that was built in 1982, has become the least productive plant in the company, and will either need to be closed down or totally overhauled within two years. Obviously, this economic life of twenty-four years (assuming we are in 2004) does translate into a linear depreciation of 1/24, or 4.15 per cent per year. But this financial language is advantageously replaced by its economic equivalent: it is more helpful to economic analysis to say that, for instance, an ethylene cracker has an average economic life of twenty-four years.

Asset lives will also ensure that similar companies are analysed in a similar way, regardless of their accounting depreciation. There are few instances of perfectly comparable businesses, but airlines provide such examples. It can be said without fear of approximation that British Airways and Lufthansa do the same thing, economically; they move people and goods in planes all over the world. Yet, the ratio of depreciable assets to accounting depreciation is much smaller for Lufthansa than for BA, suggesting that the German company has chosen to depreciate its assets more quickly than has its British competitor.[1] Whatever the accounting reasons, this is likely to confuse the analysis and is economically misleading, unless Lufthansa has a substantially larger fleet of shorter-lived planes, which is unlikely. What is more likely is that both companies have exactly the same economic life.

There are various ways of estimating the economic life of an asset/company. The ratio of gross depreciable assets to depreciation will give the accounting life, as shown above. A useful and more 'economic' variation is the ratio of current cost accounted (CCA) gross assets to maintenance capex. CCA assets are inflation-adjusted, as described in Chapter 3. Maintenance capex is the amount of *real* investment necessary to keep the company in steady state. This is not a concept that is defined without difficulty for all industries, but it is relatively easy to work out for most of them, especially for capital intensive businesses with a low or a well-defined (i.e. that can be modelled) growth pattern. Such industries would include Semiconductors, Telecom Services, Retail, plus the traditional capital-intensive industries such as Chemicals, Cement, Steel, Pulp & Paper, etc. The Materials sector, which includes all the previous four industries, had a capex to depreciation ratio of $1.68\times$ in 1990, and slightly less than 1 in 2002. This sector does not grow very fast, at best in line with GDP; this means that capex is mainly going to concern the replacement of existing assets – i.e. be *maintenance* capex. This view is reinforced by the observation that the average ratio of net to gross assets is 45 per cent, suggesting that the average asset is slightly older than half-life. Therefore, capex is going to be a very good proxy for CCA depreciation. But which capex figure? We can already discard the low numbers of around 1 time depreciation (depreciation is historically cost accounted, and we are looking for the *real* amount, which has to be higher, because of inflation). We can also discard the high numbers of the early 1990s, because economic history tells us that a lot of new capacity was being built at that time, especially in chemicals. The capex figures of this period are bound to include some capacity expansion, which we do not want to capture. This new capacity, incidentally, was partly responsible for the 1992–1993 recession. Excluding these two periods, the ratio of capex to depreciation comes out at $1.3\times$, which can perhaps be reduced to $1.25\times$ to weed out any creep capacity. This would be the basis for an estimate of maintenance capex in this particular industry.

Alternatively, an analyst can relatively easily break down a company's assets into clusters according to their economic lives: commercial buildings; industrial buildings; heavy, medium and light equipment; IT equipment etc. Generally, there is enough information about assets in the annual report, and most companies will 'fit' into these basic categories. Exceptionally, one or two must be added, such as 'exhaustible resources' (for mining companies) or 'long-term infrastructure' (for the Victorian pipes that UK water companies are still using). An harmonic average of these categories will give quite a reliable approximation for economic life.

Once gross depreciable assets have a life, intangible assets and non-depreciable assets (mainly net working capital and land) are added to create gross capital invested (GCI). The IRR is then calculated as the rate of return that equalises the value of GCI and cash flows over the life. Schematically, this is represented by the familiar 'up and down' arrow chart (Figure 4.7). Note that the last arrow is bigger than the previous ones, as this last cash flow contains all the non-depreciable assets which, by definition, still have a value once depreciable assets are extinct.

Confusion often arises between this calculation and a forecast. The CROCI calculation does not 'forecast' cash flows 'n' years out, 'n' being the economic life of the assets. It is a spot calculation, representing the average of what all projects in the firm earn today (this year). Because it is computed as an internal rate of return, it needs to simulate periodic inflows during the average economic life of all the projects, which it takes as the cash flow of the year for which the CROCI is calculated. The issue of fade (or erosion) of the marginal return on investment is a separate issue altogether. We discuss fades in the following section, as well as in Chapter 6.

As we routinely point out, all our work is driven by a sole objective: to achieve a relevant economic representation of financial markets in order to enhance an

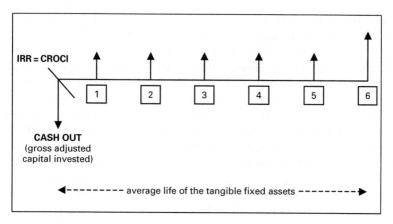

Figure 4.7 Schematic calculation of the IRR of an asset.

investor's ability to select stocks. We readily admit that applying Hotelling to an entire firm in order to calculate the CROCI can appear as a theoretical stretch to some, due to the inherent simplifications that this application entails. *However, it is relatively easy to check how good CROCI is as an approximation of the economic return of an investment.* At the most aggregated level, i.e. taking the average of roughly the 700 largest companies in the world, the cash return on capital invested should be very close to the long-term real total investment return in equity markets. Figure 4.8 shows the aggregated CROCI of these 700 stocks between 1989 and 2005. There is clearly a cycle which corresponds to the business cycle, with the 1991 and 1993 recessions, the setback of 1998, the peak of 2000 and the mini-trough of 2002. The average CROCI for this seventeen-year period comes out at 5.53 per cent.

The highly informative *Triumph of the Optimists, 101 years of Global Investment Returns* (Dimson *et al.*, 2002) contains the real investment return for twelve countries in the twentieth century. Given that the weight of each market has varied

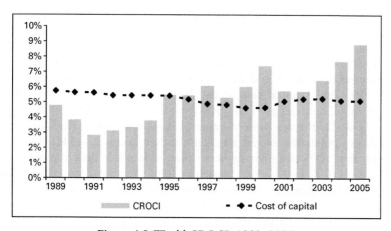

Figure 4.8 World CROCI, 1989–2005.

considerably during this 100-year span, it is very difficult to aggregate these data into a single number. An unweighted average gives a figure of 5.5 per cent. Ascribing a 35 per cent weight to the US, 20 per cent to the UK (once the biggest economy in the world) and 20 per cent to Japan, with the rest (25 per cent) being equally distributed between Canada, France, Germany, Italy and The Netherlands, produces a very similar number – 5.58 per cent. The authors' own world figure is 5.4 per cent. *Thus, CROCI approximates, to within a handful of basis points, the real long-term return of equity investment* – and this despite the fact that the last fifteen years have seen abnormal levels of returns in both Japan and the United States. Japanese companies have returned an average 3.2 per cent in the past fifteen years, a level of economic return that would not be sustainable for an entire century. Similarly, the US has enjoyed a recent period of super-returns, close to twice the cost of capital – an equally unsustainable situation. Somehow, the world return on economic capital does not seem to change over the long run, even if regional ones vary widely.

Hitherto, we have been able to reconstruct a full market value (enterprise value) of assets and approximate the replacement value of economic assets. With CROCI, the real economic return on capital invested, ends the construction of the third pillar of our four-posted edifice, the equivalence between the asset multiple and the relative return. It remains to address the fourth and last prop, the cost of capital.

The cost of capital: an implicit calculation – fading and failing

The issue of the cost of capital is a thorny one, and endless debates tend to erupt in research departments about it. There is discussion, if not confusion, about the cost of capital, the discount rate, the expected return, the cost of equity capital, the weighted average cost of capital, etc. The stakes are high, since this figure will determine whether a firm creates or destroys value. This, in turn, will have immense consequences on the acceptable economic growth rate of the firm. It is worth rehearsing right away a few situations where the cost of capital plays a major role in the assessment of a corporate strategy by shareholders. First and foremost, from their point of view, a firm below the cost of capital must not grow in real terms, since any capital invested is automatically valued by the market at a discount to its original cost, by application of the Equivalence principle. By way of example, a firm with a cash return of 4 per cent, investing with a cost of capital of 5 per cent, will immediately see a 100 investment valued at 80, or the ratio of 4 per cent over 5 per cent. Alternatively, it can be said that this firm loses 1 per cent (of assets) of value, on average. Thus, 100 invested will be worth (1) the full value of the assets plus (2) the net present value of economic profits (EP), or economic value added, in application of the RI formula: Net assets + (EP/d). In this case, we find again that 100 is immediately transformed into 80, since the market value will be 100, plus $100 \times (-1\%/5\%)$, which is -20. Of course, no consideration is given here to the fact that the new investment might yield a higher cash return than the existing business. Under rare circumstances, it is possible for some companies to find new, more profitable investments. The German company Mannesmann, an industrial conglomerate involved in engineering and building materials, is such an example. In the early 1990s it invested in mobile telephony; it became the second largest operator in Germany and was eventually taken over by Vodafone, which span off the non-telecom services businesses. However, such success stories are rare. Générale des Eaux, a French water utility, followed the same course with investments in mobile telephony and media, only to collapse under the weight of its debt. Management of businesses returning cash below the cost of capital had better be warned; a growth strategy will be taken with extreme scepticism by investors, and will result in a market value at an immediate discount to the replacement value of these investments. Should management prove the market wrong, and succeed in investing in higher returning assets, then the market will be more than happy to re-rate the company accordingly. But, as far as the law of economic profits is concerned, the correct course of action for a business below the cost of capital is to shrink it, disposing of the lowest returning parts or reducing the overall capacity in value-destroying areas. The most spectacular illustration may well be provided by Itochu, a small but typical Japanese conglomerate involved in just about everything – media, cars and tyres, industrial machinery, health care, energy services, etc. Its profile of economic capital invested is illustrated in Figure 4.9.

Clearly, management came to the conclusion that too much capital was involved in too many operations, and reduced the company's consumption of capital accordingly. This transformed the cash return profile of the company as shown in Figure 4.10.

Most of the time, companies with cash returns below the cost of capital trade at around their replacement value, with the average asset multiple coming out at 1.1× over the 1989–2005 period for our universe of large capitalisations, which includes an extravagant 1.76× in 1999, the year of the equity bubble (even low-returning companies were buoyed by this tide). However, once these management teams decide to manage their assets in the way suggested above, investors will tend to respond enthusiastically. Du Pont, the venerable US chemical company, offers an amusing symmetry between the amount of capital reduced by the management and the appreciation of its market value. Net capital invested went, on our numbers, from approximately $40bn in 1989 to $25bn in 2004. Management has reduced

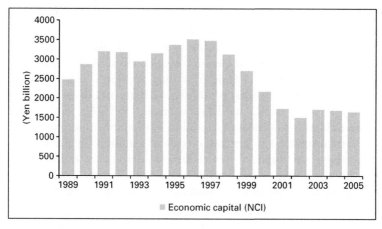

Figure 4.9 Itochu: profile of economic capital invested.

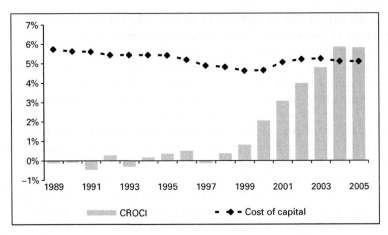

Figure 4.10 Itochu: transformed CROCI profile.

economic capital invested almost every year since 1989. The market capitalisation went in exactly the opposite direction, from $25bn in 1989 to $43bn in 2004! We would not take this one-for-one rule for granted. In any case, though, like in the case of Itochu, DU Pont's profile of cash return, whilst remaining cyclical (the trough of 2001 was as bad as in 1992–1993), did improve peak-to-peak as a result of a lesser consumption of capital, and shareholders duly adjusted the valuation.

The cost of capital, the hurdle rate of value creation and destruction, is therefore a crucial number for assessing the performance of a company. Our purpose, here again, is to present a practical solution to this difficult calculation, as well as to demonstrate that this solution is grounded in a sound economic foundation. Some obvious points are often overlooked by financial analysts. The cost of capital, for a firm, is the return that its capital providers (all providers, for all capital) expect from their investment. It is also, by definition, its discount rate. Because we analyse here the firm's value (or enterprise value), the appropriate cost of capital is a Weighted Average Cost of Capital, usually abbreviated WACC. And, finally, the analysis of the cost of capital conventionally breaks it down into a risk-free rate and a risk premium, the latter remunerating the extra risks (volatility, financial distress, sustainability of the firm's competitive advantage period) taken by equity investors.

We have already dismissed in Chapter 2 the calculation of the cost of capital as the inverse of the PE ratio; this simple trick only applies to a handful of special cases. In his reference book *The Cost of Capital*, C. Patterson distinguishes between explicit and implicit cost of capital models (Patterson, 1995). An 'explicit' model is a model where an estimate of the cost of capital is 'built up' from separately estimated components, with respect to a general theory of equilibrium pricing in capital markets. Conversely, an 'implicit' model directly derives an estimated expected return for investors, without undue consideration to the components of this return. Here is not the place to review all these models, but it is a good opportunity to make once again our 'theory versus practice' point: *a quantitatively-minded practitioner will always prefer an implicit approach*. The reason is that share prices do not adjust from 'the truth' (even assuming that such a definitive concept exists in financial markets), but from what is discounted by investors. It is always preferable, therefore, to start any financial analysis from what the market is pricing; this is as true for the cost of capital as it is for other financial variables and concepts, such as expected growth or margin.

The genes of almost all explicit models are to be found in the CAPM, Capital Asset Pricing Model, or APT, Asset Pricing Theory. The CAPM was invented by William Sharpe in the 1960s, himself a student of Harry Markowitz, another very important figure in financial theory, who we will meet in Chapter 9. Let us leave it to Benoit Mandelbrot to argue with Professor Sharpe (Mandelbrot and Hudson, 2004):

> Recall that, under CAPM, the return an investor should expect to receive from a stock is just the T-bill rate [i.e. a risk-free rate], plus some proportion of the stock market's overall performance; that proportion is the crucial 'beta' value, which varies from stock to stock. Under the orthodox theory, nothing else should be going on. No need to study the fundamentals of the company in question [. . .] Just calculate the beta, check the T-bill rate in the newspaper, and make a broad economic forecast about how the stock market overall will do. End of story.

Although this is a simplification of the legacy of Professor Sharpe, the criticism is accurate. In a slightly drier style, C. Patterson explains CAPM like this (Patterson, 1995: 35):

> if [the non-systematic risks] are uncorrelated across securities, and the number of securities is sufficiently large, the variance of the portfolio's total return is determined *only* (our emphasis) by the systematic risks of its components securities.

The latter is the portfolio beta, or the average of the betas of the components. Arguments in favour of and against the CAPM have been going back and forth since the 1970s, so the issue is not exactly new. In 1992, Professors French and Fama published a very important article showing that fundamental variables such as book value ratios or earnings ratios (even though these are accounting-based ratios) can explain a large part of the performance of one stock relative to another (French and Fama, 1992). This was in itself enough to cast a shadow of doubt on the validity of the CAPM model as an investment tool.

Implicit models, still according to Patterson, include the observation of the historical risk premium, as well as DCF and '"q" ratio-derived' calculations. Although the first option seems to be the easiest and the most straightforward, a rigorous measure of the historical risk premium does create serious practical difficulties. An excellent analysis of the historical risk premium in the US was provided in 2002 by Robert D. Arnott and Peter L. Bernstein (the very same from the introduction of this book), in an article published in the *Financial Analysts Journal* (Arnott and Bernstein, 2002). The authors point out that 'the *observed* excess return and the *prospective* risk premium [are] two fundamentally different concepts that, unfortunately, carry the same label – risk premium'. In other words, only the *ex ante* expectation constitutes a true measure of the risk premium. Unfortunately, because it is easier to measure what has happened rather than what was expected to happen, it is the *ex post* achievement, i.e. the realised performance, that is commonly used as the basis for the calculation of the historical risk premium.

We prefer to use a DCF-based model to calculate our discount rate because it seems to be the methodology where assumptions can be pinned down most easily, especially if implemented implicitly on a spreadsheet, as opposed to an explicit and rambling mathematical formula. The mathematical principle of a DCF-based model is straightforward enough, and is a simple rearrangement of the FCF/d formula. Evidently, if the discounting of free cash flow to infinity gives a market value, this can be re-written so that an observed market value (MV) gives a discount rate, where $d = FCF/MV$. But this suffers from the same problems as those identified in Chapter 2: free cash flow is a volatile measure, and this static discounting exercise ignores growth. A partial response to these objections would be to introduce growth (g) in the discounting formula, which becomes $FCF/(d - g)$. Extracting the discount rate from the formula would give $d = (FCF/MV) + g$, which is the basic DCF-based cost of capital formula, usually expressed, for the cost of equity only, as dividend yield plus expected growth. This makes perfect sense; the expected return of an equity investor has to be the current dividend yield plus growth expectations, be it of the dividend stream or of the share price, depending on the assumptions taken on the pay-out ratio. But this model only works when $d > g$; growth is understood as the *sustainable* long-term growth rate.

This brings us to a familiar problem, namely the impossibility of predicting, with any level of accuracy, the shape of the stream of income (dividend, or free cash flow) to be discounted in the *immediate* future, say the next two business cycles – a frustrating issue in financial modelling. The reason is that it is not possible to predict how the competitive advantage period of the firm will evolve over time. We define the competitive advantage period as the period during which the firm earns a return above the cost of capital. It appears that this economic characteristic is largely random, with some companies defying the laws of competition and reinventing themselves constantly, whilst others fail mysteriously overnight. Consider the following example of two companies both selling consumer goods: Colgate and Nike. In Figure 4.11, it can be seen that Colgate has been able not only to sustain but also to increase its cash return almost every year since 1992, in what is otherwise a cut-throat business.

Looking at Figure 4.12, Nike, another very successful global provider of consumer goods, appears to have given up a significant portion of its excess return in 1997, without any obvious reason other than a very substantial investment programme, and certainly independently of any corporate event (acquisition, disposal) or macroeconomic event.

Furthermore, it is difficult to distinguish between 'fade' – a *permanent* loss of competitive advantage translating into a lower marginal return – and what can only be a cyclical loss of return. In the case of Intel, shown in Figure 4.13, the pattern of cash return between 1989 and 2000 does suggest a fairly orderly cyclical pattern, possibly with a slight upward fade. With the technology recession of 2001, are we

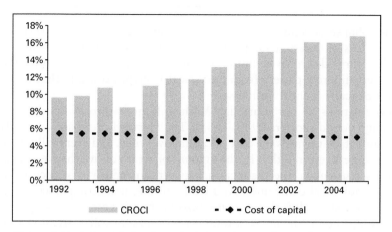

Figure 4.11 Colgate-Palmolive: CROCI and cost of capital, 1992–2004.

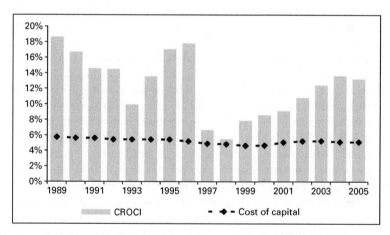

Figure 4.12 Nike: CROCI and cost of capital, 1989–2005.

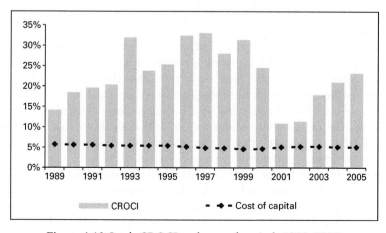

Figure 4.13 Intel: CROCI and cost of capital, 1989–2005.

to read the collapse of return of that year as an unprecedented cyclical trough, or as an abrupt loss of excess return? The following years suggest that it might be a bit of both; returns did recover, but at a slower pace. The cash return profile also followed a very different pattern from the typical V-shaped recovery that we usually observe in classically cyclical businesses.

These observations do not contradict Michael Porter's theories on the competitive advantage period (Porter, 1980, 1985). The Harvard professor contends that *industry* returns fade towards the cost of capital over time, and eventually *industries* lose all their excess return – that is, the amount of return above the cost of capital. But investors must make the distinction between an industry, or sector, and its components, individual companies. And whilst sectors fade, companies *fail*, as the last few examples show. It is therefore not possible to calculate the cost of capital of individual companies as the internal rate of return of an explicit stream of income (say free cash flow). Eventually, a company's return *will* get close to the cost of capital, but we have no way of knowing how and when it will get there, and all the empirical evidence shows that this path is unpredictable. We will address this issue more comprehensively in Chapter 6, when we analyse the different patterns of CROCI profiles.

Yet, evidently, the internal rate of return which reconciles the market value of the firm and its stream of cash flows *is* the expected return of its capital providers, and thus the real cost of capital. However, what is not possible to be predicted at a company level, or even at a sector level (i.e. what is the competitive advantage of the energy sector relative to the rest of the economy?) *is* possible to implement for the market as a whole, *because there is no fade at the level of the economy*. In truth, it could be argued with some success that this is not entirely accurate. National economies gain or lose competitive advantage relative to the world economy through their exchange rate, for instance, or through the fact that they own certain mineral resources. By implementing a more or less liberal economic policy, countries will gain or lose a certain advantage in world trade. Investments in the education system can be seen as a competitive advantage leading to a dominant position in certain industries. However, none of this appears to be enough to inflict long-term damage or to procure a long-term advantage for national economies, at least those of the US, Europe and Japan, which represent the vast majority of the investable universe of an equity investor.

As a result, the issue of fade can be ignored altogether at the most aggregated level, and it is possible to model explicitly a stream of, say, 100 cash flows (the net present values after the 101st cash flow are so small that they can safely be ignored) for the entire market. We are looking for a *weighted average cost of capital* here; therefore, we need to model *operating* and *free* cash flow, and calculate the IRR which equalises the net present value of these 100 cash flows to the aggregated 'enterprise value' of the market – that is, put more simply, the combined total market value of equities, financial debt and economic liabilities.

Free cash flow is given by the after-tax cash yield on asset (CROCI × net assets) minus the net growth in assets, which includes maintenance as well as expansion capital spending. In our experience, it is much easier, and more accurate, to model free cash flow in this manner, because it allows the analyst to focus separately on the two cycles that influence the company's FCF: the cash return cycle, and the growth cycle. We suggest modelling them independently, and combining them to form the stream of FCF. Let us deal first with the cash return. As we have seen previously, we can assume that there is no fade in returns for the market as a whole, which means that the trend cash return will be at the cost of capital – itself approximated by the long-term average cash return of the region in question. In the case of the US economy, the average cash return between 1989 and 2005 comes out at 6.53 per cent (remember that this is an inflation-adjusted number). This is remarkably close to the long-term averages that others have calculated (see Dimson *et al.*, 2002) over different time horizons, which proves that fade in returns is not a meaningful concept at the level of an economy. However, the cash return in 2004 was 9.3 per cent, some 280 basis points above this trend. Given the lack of fade assumption (upward or downward), this discrepancy can only come from the business cycle. In practice, even with no change in the long-term, or trend, cash return of an economy, cycles come and go, pulling the yearly cash return up and down around the long-term mean. In Figure 4.14 the US business cycle is very conspicuous, with the lows of the early 1990s and the peak of the late 1990s.

It will therefore be necessary to model a standardised business cycle, with its peak, trough and period. This can be constructed from the observation of history. Similarly, net growth in assets will follow a fade-free trend, naturally quite close to trend GDP, but with accelerations and decreases in the rate of accumulation of assets, again quite closely correlated to the macroeconomic business cycle. We show in Figure 4.15 the aggregated variation of growth in assets for the full universe (700 or so global companies) under CROCI coverage since 1989. The average comes out at 8 per cent, twice the global GDP growth, but is distorted by three factors. First, economic capital includes mergers and acquisitions, which is not part of trend growth. Second, this universe of large capitalisation stocks represents, by definition, the most economically successful companies in the world, the growth rate of which is bound to be higher than the average of the world economy. And third, it excludes the less dynamic, i.e. non-market-related parts of the economy. But the highs and lows of the global business cycle can clearly be recognised. See

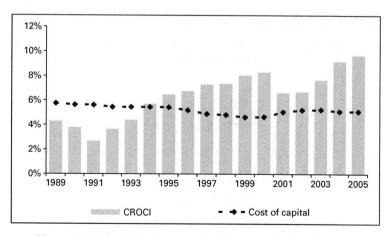

Figure 4.14 The US business cycle: CROCI and cost of capital.

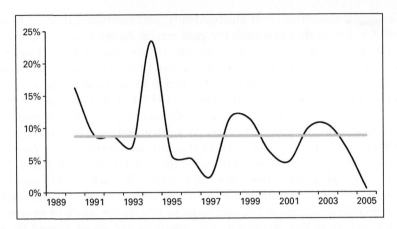

Figure 4.15 Full universe under CROCI coverage: change in economic capital (NCI) percentage, 1989–2005.

especially the 1991–1993 Europe/US recession, the (strong) 1995–1996 recovery, the Asia-induced 1997 trough, the 1999 peak, and the more recent 2000–2002 technology-driven slowdown.

Combining the cycle of cash return with the cycle of growth in assets will produce a stream of FCF going far enough into the future to calculate an internal rate of return (IRR) on the observed market value of assets (the aggregated enterprise values). This discount rate is an approximation of the expected return of investors on this particular market – in other words, the average cost of capital prevalent in this economy. Because the cash return is inflation-adjusted and net assets are at replacement value, the IRR will be the real expected return.

An empirical calculation with multiple uses

This empirical calculation has got numerous practical applications, and provides invaluable information about the state of market expectations. First and foremost, this cost of capital figure closes the study of the relative return – that is, the cash return relative to the cost of capital, itself the second part of the Economic Equivalence identity:

$$\frac{\text{Value}_{\text{market}}}{\text{Value}_{\text{replacement}}} = \frac{R}{d}$$

or, in the jargon of this book:

$$\frac{\text{EV}}{\text{NCI}} = \frac{\text{CROCI}}{\text{CoC}}.$$

As we have seen in Chapter 2, the economic equivalence is the bedrock of mean-reversion in financial markets.

Second, this expected return/discount rate figure can naturally be used as the hurdle rate of value creation for individual companies, sectors or indeed markets. Readers familiar with the CAPM will legitimately question the use of a single figure applied to hundreds of different companies. Traditionally, the computation of the cost of capital is taught as a weighted average of the cost of debt and equity, by definition a number depending on the financial gearing of each individual company, the rating of the local market and the local cost of debt. Whilst this is undeniably true, there are also some benefits in applying a global cost of capital to all companies, and the idea is not as outlandish as it may appear. We apply the CROCI model to a small group of very large companies only, the 700 to 800 largest companies in the world. All these companies have access to global capital markets, and can swap interest rates and currencies as they please. Moreover, there does not seem to be much evidence that investors are discriminating against indebted or risky companies within the big firms bracket by demanding a higher return. We will show in Chapter 7 that it is always possible to release this simplification, especially in the case of heavily indebted companies.

Finally, the calculation presented here can be used to extract the risk premium that investors are willing to receive for a pure equity investment. This approach has the advantage of addressing the confusion between realised and expected risk premium, perceptively identified by Arnott and Bernstein (2002). By using the IRR of the market, the calculation is, by definition, forward looking, contrary to the traditional way of measuring the risk premium, which is simply the observation of the realised excess return of equities over bonds, annualised. The drawbacks of the latter approach are substantial. To name two, there is, first, a strong survival bias in equity indices, which will flatter the total return of equities relative to bonds, and inflate the observed risk premium. Second, this measure is *ex post*, and only gauges what it says, namely the excess return of equities over bonds. This number is not equivalent to the *ex ante* risk premium that equity investors were willing to receive for their commitment at the beginning of the period. In other words, an *ex post* measure gives the original risk premium *plus* deviation from expectations, be it disappointment or the reverse. Since there is no way of knowing, this measure is, at best, a poor approximation of the actual historical risk premium, and an even poorer guide for what the risk premium should be on equity investments going forward. In reverse, extracting the risk premium from the implied expected return on equities should give a fairly good approximation of the *ex ante* extra remuneration required by investors for equity financing.

As already seen, the market's internal rate of return, which in our case is based on the enterprise value, is equivalent to a weighted average cost of capital. It can therefore be written according to the following formula:

$$\text{WACC} = \frac{E}{EV} \times \text{CoE} + \frac{D}{EV} \times \text{CoD} \times (1-t).$$

where E is the market value of equity and CoE the real cost of equity, D is the market value of debt and CoD the real cost of debt, and t is the marginal corporate tax rate. The proportion of equity and debt value within the enterprise value is directly observable; let us call them e and d, such that $e + d = 1$. The real cost of debt is approximated by the BBB bond yield (BY), which is the credit rating of the market, on average, minus inflation expectations. The WACC is the IRR of the market, and the corporate tax rate is estimated at 30 per cent. Thus, the real cost of equity is:

$$CoE = \frac{IRR - 0.7(dBY)}{e}.$$

This figure comprises the risk premium and the real risk-free return. A number of simplifications are required in order to extract the risk premium from it. Theoretically, the real return on risk-free securities ought to be given by the return of inflation-linked bonds, such as the TIPS in the US, the index-linked bonds in the UK, the OATi in France, etc. In practice, using the return from these securities can be misleading. These bonds tend not to be very liquid (although the liquidity situation has improved dramatically since their launch), and it is difficult to know whether their yield conveys a genuine price, or is also a function of investors' appetite in the face of an illiquid market. These issues also lack long history, which prevents the calculation of meaningful averages. It is a good idea to calculate the real yield with the nominal bond yield minus inflation expectations as well, by way of comparison. However, volatility in the series can also create some problems. A third solution would be to assume that the real yield on risk-free securities mean-revert to 2.5 to 3 per cent for long periods of time, which it does, observably,[2] and deduct this amount from the calculated cost of equity, to arrive at the implied, or *ex ante*, risk premium.

Notes

1. 'Fleet is generally depreciated over periods ranging from 15 to 25 years, after making allowance for estimated residual values' – BA Annual Report; 'New aircrafts and spare engines are depreciated over a period of twelve years to a residual value of 15 per cent' – Lufthansa Annual Report.
2. In order to observe the real yield of government bonds (i.e. quasi risk-free) over long periods, the study of UK Gilts, which go back a few centuries, is particularly useful. Throughout the nineteenth century and up to the Second World War, inflation was almost unknown for long stretches of time, and therefore nominal and real yields were the same. In this period, there is strong mean-reversion of the nominal yield around the 3 per cent mark. It can also be observed that 3 per cent is more or less in line with global GDP growth in modern times.

References

Arnott, R. and Bernstein, P. (2002). What risk premium is 'normal'? *Financial Analysts Journal*, **March/April**.

Dimson, E., Marsh, P. and Staunton, M. (2002). *Triumph of the Optimists, 101 years of Global Investment Returns*. Princeton University Press.

French, K. R. and Fama, E. F. (1992). The cross section of expected stock return. *Journal of Finance*, **47**(2).

Hotelling, H. (1925). *A General Mathematical Theory of Depreciation*. American Statistical Association, pp. 340–353.

Keynes, J. M. (1936). *The General Theory of Employment*. Harcourt Brace.

Mandelbrot, B. B. and Hudson, R. L. (2004). *The (Mis)behaviour of Markets: A Fractal View of Risk, Ruin and Reward*. Basic Books.

Patterson, C. S. (1995). *The Cost of Capital: Theory and Estimation*. Quorum Books.

Porter, M. E. (1980). *Competitive Strategy: Techniques for Analyzing Industries and Competitors*. The Free Press.

Porter, M. E. (1985). *Competitive Advantage*. The Free Press.

Tobin, J. and Brainard, W. C. (1977). Chapter 11: Asset markets and the cost of capital. *Cowles Foundation Paper 440*, reprinted from *Private Values and Public Policy, Essays in Honor of William Fellner*. North-Holland.

5 The price of growth

The stuff of dreams

We have seen in Chapter 4 how difficult it is to deal with growth; there are subtle differences between *free* and *net* cash flow, and it is fiddly to introduce growth explicitly in the Hotelling model of depreciation. As a result, the economic Equivalence between the asset multiple and the relative return ends up with two limiting assumptions; both the level of cash return (CROCI) and the level of economic capital (NCI) are deemed constant. Strangely, the assumption of constant returns does not seem to bother investors much; it does however need to be analysed in some detail, which will be the subject of the next chapter. On the other hand, they often seem concerned about the assumption of constant Net Capital Invested (NCI), because it is perceived to be equivalent to a 'static', or no growth, assumption. This needs to be qualified. Net capital invested represents an approximation of the real value of assets, at replacement cost. Assuming that NCI remains constant is not quite the same as assuming that the asset base is left untouched. Every year there is an amount of new capital invested in the business, which exactly replaces an amount of capital which has become obsolete, and so does not produce any more economic profits. If the replacement cost of this extinct capital goes up, so does the level of NCI – and vice versa. However, it is true is that the Equivalence does not take into consideration the *expansion* of the capital base, for instance to accompany the future expansion of a rapidly growing core business or to venture into new areas. As such, it does represent a simplification of the economic reality.

Given that growth is the stuff of dreams in financial markets, it is understandable that the simple economic Equivalence should be seen as a somewhat limited valuation model, a concern which deserves the consideration of the current chapter. Growth is a difficult concept to pin down. It represents an exponential progression (it compounds) but is often expressed as a perpetuity calculation (a ratio) for the sake of simplicity. For a more accurate calculation the maths quickly gets a bit complex, because you have to deal with intricate, non-linear relationships admitting of no shortcuts, unless you are comfortable manipulating integrals in your sleep. Not that this would be beyond the means of any numerate postgraduate and his computer. The problem is that the number of explicit assumptions escalates very quickly because nothing can grow at a constant rate forever, and the usefulness of a model is generally inversely proportional to the number of assumptions required. In order to limit the number of explicit assumptions, then, growth has to be understood to be 'at equilibrium', which in practice means that 'g' must be smaller than 'd', since the discounting factor is d minus g, with a result which obviously cannot be negative. There is nothing wrong with this simplified model, except that the additional amount of information that 'growth at equilibrium' brings is probably quite small – not least because, in theory, g can only be a small number, normally close to zero (perhaps 1 per cent or 2 per cent). Finally, growth is tricky because no one seems to agree on what is actually growing, although by default everybody uses reported earnings growth. In this chapter, we focus on the three important issues to the analysis of growth. First and foremost, growth of what? Since reported earnings are hardly the most relevant item for investment analysis, it is highly dubious whether the *rate of change* of reported earnings could be either. Second, how to measure growth? Explicitly or implicitly? We will touch on the debate of the relative importance of what an investor *thinks* against what the market *prices*. And finally, we will offer a quantitative framework for measuring how much growth expectations matter in the pricing mechanism.

CROCI and the Big Mac

So what is 'growth'? Sales growth? Earnings growth? Asset growth? Since an economy moves upwards, on a trend basis, everything in an economic entity – sales, assets, profits – will have a tendency to grow, unless this entity's relevance to the economy is fading, or it is itself dying, perhaps because of bad management. According to the divide between investment and speculation, *dividend* growth is what should exclusively matter to an investor. However, this is not always what is observable, even over very long periods of time. Microsoft started to pay a dividend only in 2003, some seventeen years after its Initial Public Offering, and it still saw its share price going up nearly 263 times over this period. The argument that, for almost 4000 days of trading, investors always found a 'speculator' to whom they could sell on their shares is unquestionably technically true, given that nobody bought these shares for income. But it is on the verge of being spurious. Obviously, investors are sometimes quite happy to see their due, the dividend, left with the company in the form of retained earnings. Since every Finance Director knows that retained earnings are the cheapest source of financing, this means that investors are sometimes quite happy to fund cheaply the left-hand side of the balance sheet – in other words, to fund the asset expansion of their company. This can only mean that investors view *asset growth* as being almost as important as dividend growth.

Warren Buffet would embrace this argument wholeheartedly. In his view, a high dividend payout ratio is tantamount to the admission that the company has run out of investment opportunities. More conservative investors argue that management should let their shareholders decide where they want to invest the fruits of their capital by 'giving them their money back'. To stick to the Microsoft example, this would imply that Microsoft should not have invested, for instance, in the X Box business, but returned money to shareholders earlier (with dividends or share buy backs). Those investors who then wanted to invest in a computer games business would have done so more efficiently, the argument goes, by buying Sony or Nintendo shares. The debate is endless and, all considered, not very interesting, because it is difficult to draw general conclusions from it. That said, there is, however, abundant academic literature on the subject. It is accepted that a dividend change may convey important information to shareholders even if managers are not explicitly trying to use dividends as a signalling tool. The dividend change is interpreted as evidence of increased or decreased cash flow. When firms announce dividend increases, their stock prices generally increase by about 2 per cent (Aharony and Swary, 1980). However, the relationship is loose. Lintner (1956) discovered that individual firms tend to smooth their dividends. He found that managers aim to have steadily increasing dividends, and as a result only slowly adjust dividends to increases in earnings. This explains the major differences in the dividend policies of various types of firms. The high-tech growth firms have both low dividend yields and low payout ratios, and Microsoft is not the sole example. Companies like Dell and Cisco Systems declare no or low dividends despite having net profits in excess of 2 billion US dollars. Dell's net profit for 2003 was $2.6 billion, while Cisco Systems declared a net profit of $3.6 billion in 2003. Utilities, on the other hand, usually pay out a sizeable portion of their earnings in dividends. Duke Energy's payout ratio in 2002 was 75 per cent.

What is beyond doubt is that asset growth is indeed the *only* form of growth that matters economically, i.e. for the production of economic profits, residual income or economic value added. The cash that is produced from the value-added process of a company is defined as:

$$(CROCI - CoC) \times NCI,$$

with CROCI the rate of cash return on asset, CoC the cost of capital, and NCI the net capital invested, or net economic assets. Thus, only three variables can affect the rate of production of economic profits: asset growth, a change in the level of return on assets, and a change in the cost of capital. Of these three, it is clear that only the first one is a true measure of economic growth for a company. And yet, for most investors, 'growth' will almost always refer to earnings growth. If this is accounting earnings growth, it is in most cases more or less meaningless. If this is *economic* earnings, though, it carries some meaning. After all, it is the rate of accumulation of value added. Yet measuring this accumulation is not a very insightful piece of analysis. According to the formula above, earnings growth is the product of asset growth and return expansion, and it is crucially important to differentiate between the two. The Big Mac example that follows illustrates the interplay between asset growth and cash margin, and explains why.

In 2002, McDonald's achieved a cash return on economic assets (CROCI) of 8 per cent. In the long run, McDonald's appears to be approximately a 10 per cent CROCI business, but the company went through a rough patch between 2000 and 2002, and saw its cash return drop by 200 basis points (this was the time when various lobbies had identified McDonald's as the symbol of unhealthy eating habits, and top line was starting to be hurt. A radical change in the offering followed, with the introduction of new products such as salads, fruit and yoghurts). We estimate that the NCI of the company was in the region of $23.3bn in 2002, which, assuming a real cost of capital of 5 per cent, translates into an economic profit of $(8\% - 5\%) \times 23.3bn \approx 700m$. In 2003, management succeeded in turning the fortunes of the company around, and the CROCI improved to 9 per cent. NCI grew by about 6 per cent to $24.8bn, producing an economic profit of approximately $990m. Now, the really important question: had CROCI stayed at 8 per cent, by how much would economic assets have needed to grow to achieve $990m? The answer is: by 42 per cent. Indeed, for a 3 per cent excess return to generate $990m, it must be applied to an asset base of $33 000m – a 42 per cent jump from McDonald's level of NCI in 2002. In some way, this is a mathematical illusion. The reason why a 100 basis points improvement in cash return is equivalent to a 42 per cent increase in the asset base (in the Big Mac case) is because of the leverage effect of the cost of capital. It is the *excess return*, i.e. the return above the cost of capital, which produces economic profit, not the absolute level of CROCI. In other words, generically speaking, for an 8 per cent CROCI company with a cost of capital of 5 per cent and an asset base of 1000, it is the 3 per cent excess return applied to this asset base that will produce 30 of economic profits. In order to produce 40 with the same asset base, the excess return has to expand to 4 per cent; in order to produce 40 with the same excess return, the assets have to grow to 1333. In both cases, there is an increase of one-third.

Same earnings growth, different valuation

However, this 'illusion' has very real consequences for shareholders. What matters more for investment analysis and valuation is *how*, not how much, the company grows its earnings – by margin expansion or asset growth. In the case of an expansion of cash return on an unchanged capital base, the source of earnings growth is cost containment, achieved either directly by cutting costs or indirectly by letting costs grow less quickly than revenues. In this case, there is no need at all for shareholders to ask anybody any questions: the benefits flow directly into their pocket. In the case of an increase in economic profits via growth in assets, it is almost the reverse; management need first to consume capital, a costly commodity, with the promise that returns will follow. Here, shareholders have every right to be inquisitive.

Needless to say, the market has no qualms about applying a different valuation to each case. In 1995, Tomkins, a global engineering group based in the UK, and Ecolab, a global service company based in the US, were trading on almost identical PE ratios: 18.7× and 19×, respectively. Investors knew what they were doing, since both companies grew economic profits by 31 per cent in the following few years. Yet by 1998 Tomkins was still trading on a virtually unchanged multiple (20×), whilst Ecolab was trading on an economic PE ratio of 29×. What could possibly explain this large difference in rating? The fact that the two companies are quoted in different markets might seem the obvious answer. As it happened, the US market went from an economic PE of 22× to one of 33× in the period. This could, roughly, account for the multiple expansion of Ecolab. However, the UK market went from an economic PE multiple of 22× to more than 37×. So not only did Tomkins' valuation diverge from Ecolab's, despite exactly the same earnings growth, but it also suffered a massive de-rating relative to its own equity market. In reality, the two companies grew their economic profits in a very different way, which is the reason behind this apparent valuation anomaly. Ecolab's CROCI went from 14 per cent to 18 per cent, whilst Tomkins' went from 8.4 per cent to less than 9 per cent. Ecolab was able to grow EP 'the virtuous way', by cash margin expansion, whilst Tomkins grew EP 'the expensive way', by adding capital (in fact, mainly by acquisitions).

Although investors did not penalise Tomkins by actually applying a lower multiple to its economic profits, they denied the company the benefit of multiple expansion, despite its returning the same 30 per cent or so economic profits growth that Ecolab delivered. As it turned out, investors were right. Tomkins' management had to back off from their acquisitive strategy in 2000 and made substantial disposals, for which the company fell into the investors' sin bin for a few years.

There are those who will probably be outraged at the 'simplicity' of the above analysis, shamelessly comparing two companies in different sectors and different markets. Admittedly, it is hard to give it more than anecdotal value. A more sophisticated statistical analysis is difficult to carry out, because of the difficulty of finding homogeneous groups of companies with similar growth rates; however, the tests that we have done show that the correlation between multiple expansion and cash return expansion is significantly better than between multiple expansion and asset growth. This is hardly surprising. Beyond the obvious fact that an 'asset strategy' consumes capital, it is generally more complex to pursue than a 'simple' cash margin expansion. Earnings growth will only come through if the marginal return on new capital is not significantly lower than that of the existing business. Specifically, growing assets whilst accepting a lower marginal return can also 'work', i.e. generate additional value, but only if

$$\frac{NCI_1 - NCI_0}{NCI_0} > \frac{CROCI_1 - CROCI_0}{CROCI_1 - CoC}.$$

In other words, it is possible to accept a fade of CROCI whilst growing assets, but only insofar as the loss of cash margin, as a percentage of the new excess return $(CROCI_1 - CoC)$, is smaller than the increase in net economic assets. In practice, this means that the fade in return can only be very small for the company to keep on growing its EP, because it is difficult to grow assets very fast for a very long time. The retail sector is a good example of such cases. Retailers can grow assets aggressively for some time, as they expand abroad or complete their geographical coverage at home. Once the prime locations get saturated, they move progressively into less and less attractive second-tier locations, where the cash return is lower because of lower frequency, less affluent neighbourhoods etc. If their expansion strategy is aggressive enough, they will compensate for the loss of cash return with a bigger asset base, if the rule above is respected. Such examples exist in the United States, for instance, where the expansion strategy of a retailer often aims at covering the country from one coast to the other, which gives very aggressive growth profiles. Walgreen, a US pharmacist, is such an example. In Figure 5.1, we show the net (economic) capital invested (NCI) of Walgreen since the late 1980s. As shown by the line, the average year on year growth rate is around 15 per cent per annum, or approximately four times GDP.

However, at the same time, the company accepted a lower marginal CROCI. Its cash return went from above 9 per cent in the early 1990s to as low as 7.8 per cent in 2001, to recover slightly after that. According to the formula above, a loss of, say, 10 basis points in cash return per year at these levels has to be compensated by a growth in assets of approximately 3 per cent – a hurdle that Walgreen was easily able to surpass. As a result, economic profits carried on growing, as shown in Figure 5.2.

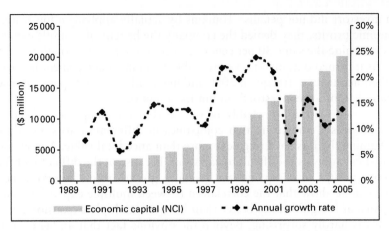

Figure 5.1 Walgreen: net economic capital (NCI), 1989–2005.

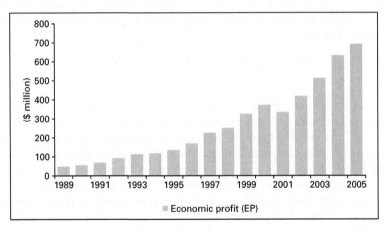

Figure 5.2 Walgreen: economic profit, 1989–2005.

Bear in mind that the above is only an *illustration* of the trade-off between growth in assets and cash return, not an apology for growth over cost management. In reality, many retailers try to implement this strategy but lose too much cash return too quickly and end up bankrupt. The latest example was that of Kmart, another US retailer that went under the protection of Chapter 11 in January 2002. However, one of the most infamous examples to choose here is probably Enron, the sadly well-known oil services company. Between 1996 and 2001, the average real growth in economic assets was more than 21 per cent per annum. It was, undisputedly, a 'growth story'. But the average cash return over the same period was a mere 5 per cent. Enron was growing its capital base way beyond its cash means, which prompted the management to find less and less legal ways to fund it, as it turned out. The Enron case illustrates better than any argument the other issue about growing EP with asset growth. Not only does the company need to maintain the marginal cash return level, or accept a very limited fade; it must also *fund* that asset expansion. Here, the rules are simple enough. If the cash return is lower than the net growth in assets, there is a funding gap that cannot be financed out of the company's own means. Either the company accumulates debt, or it needs additional equity capital.

Talking of 'earnings growth', even *economic* earnings growth, obfuscates some important issues behind the scenes that cannot be ignored by investment analysts. How the company grows its profit line is always at least as important as the rate at which it is growing it. And, as a general rule, *the level of cash return is a significantly more important variable than the growth in net assets.* We will, later on, provide some statistical evidence that this is indeed the case in the market; but the analytical route leads to the same conclusion. Asset growth can easily fall from 10 per cent to 1 per cent and jump back up again to 10 per cent, without affecting the survival of the company. It is in fact the sign of good management to be able to adjust capital spending to cash flow and the business cycle. This volatility makes it a difficult variable to analyse and predict, at best yielding not very much insight. A similar bounce in CROCI, moving from 10 per cent to 1 per cent and back to 10 per cent again, would be equivalent to a 'Black Swan' – a six sigma event, something that, for all intents and purposes, is a very rare occurrence. In all likelihood, if a company were to be hit so hard as to see its cash return melt away from 10 per cent to 1 per cent in a single year, it would probably never be able to recover its 10 per cent return any time soon. The explosion of the technology bubble provided many examples of such a 'loss of substance', where the cash return plummets to such a low level that it triggers a severe accumulation of debt and, furthermore, prevents the company from growing out of its troubles, since the maximum growth rate achievable without debt accumulation is equivalent to the CROCI. Alcatel, the French conglomerate involved in telecom equipment, cables and the manufacturing of high-speed trains (the 'TGVs'), fell into such hardship, as is clear from Figure 5.3.

Faced with such a situation, a company has only two choices. Either it accepts its fate, restructures its debt and lingers with no growth prospects, hoping to be bailed out by the cycle, or it reinvents itself and aggressively sells assets, accepting this 'loss

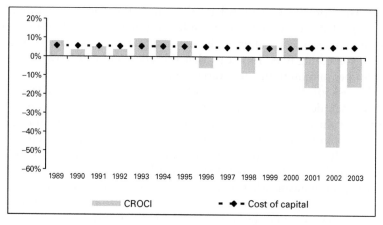

Figure 5.3 Alcatel: CROCI and cost of capital, 1989–2003.

of substance' and becoming a much smaller company. Practically, this translates into asset impairments (the recognition that some assets have become worthless) and asset disposals. This is the course that Alcatel chose post-2002, and its asset base went down by more than €2.5bn as a result. This allowed its CROCI to recover to previous cyclical peaks, and the company to be 'saved'. In 2005, Alcatel's excess return (the amount of cash return over the cost of capital) was back to a healthy 400 basis points, like it was in 1993. However, its production of economic profits is now substantially lower; in 2005 we estimated that the company had less than €8bn of economic capital, against €14.5bn twelve years ago. Needless to say, its market value has fallen in proportion.

Do *you* think what *they* think?

The second issue about growth is a classic conundrum of investment analysis; how should it be measured? In 90 per cent of the cases, forward asset or earnings growth is an *explicit* forecast or prediction issued by companies or financial analysts. Yet, consider the following argument. Most professionals agree that future price movements are, by and large, unpredictable. Moreover, it is equally undeniable that these prices are largely influenced by fundamental data such as the level of FCF. So, arguably, predicting FCF accurately should be almost as impossible. This does not prevent the whole industry from spending millions of hours a year trying to forecast FCF and all sorts of other things ... There is more than a small inconsistency here! Yet it is not difficult to see where all this is coming from. From the point of view of the company, growth is the pace at which the Chief Executive has decided to expand assets, on the three- or five-year plan. This expansion programme is based on some management consultants' analysis of the company's strengths and weaknesses, the competitive landscape and so on, so that, from the point of view of a company's management, it is natural to think about growth in these explicit terms as well. This is, of course, not irrelevant information, since free cash flow is broadly gross cash flow minus total net capital spending. In other words, the pace of expansion largely dictates the level of a key variable in the valuation of assets. The question is whether explicit forecasts from *stock analysts* have the same value. Here, growth means the pace of earnings that they decide is the most likely going forward. It is an important part of an analyst's job to stand up in the morning meeting and declare, preferably convincingly, something like: 'I forecast that this company will grow [its earnings] at 12 per cent per annum in the next three years'.

Taking the risk of alienating many professional analysts, it is a fact that the 'explicit' approach described above has never appeared to generate a lot of useful information for valuation analysis, at least in our work. This is a fundamental point to which we will come back towards the end of this chapter, as well as during Chapter 7, largely dedicated to the *implicit* measure of growth. Explicit growth forecasts rarely indicate whether the shares are a buy or a sell, because the market is a discounting mechanism; what matters is what is already priced in, rather than what analysts think is going to happen. In practice, most investment professionals have figured this one out, and the common yardstick tends to be earnings estimates revisions – in other words, *the rate of change* of growth expectations. If the rate of change is positive and big, the share price is supposed to react in a commensurate manner and *vice versa*. In practice, this can work. If some estimates are downgraded by 20 per cent, it is not unusual to see the company's share price falling by approximately the same amount, especially in large liquid markets like the US. However, there is a strong assumption behind this practice; namely, that prior to the change in estimates the shares were priced fairly, and reflected exactly the previous set of expectations. This assumption is as likely to be correct as the market is efficient, which we know is only 'approximately, and most of the time'. Of course, in order to calculate an implicit forecast, someone has to produce some explicit ones! I admit that pointing out the relative usefulness of forecasts for stock selection purposes whilst recommending the calculation of implicit ones, is slightly disingenuous. Fortunately, human psychology bails us out; there are enough forecasters out there who are convinced that they will get it right for us to be able to calculate implicit growth rates for many years to come.

There are many techniques to extract implicit information, but they are all based on the same principle; the market value of the asset contains the data. Analysts have to build what is sometimes called 'a reverse DCF', where the unknown variable is not the value of the assets, but the stream of FCF. Of course, a number of simplifying assumptions have to be taken, as there is an infinite amount of FCF paths whose net present value would equal to the market value. In the majority of cases implicit information will not be radically different from explicit forecasts, or too close to them for their analysis to be conclusive. The value of implicit information is often in the tail of the distribution, when investors are either too pessimistic or too optimistic. We will see some examples of such situations in Chapters 7 and 8.

Growth matters . . . sometimes – some disturbing news for growth managers

The growth/return interplay is a crucial relationship that investors had better watch carefully, if only because valuation will immediately and accurately reflect the management's growth/return strategy. For instance, shareholders may suffer financially when management grows assets irrespective of the level of cash return. At least, they are asked to support and fund a gamble – namely, that all this additional capital will earn at least the cost of capital. Such a strategy is a likely trigger for a valuation discount (remember Tomkins) or worse (remember Enron). Equally, a high-return, low-growth business is not a very attractive proposition, unless a large chunk of the excess profit is returned to shareholders. In this case, the firm is likely to be priced like a bond, which will inevitably raise complaints from its management. Without the return of excess cash to shareholders the company will accumulate cash, and will be open to criticism for its lack of strategic foresight.

This is by no means a theoretical case. In early 2000 in Japan, the deflationary environment meant that companies were extra cautious about their investments. It was not unusual to find companies with a third of their enterprise value in cash. Eventually, foreign shareholders in particular became exasperated by such meek corporate strategies, and an increasing number of them took the unprecedented step of valuing cash as an asset, *circa* 2003. The consequences of this expedient on valuation are dire. Imagine a company with net assets of 1000, a market capitalisation of 800 and net debt of 200, made of 700 of gross financial debt and 500 of cash. Assuming that the assets are priced correctly, this asset multiple (1× exactly) implies that the business is returning exactly the cost of capital, say 5 per cent. With CROCI at 5 per cent, free cash flow is 50 (50 divided by 1000 is 5 per cent). Investors in Japanese equities, such as in our example, started to add 500 (the cash) to net assets, and took the *gross* amount of debt (i.e. 700) for the calculation of the enterprise value. This did not change the asset multiple; the enterprise value went up to $800 + 700 = 1500$, but so did net assets, $1000 + 500 = 1500$. However, the cash return collapsed. Free cash flow remained at 50 or so. Strictly speaking, the financial income on 500 of cash should have been treated as 'operating income', since this cash was considered an operating asset. However, Yen money market yields were close to zero. Even assuming that this cash was invested in foreign currencies at 2 per cent after tax, FCF would have increased to 60 only ($50 + 500 \times 2\%$). This was not enough to prevent the cash yield from falling to 4 per cent (60/1500). This, in turn, meant that an asset multiple of 1× was no longer appropriate, and should have been 0.80×, in application of the Equivalence principle. The EV should therefore have fallen by 300, which represents a cool 37.5 per cent of the market capitalisation.

From the point of view of the principles of corporate finance, this is of course a heresy. Cash is, unquestionably, 'negative debt'. A company with net cash equal to its market capitalisation is really free for an acquirer. Whether cash is assumed to be on the asset or the liability side (with a negative sign) of the balance sheet by investors, all the acquirer will be asked to pay for will be the market capitalisation. He will then immediately pay himself with the cash, and all other assets will therefore be free. But investors chose to move cash on the asset side because they wanted to penalise the valuation of companies holding large amounts of cash in a situation where the yield on this cash was close to zero. Their objective was to force these companies to rethink their dividend and share buy-back policies. The growth/return interplay does have an impact on valuation, but one that is not necessarily visible through the analysis of 'earnings growth'.

The above proves, at least empirically, that valuation is influenced by the growth strategy of management, and therefore by growth expectations – but by how much, and under which circumstances? In Chapter 2, we have already met the special case of the firm for which growth does not matter at all. It is the firm which returns exactly the cost of capital. By definition, such a business does not produce any excess return or economic profit (the cash return, or R, minus the cost of capital/discount rate, or d, is always zero), no matter how much capital is ploughed into the company. Therefore, irrespective of the growth rate, the enterprise value will always equal the value of net capital invested (net assets), and the asset multiple will be constant and equal to 1. Put another way, since

$$EV = NCI \times \left(1 + \frac{R - d}{d - g}\right)$$

when $(R - d) = 0$, then $EV = NCI$.

It follows logically that it is the level of return which 'unlocks' the impact of growth on valuation. A cost of capital business growing at 20 per cent per annum will trade at $1\times$ capital invested, but this will change if the return shifts by 10 basis points above (or below) the cost of capital. And what if it shifts by 5 percentage points? Is the change in valuation commensurate? The answer is that it is not. Growth matters; just a little bit for a firm with a small excess return, but a lot more for a high CROCI business. Although this may be intuitive to some, the best way to prove this is to use some simple mathematics. Let us take the example of two businesses, with a 20 per cent (i.e. very high) and a 6 per cent (i.e. just above the cost of capital) CROCI, respectively. Given the relationship above, the value of the firm, EV, will change with $(R-d)/(d-g)$. With $R = 6$ per cent and $d = 5$ per cent, this factor will become $1/(5-g)$. Measuring the rate of change of one variable (EV) with respect to the other – $(R-d)/(d-g)$ – will give us how much the latter, i.e. the return/growth combination, matters for the valuation of the assets. The rate of change is given by the *slope* of a constant, linear relationship between EV and $(R-d)/(d-g)$. This slope is measured by the derivative of the factor[1], which is $1/(\{5-g\}^2)$. It is immediately obvious that, with CROCI at 20 per cent, the slope becomes $15/(\{5-g\}^2)$. In other words, the rate of change of the EV to a change in the growth rate is fifteen times faster when CROCI is 20 per cent than when CROCI is 6 per cent. *Growth matters fifteen times more for the valuation of a high CROCI business than for that of a 'slightly above the cost of capital' business.* In short, growth matters, but only for high-return businesses. Put in another way, the *one* factor that applies in all cases is the level of cash return.

This is a point that is surprisingly under-researched in the economic literature, but has not gone totally unnoticed either, and was tested by no less than the father of 'q', Mr James Tobin himself. In their 1977 paper, Tobin and Brainard run a cross-sectional regression analysis (a statistical study that measures the influence of a variable on an observation, independently of any other variable that might also affect that observation; here, the observation is the market price of an asset) on nine factors supposed to affect the 'q' ratio between 1960 and 1974 on a universe of US stocks. Among these factors were past growth in earnings, cyclicality of earnings, volatility of earnings, economic earnings yield (defined as the ratio of earnings to replacement value of the firm), default risk, etc. The factor explaining the largest chunk of 'q', by an overwhelming margin, was economic earnings yield, or E/V in Tobin's notation. This is, of course, nothing more than a measure of cash return. Tobin noted that 'the importance of E/V is, of course, to be expected', but without saying why. In contrast, the effect of growth on valuation was marginal, up to ten times less than that of economic earnings. We ran a comparable test for the 1989–2004 period, replacing Tobin's definition of economic earnings yield with CROCI, and replacing his two default risk criteria (which we found not to be statistically significant for that period) with financial gearing (which was very significant). The result is shown in Figure 5.4.

As in Tobin's work, the overwhelming marginal factor contributing to the asset multiple is CROCI, or economic earnings rate in Tobin's language. This measure accounts, on average, for 77 per cent of the 'q' ratio in the US during that period. In contrast, growth has a mere 12 per cent weight in the make-up of an average 'q' ratio. Note, incidentally, that financial risk (gearing) and earnings volatility have a negative contribution, as would be expected. The interpretation of these two studies is clear; the market is perfectly aware of the relative importance of

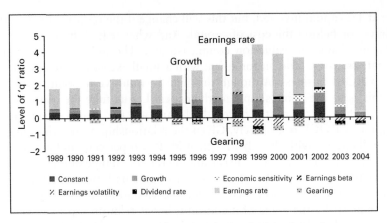

Figure 5.4 Factors influencing the level of the 'q' ratio.

earnings yield (CROCI) and growth for the valuation of equities. As Tobin said, it was to be expected, and the contrary would have been a blow to the Efficient Market Hypothesis. The market is also aware that the imbalance in the explanatory power of the two factors for the overall universe of stocks comes from the fact that growth only really matters for the valuation of the smaller universe of high CROCI companies. This can be verified by computing the same regression analysis for two sub-groups of the universe, the low and the high CROCI companies. If the theory is verified, then the marginal contribution of the growth factor should be higher for high CROCI businesses than for low CROCI ones. This is indeed what can be observed. For the 2004 sample, the market attributes almost no explanatory power to growth in the making of the 'q' ratio for low CROCI companies, against a more noticeable 9 per cent for the high CROCI group[2].

The reason why economic growth only matters for the valuation of high CROCI businesses is easily explainable and has been a thread throughout this chapter: *only high CROCI businesses can fund growth internally.* As we have shown in the previous section, the cash return measures the cash available to the management of a company to fund the expansion of its capital base. If the cash return is so small that capital expansion becomes insignificant, then investors will logically not price any growth assumption in the value of the firm. And in the end, growth (in assets) of course matters, but nowhere near as much as the average investor thinks. This bears obvious but important consequences for the Equivalence as a stock selection model, namely that the asset multiple and the relative return *can* be used in an efficient and successful way for most of the universe, despite ignoring growth in assets, in a manner most disturbing for growth managers.

The third dimension – the Market Horn of Plenty

The previous section showed that growth is a lot more complex to analyse than plain earnings growth would suggest. Yet the latter is a subject that occupies an unduly large amount of time in an average research department or fund manager's mind.

We recommend that any valuation work should always start without any reference to growth, especially *explicit* growth expectations, in our case by using the Equivalence as a guide. It is always possible to refine the analysis further. However, even if one did nothing else and selected stocks on that basis, the worse that would happen is that genuinely high-growth businesses would appear more expensive than they should. Granted, this could be an opportunity cost, but this would never lead to a situation where growth stocks are entered at the wrong price in a portfolio or, worse, some stocks are taken for what they are not. So you have missed the next Microsoft, but you don't have Enron in your portfolio. Which situation would you rather have – this one, or the reverse?

And yet we know that growth in assets significantly influences the valuation of high return companies in particular. There will be, therefore, certain instances where it is necessary to have a three-dimensional model, incorporating value, return and growth. It is entirely possible to build such models, but the results will only be relevant to a systematic stock selection process if the growth variable is 'implicit', in other words extracted from the current valuation, rather than 'explicit', in other words the result of a specific view from the investment analyst. That's because what matters to an investor is what the market is pricing, not a random view on growth by some analyst, however insightful. In the following sections, we present various ways of capturing this third dimension.

Let us start with an observation. If we arrange a global universe of stocks according to their asset multiple and their level of cash return, thereby creating a picture of their economic PE ratio, the shape of this cloud of points is not random. The companies are arranged in a horn shape, which we will call the Market Horn of Plenty. The small end of the horn is pointing towards the origin of the chart, i.e. low asset multiple and low cash return. The mouth of the horn, in the opposite direction, is pointing towards the sky (Figure 5.5).

This is, however, an optical illusion, because such a chart can only represent two dimensions. The companies are, in reality, arranged on an upward-sloping surface inside a cube, whose depth is the third dimension – in other words, the growth rate

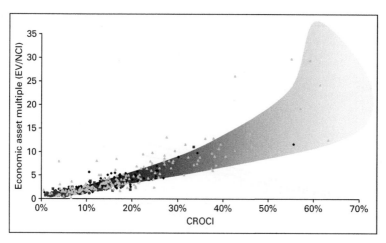

Figure 5.5 The Market Horn of Plenty (1).

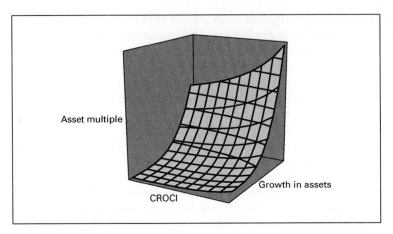

Figure 5.6 The equity market surface.

in assets. The other dimensions are value and return or, in this framework, asset multiple (EV/NCI) and CROCI (Figure 5.6).

On the usual two-dimensional chart, the companies appearing in the mouth of the horn are in fact the furthest away (inside the cube), and are those with the highest growth rate. It is possible to improve the 3D visual impression of the horn slightly by adding the regression line for each tercile of cash return (Figure 5.7). Unsurprisingly, the higher the cash return, the higher the slope of the regression line – i.e. the higher the expected growth rate. This is an observation that illustrates nicely the mantra of this chapter: only companies with high CROCIs can grow without recourse to external funding.

Another crucial observation for the benefit of growth-spotters is that if growth expectations were always irrelevant to valuation, then all the stocks would be on the same PE ratio. The equivalence between asset multiple and relative return, in

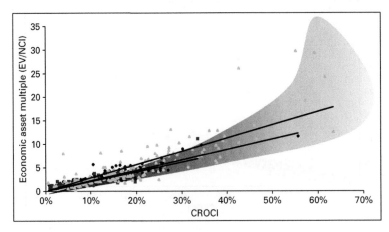

Figure 5.7 The Market Horn of Plenty (2).

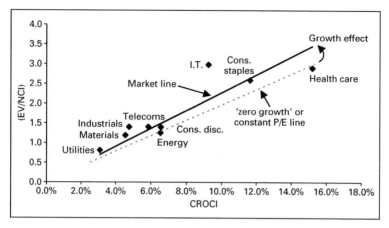

Figure 5.8 Market line and constant PE line.

other words, would be constant, and all equities would be nicely arranged along a 'constant PE line', which would happen to be the inverse of the cost of capital. In Figure 5.8 we show such an imaginary line, as well as the regression line that best fits an actual global universe of stocks.

It is clear from this chart that, in the real world, two factors modify the imaginary constant PE line. First, because the real universe of stocks will have an average growth rate of more than 0 per cent, the line is shifted upwards; for a given level of return the investors are required to pay slightly more than in the imaginary no growth world, and that 'slightly more' represents the price of growth. Furthermore, in the real world the gradient (slope) of the regression line is steeper than just the 45 degrees of the imaginary PE line. This is because of the higher price of growth at higher CROCI levels, as we have seen previously. These modifications (to the constant PE line) encapsulate the impact that expected growth in assets has on the value of equities.

It is therefore perfectly possible to extract the third dimension (e.g. growth) from the market, and know exactly how much investors are paying for one unit of growth, at any point. In Figure 5.9, we plot the price of growth for a global universe of stocks, since 1989.

The technology-driven bubble of 1995–2000 is very conspicuous – its build-up phase as much as its abrupt end. The aberration of this period is made all the more obvious by the magnitude of the change in the price of growth, which on this scale went up more than fivefold. It is worth noting as well that, outside of this period, the price of growth is almost a constant variable in the pricing mechanism. A similarly shaped chart is obtained by plotting the price of a 4 per cent growth rate through time, which is a good approximation of GDP growth for the quoted sector. This means that, on average, investors are rarely willing to take a bet on growth, which they tend to view, it seems, as a stable (albeit cyclical) variable. Once more, what really matters is the level of cash return.

We know by now that investors are willing to pay more for one unit of growth if it is coming from a high-return business, and that this hierarchy is theoretically correct. Although this observation already gives great insight into the relevance of

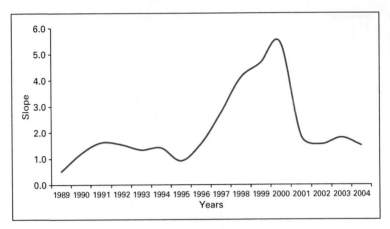

Figure 5.9 The price of growth through time.

growth for the pricing of assets, it is possible to take the analysis one step further, and build a generic pricing function for *all levels* of growth. The first stage of this analysis is to segregate the companies of a global universe by growth rate, for instance into deciles. According to the Horn of Plenty theory, each group will display a specific relationship between value and return, with investors paying more and more for a given level of return as we progress through the groups towards the higher growth ones. Thus, the preparatory work will produce ten 'slopes', or value/growth relationships, for each of the years of the test period. By way of example, Table 5.1 shows the slopes associated to the ten growth rates for the year 2004.

Note that the price of growth does not always increase with the growth rate. Some statistical noise in decile 3 and decile 5 makes the price of 1.5 per cent and 2.9 per cent growth, respectively, cheaper than the previous category. However, the general direction is right; in eight cases out of ten, the slope gets steeper (therefore, the price of assets increases, at constant return) as the growth rate gets higher. With these data it is now possible to define a function, which we will dub 'the Price of Growth'. This function relates the *average* slope of the yearly observations with their growth rate. This relationship is shown in Figure 5.10.

Figure 5.10 gives some invaluable insight into the way investors price growth on average. Strikingly, the function is not exponential, as maybe could have been intuitively assumed. In other words, at some point, additional growth does not produce additional valuation. Investors in aggregate know better. They know that companies routinely attempt to get near the sun (i.e. grow very fast) and burn their

Table 5.1 The 2004 gradient of growth

Decile	1	2	3	4	5	6	7	8	9	10
Average growth (%)	0.0	1.0	1.5	2.0	2.9	3.1	4.2	5.3	6.9	11.4
Slope	14.9	17.4	14.3	26.1	20.6	21.8	21.7	21.5	26.8	33.5

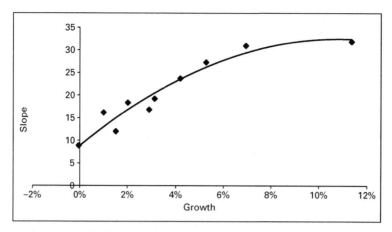

Figure 5.10 The 'price of growth' function.

wings, mainly by accumulating too many financial liabilities. They also know that a real trend growth of more than 10 per cent per annum is already close to three times GDP, which may as well be called breakneck speed. Anybody (in this case any company) attempting to achieve much more than this may well not be very credible, or at least not for very long. In the end, the market's conservatism in the price of growth is probably entirely justified. Note as well that the 'price of growth' function flattens out quite rapidly, maybe as early as the 'GDP mark', which we put around 4 per cent for a global universe. Investors seem to be incredibly cautious about the sustainability of above GDP growth rates. It is hard to think of anything more sensible to do in investment analysis.

But of course, this last comment is only true 'in aggregate'. Applied to individual situations, almost the contrary could be written: the asymptotic nature of the price of growth function means that genuine growth stocks may be penalised by this market pricing. Growth managers will find some support here for their art. Perhaps the best example in this instance is Apple. Pre-iPod, Apple was a fairly ordinary company; its average CROCI between 2000 and 2004 comes out at 6.3 per cent, barely above the cost of capital. Post-iPod, Apple takes on another gloss; its cash return reached 56 per cent in 2005. As for its rate of accumulation of economic assets (remember that R&D and marketing costs are capitalised into economic assets), it is so fast that it is really anybody's guess – 10, 20, 30 per cent, or more. The firm could certainly afford 56 per cent! Yet, strikingly, on the assumption that Apple's competitive advantage can sustain such a level of cash return for the next few years, the implicit (i.e. as priced by the market) expected growth rate in economic assets is mid-teens, at a market capitalisation of about $40bn (we have used here the value-to-trend technique, which is explained in detail in Chapter 9). This is very characteristic of the way in which a very high growth business is priced, according to the price of growth function. But it could be seen as understating the 'true' economic growth potential of the company. Even iconic companies such as Apple do not escape the rules of the price of growth.

Note

1. For those who really need to know:

$$\frac{d}{dg}(5-g)^{-1} = -1 \times (5-g)^{-2} \times (0-1) = +1 \times \frac{1}{(5-g)^2}.$$

2. The price of growth was quite low in 2004, which explains why growth only accounts for 9 per cent of that year's 'q' ratio.

References

Aharony, J. and Swary, I. (1980). Quarterly dividend and earnings announcements and stockholders' returns: an empirical analysis. *Journal of Finance*, **35**(1), 1–12.
Lintner, J. (1956). Distribution of incomes of corporations among dividends, retained earnings, and taxes. *American Economic Review*, **46**, 97–113.
Tobin, J. and Brainard, W. C. (1977). Chapter 11: Asset markets and the cost of capital. *Cowles Foundation Paper 440*, reprinted from *Private Values and Public Policy, Essays in Honor of William Fellner*. North-Holland.

Drawing Up the Plans: Analysis of Economic Profits

6 The fundamental analysis of economic characteristics

The storytellers – fundamental and investment analysis – the special case of financial groups

Although accounting-based numbers will tend to generate misleading noise for the purpose of investment, that noise is certainly not the sole reason for the lack of alpha in traditional active fund management (on average of course). Investing by numbers is not the favourite technique of investors, who like nothing more than a good story. With a hint of conspiracy if possible... The fact that human beings love good stories is a well-identified topic of research in sociology, including the belief in political conspiracies regarding popular stories such as the death of Princess Diana or the assassination of John F. Kennedy. In the world of finance, this human characteristic leads laymen to view the stock market as a vast battleground where downfalls are decided, plots are done and undone, and superior strategic alliances sealed. By whom? By 'them'. 'Somebody out there knows something about it'. But nobody else, except for my well-informed friends or clients, know that they know ... I routinely explain to those that ask that buying just one stock, even tipped by the best of sources, carries an enormous specific risk, regardless of the appeal of the story. I readily confess to them that I have no idea of where the market is going in the next few weeks, or even few months. I meekly use the line of Peter Lynch, the legendary manager of the Magellan fund: 'if you are not prepared to see your investments go down 30 per cent at some point, then equities are not for you'. But the more the story-lovers are put off, the more counterproductive it becomes; eventually, they become convinced that I refuse to share with them the secret of the next corporate battle.

This would not be so bad, indeed it would be funny, if this romantic view of the stock market were confined to the layman (except for the fact that 'somebody out there' must be losing a lot of money on his investments). Unfortunately, it is my experience that many professional investors, whilst more educated in the ways the market works, are equally in love with good stories. This is far more dangerous than the inevitable after-dinner conversation, because a professional's story will carry more weight. He or she might have met with the management of this particular company. The professional investor will also have met with a 'well-informed' professional analyst, 'who is very close to the company', and he will sprinkle his demonstration with figures and historical references: 'I don't know if you remember, but last time Greenspan said something like this, the sector did +20 per cent in three months ...' Be it the professional or the layman, though, both suffer from the same misbelief; namely that they know something that the market does not, which is *very* unlikely.

More precisely, human beings will tend to make 'something out of nothing' due to the misperception and misinterpretation of random data. They will tend to infer 'too much from too little', from the same misjudgement, and will have a strong propensity to 'see what they expect to see', with their biased evaluation of these ambiguous and inconsistent data. These three characteristic modes of behaviour have been identified by Thomas Gilovich, a researcher in cognitive psychology, in his book *How We Know What Isn't So* (Gilovich, 1991). Their description is strikingly well suited to a typical investor, despite the fact that Mr Gilovich's book does not once address the issue of behavioural finance, his brief being a much more general one. In short, human beings appear to love to speculate (the term could not be more appropriate in a financial context) much more than they love to analyse. There is of course nothing wrong with this, except that our brain seems to be exceptionally poorly equipped for this exercise. Speculation implies weighing probabilities, and it does not seem to be able to cope with them, as the early behaviourists discovered.

The framework of an economic model will offer exactly the contrary of this universal human trait; it reduces the possibilities of speculation to a minimum, and frames investment analysis within a narrow field. An economic model will characterise a company, *any* company, except financial groups, with three endogenous and two exogenous variables: an amount of invested capital, a real growth rate and a real cash return associated with this capital, complemented by an ambient expected return (cost of capital) and a market price. This chapter deals primarily with the three endogenous variables, whose study we call 'fundamental analysis'. Linking these endogenous variables with the two exogenous ones is what we call 'investment analysis', which is the subject of the following chapter.

First, though, a word on the exclusion of financial groups, banks, insurance companies and diversified financial services (e.g. mutual fund companies, brokers, etc.). This stems from the fact that a successful economic analysis depends largely on the accuracy with which economic capital is identified. Financial groups carry large amounts of what could be called 'third party capital' – in other words, capital that does not belong to shareholders, and is not provided by lenders. These are the assets deposited by the clients of these companies; bank deposits, for instance. Due to the complexity of these groups, accurately segregating only the capital financing the company's own assets is nearly impossible, especially since most of these assets are 'marked to market', in other words revalued every day at their market value. In the case of a life insurance company, this generates a controversial and well-rehearsed debate about who owns the capital gains on third-party capital: policyholders or shareholders? The use of derivative instruments, which lay off risks associated to an asset onto other market participants in exchange for a premium, blurs the picture some more. In his unauthorised history of LTCM, Roger Lowenstein (2002: 104) explains how the first 'swap' of interest rates was engineered in 1981, and what happened after this *premiere*:

> The business grew { . . . } exponentially. Soon, banks were swapping obligations for currencies, interest rate payments, equities, any future stream of cash that could be traded for another. { . . . } One offshoot – largely unintended – of this tremendous growth was that banks' financial statements became increasingly obscure. Derivatives weren't disclosed in any way that was

> meaningful to outsiders. And as the volume of deals exploded, the banks' balance sheets revealed less and less of their total obligations. By the mid-1990s, the financial statements of even many mid-sized banks were wrapped in an impenetrable haze.

Although further regulation, and the Basel II agreement in particular, has put some order in this jumble, it is not clear that enough has been done to reveal the true economic picture of a bank's balance sheet.

Furthermore, there is an analytical issue on top of the disclosure issue. Segregating capital and identifying cash flow for financial groups is difficult because, fundamentally, these businesses do not produce profits in the same way as non-financial groups. The latter simply add some value, via a proprietary process, to a certain amount of operating costs, and sell units (goods or services) of the total cost to its clients. The former capture capital flows, often thanks to a high financial gearing (partly from debt, partly from 'third-party capital'), transform them and clip a remuneration for this process. Even if it were possible precisely to identify cash flows and economic capital for financial groups, the difference in balance sheet gearing would demand the calculation of an expected return ('cost of capital') specific to them. Having tried various ways of dealing with all these issues, we have not found the exercise to yield any particular insight into the pricing of financial groups, which is why they are usually excluded from economic profits models. However, as we will see later, excluding them from the universe of investment is at worst neutral, and, in fact, often beneficial to the performance of a portfolio.

Missing something? The right chemistry

Although the storytellers will shiver at the idea that any company can be shrunk to three endogenous variables, it is not clear what other relevant information analysts are missing through their careful study. Critics often mention management skills as one obvious area for economic analysis to fall short. This appears to be more an example of Thomas Gilovich's 'too much from too little' inference. True, the fundamental analysis that we suggest does not require regular contacts with management – in fact, it requires none at all. But saying, as a result, that it is not possible to judge the skills of management implies that this assessment can *only* be achieved through regular contacts and conversations. This, in turn, implies that financial analysts are very skilful psychologists, and that they have an above normal ability in the field of capacity assessment. And yet anybody who has been involved in recruitment, for instance for graduate programmes, knows how difficult this assessment is. The evidence is that the hit ratio, in other words the ability to detect the 'right person', is not much higher than 50 per cent – i.e. random. As an analyst, it is not the invitation to the corporate golf day of your favourite company that puts you in a better position to assess the management skills of the directors.

Now, observe Figure 6.1, which plots the cash return of a large European chemical company between 1989 and 2005.

The business cycle is easily recognisable, with two distinct troughs; one in 1991–1993, the last period of global, economy-wide recession, and another in 2001.

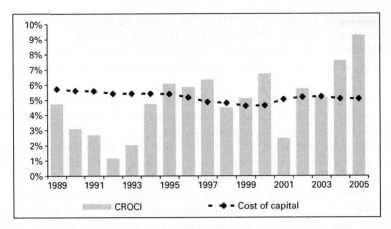

Figure 6.1 A large European chemical company: cash return, 1989–2005.

The second trough is about as depressed as the first one, with a CROCI of 2.5 per cent, against a yearly average of 1.9 per cent during the first slowdown, but it is much shorter, with only one year down against three a decade earlier. Over the entire seventeen-year period, the average CROCI is 4.86 per cent, below the cost of capital. This is clearly a value-destroying business over the cycle – not really a surprise for such a tough sector, plagued with overcapacity in the early 1990s (see how depressed returns were at the beginning of the period) and faced with severe competition from Asia.

Figure 6.2 plots the cash return of another large chemical company, this time from the US, with business very similar to the first one. Witness the average CROCI over the seventeen-year period, 4.72 per cent – almost exactly the same as chemical company number one. Incidentally, given the amount of adjustments to cash flow and assets that are made to derive these figures (remember that CROCI is the IRR of gross economic assets and gross cash flows over an average asset life), the fact

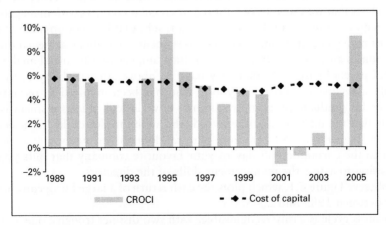

Figure 6.2 A large US chemical company: cash return, 1989–2005.

that these two averages are so close is really remarkable. It shows how accurately an EP model can measure the economic reality of an industry.

Comparing the two figures, it is clear that there is a resemblance in the pattern of cash return, with a similar cycle in the early 1990s and again in the early 2000s. Yet, despite the fact that the long-term average CROCI is the same in both cases, company number one appears in better shape than its competitor, for the following three reasons. First, it has improved its cash return by almost 400 basis points between the cyclical peaks of 1989 and 2005. It moves from a paltry 4.75 per cent in 1989, to more than 6 per cent in 1995 and again 1997, and finally 8.6 per cent in 2005. In the same year, company two, on the other hand, has only been able to match the performance of 1989. In fact, company two has not managed to improve peak returns at all. The peaks of 1989, 1995 and 2005 are almost identical. Note, however, that company two achieves a *higher* cyclical peak (always more than 9 per cent) than company one. But the two companies are now almost neck to neck, whereas seventeen years ago, company two was returning exactly twice as much as company one (9.45 per cent against 4.75 per cent).

Second, company two has suffered severely at the hands of the 2001 recession. Whilst company two troughed at 3.5 per cent in the 1990s, at a level twice as high, again, as its competitor, company one, the situation was inverted less than a decade later. The 2001 trough saw a very weak CROCI of 2.5 per cent for company one, but a catastrophic CROCI of −1.4 per cent for company two. Negative cash returns are extremely rare, and suggest a severe level of corporate distress.

Third, company two struggled in the recovery phase. It took just one year for company one to jump back to value creation, after the recession of 2001. But company two was still in the doldrums, with another negative cash return of −0.73 per cent in 2002, and then a mere 1.1 per cent in 2003. At that point, company one was returning 5.2 per cent – more than four times the return of its US competitor.

Considering that the two companies compete in roughly the same fields, it is unquestionable that the management of company one has done a better job than the management of company two, although competitive situations are never cast in stone. Indeed, it is noticeable that during the more recent period (2003–2005), company two seems to have found its way again and is successfully fighting back. Yet, over the entire period, the difference in performance is striking, and, of course, has not escaped the attention of investors. The market capitalisation of company one went from €8.5bn in 1989 to approximately €29bn in 2005, an advance of 240 per cent. The market capitalisation of company two went from $17.2bn in 1989 to $44.5bn in 2005, an advance of 158 per cent.

What we have just conducted here is some *very basic* fundamental analysis, based on one variable only – the level of cash return on assets. We have not looked at the rate of accumulation of debt, or of economic assets. Nor have we assessed the changes in net working capital, usually a good short cut to cost management skills. We have not looked at how currencies might have impacted the performance of one or the other company. But, in spite of all these question marks, it is hard to arrive at any other conclusion but the fact that the management of company one has achieved a better result. Would regular contact with the management of both companies have achieved more? These contacts would certainly have given a sense of consistency (or lack of it) in the pursuit of the corporate strategy, a sense of reliability with respect to the delivery of promises to the market. And, for those who rely on them, they would have been helpful to construct forecasts. However, with the possible exception of turnaround situations, where leadership is paramount and needs to be assessed almost always in person, there is little doubt that a great deal of management know-how can be checked through the study of economic numbers.

Although we would never advise focusing solely on the cash return as a way of analysing a company, the study of its level, pattern, direction and volatility, as well as the comparison with peer groups, or the overall sector to which the company belongs, has to be the first port of call. We have seen in Chapter 5 that, in the studies of Tobin as well as in our own work, the level of cash return is the overwhelming explanatory factor to the level of valuation. The CROCI characteristics are the DNA of the firm. As shown in the chemical example, it helps the outside analyst in his assessment of the firm's corporate decisions. It also reveals whether the firm is creating or destroying value, indicates its competitive position, and determines the rate of growth of its economic assets.

Three CROCI patterns: a typology of corporate behaviour

We propose here a typology of corporate behaviour through the lens of three CROCI patterns. We have selected them arbitrarily, because they illustrate a point which we think is important, not because they are the only three. There would be nothing worse than trying to box all companies into one or the other. Methodologically, investors who wish to identify a return pattern will need to build enough history, encompassing at least two full business cycles. We suggest reconstructing historical data at least back to 1989 whenever possible. That year corresponds to the peak of the 1980s business cycle, as well as the peak in the cash-flow cycle (there is sometimes a lag between the two). For companies with long enough history, mainly in the US, data can be built back to 1980, which gives a picture of the full business cycle of the 1980s, with the very deep recession of 1981–1983. The period from 1989 to 2005 captures the slowdown and recession of the early 1990s (1991 in the US, 1992–1993 in Europe); the subsequent recovery; the turbulent years of the Asian crisis (1997–1998); the new peak of 2000; followed by the sometimes abrupt slowdown of 2001 and 2002, and the recovery of 2003–2005.

Pattern one: rising cash returns above the cost of capital

Leaving aside the case of a cyclical recovery (on which more later), rising cash returns above the cost of capital are usually a signal that the company enjoys a strong, and strengthening, competitive position. For instance, a young, emerging company will tend to have a sharply upward-moving CROCI, but typically for a short period of time only. This was the case for Cisco Systems, the router company, in the early 1990s. Its cash return more than doubled between 1989 and 1994, the year of its peak CROCI, but started to fall *before* the Internet revolution really began in earnest, *circa* 1995–1996 (Figure 6.3).

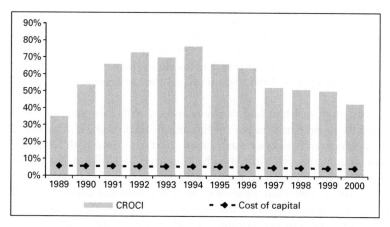

Figure 6.3 Cisco Systems: cash return, 1989–2000.

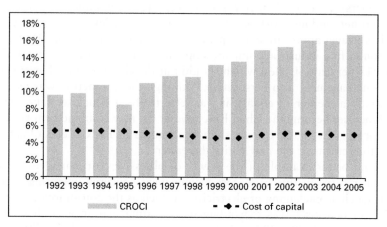

Figure 6.4 Colgate-Palmolive: an upward-moving CROCI pattern.

It is possible, but rarer, that a more established company shows a continuously rising CROCI pattern. As illustrated with Colgate in Figure 6.4, the returns show smaller incremental improvements for a longer period of time.

An upward-moving CROCI pattern, whether small and regular or large and sharp, conveys a simple message: take notice. A rising cash return means that the company is able to increase its generation of cash whilst increasing its consumption of capital at a slower rate, or even decreasing it. (Remember that CROCI can equally be calculated as an IRR of gross economic assets and gross cash flows, or as the ration of free cash flow and net economic assets. In both cases, if the flows grow faster than the economic capital, CROCI will increase.) In other words, it is a sign of improving capital productivity. In 1999, the UK consumer product group Reckitt & Colman merged with Benckiser, the German manufacturer of Calgon, a leading brand of water softeners for dishwashers, among other things. Prior to its merger with Benckiser, Reckitt could be best described as a rather sleepy, dusty company. It enjoyed a good portfolio of brands, and was returning way above the cost of capital, but returns were fading and this was just about compensated by an increase in capital invested, such that economic profits were stagnant. Its acquisitions of US brands in 1990 and 1994 had loaded the balance sheet with goodwill, but the improvement of returns was slow; the CROCI was 13.5 per cent in 1989, and 16 per cent in 1995. Not bad, but the management of Benckiser had other ideas.

As a research analyst, I had had various contacts with this company in the early 1990s, especially in preparation for its floatation. Back then, it was already clear that the management of Benckiser was a breed apart. Annoyed with German bureaucracy, it had already abruptly shifted its headquarters to Holland, for instance, and had therefore become a Dutch company, despite a long and distinguished German lineage. I remember well their obsession with net working capital, and how the Finance Director calmly assured me during one meeting that they could, and would, operate on the basis of zero net working capital. Net working capital is the aggregation of inventories, receivables (payments due from clients) and payables (invoices due to suppliers). In an ordinarily run company, receivables and payables broadly cancel each other, and net working capital amounts to the level of inventory, which historically averages approximately 7 per cent of sales. Back in the mid-1990s, it was still common to find industrial companies operating on net working capital of more than 10 to 12 per cent of sales, which should put the claim – and achievement – of Benckiser's management into perspective. Although the transaction was technically and financially a merger of equals, it was, effectively, a Benckiser takeover. Bart Becht of Benckiser became the Chief Executive of the new combined entity, and the rest is history ... In Figure 6.5 we show the returns of Reckitt & Colman up to 1999, and the returns of the new entity thereafter.

We have no better example of the power of obsessive cost management on the level of cash return. In this case, cost management concerns operating costs, i.e. input costs (such as packaging or electricity), as well as the consumption of capital. Whilst Reckitt-Benckiser was expanding its operating margin as well as its revenue line during the 2000–2005 period, it was consuming remarkably little capital,

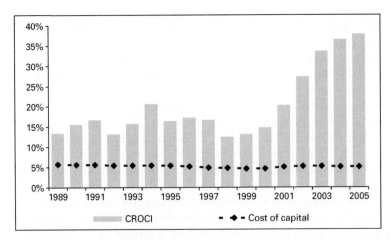

Figure 6.5 The returns of Reckitt & Colman to 1999, and of Reckitt-Benckiser thereafter.

the combination of which produced this explosive productivity of capital. Not denying management their laurels, it is important to stress that only the *combination* of cost management and revenue growth could produce these exceptional results, due to operational leverage (operational leverage describes profit growth achieved by containing fixed costs as the revenue line grows). Both Reckitt and Benckiser had a powerful portfolio of brands with the potential to grow fast. Without this, the results would have been less spectacular. Many companies cut or contain costs to accompany a decline in revenues; the results are still commendable, but they don't put these companies in Benckiser's category.

Whilst the Reckitt-Benckiser case is probably the most extreme and least predictable example of improved capital productivity, this phenomenon has been widely spread throughout the world since the mid-1990s. The world's CROCI, an aggregation of the 700 largest companies, has expanded continually since the trough of 1991, with successive peaks at 5.4 per cent (1995), 6 per cent (1997), 7.4 per cent (2000) and 8.4 per cent (2005). This appears to be the result of a double technological revolution. On the one hand, the implementation of new information technologies at ever decreasing prices has improved productivity in many quarters of the global economy. In CROCI speak, the replacement value of capital has tended to decrease in the 1996–2005 decade, due to high technological progress, reducing the consumption of capital. At the same time, financial techniques have evolved very rapidly, thanks to the emergence of derivative instruments and other securitisation techniques.[1] The latter in particular, associated with an unusually low cost of carry (the cost of 'carrying' a financial instrument by borrowing funds), has allowed companies to reduce their apparent consumption of capital, especially in net working capital management – the very same thing that was targeted by Benckiser a decade ago. The securitisation of receivables is now a routine operation; to simplify, a bank 'purchases' large amounts of receivables and packages them into an investable vehicle, such as a fund, which is then placed with investors. For a remuneration, these investors carry the risk of default of the debtors, which is statistically low due to the diversity of the credit risk, as these receivables are pooled from various economic sectors. The emergence of such techniques has resulted in working capital requirements falling dramatically. For the CROCI universe as a whole, more than 13 per cent of revenues used to be tied in working capital in the late 1980s – a figure that dropped to less than half (6.1 per cent) in 2005. More advanced companies, such as Reckitt-Benckiser, now operate with *negative* working capital,[2] a feat that used to be the sole privilege of retailers.[3] Such a revolution in balance sheet management has had a profound affect on the level of CROCI in the past decade.

What is still unresolved at the end of this decade of staggering productivity is the sustainability of this phenomenon, and the extent to which the low cost of carry (i.e. the low level of interest rates) has been an exceptional prop for such sophisticated financial engineering. But this story has yet to be written, and it is unlikely that investors will know for a few more years. Once monetary conditions normalise, perhaps companies will find it harder to fabricate rising CROCI through financial engineering. But those who can, by fair means or foul, will always deserve investors' closest attention.

Pattern two: falling or fading cash returns

Earlier, we came across Walgreen, the US retailer accepting a declining marginal return on its capital, and therefore a fading CROCI. The company was doing so because it was able to grow its capital base at a much faster rate than the difference between return on existing and new capital. So falling returns are not necessarily unmitigated bad news. However, they are usually associated with the general theory of the capital cycle: falling returns occur when capital is being added indiscriminately. The result is that supply (read *capacity*) and demand become imbalanced, in favour of supply. As we have pointed out in Chapter 3, the capital cycle theory was indirectly formalised by the early twentieth century economists in search of the rules of capital formation. Later, Michael Porter, the famous Harvard professor, wrote extensively on the subject, focusing on the theory of competition, which, by his own admission, 'has preoccupied [him] for two decades'. A handful of practitioners are using the capital cycle theory as 'an alternative investment paradigm', as Edward Chancellor puts it. This historian of markets and finance has recently edited and published a selection of investment reviews from Marathon, a London-based asset management firm whose investment strategy is strongly influenced by the study of the capital cycle (Chancellor, 2004).

We are unquestionably in full sympathy with the theory, but we doubt whether it can be applied systematically for stock selection purposes – and in that we are joined by no less than the legendary Benjamin Graham and David Dodd. Their seminal book *Security Analysis* already contains a very clear description of the capital cycle, two years before Keynes published the *General Theory*: 'A business which sells at a premium does so because it earns a large return upon its capital; this large return attracts competition; and, generally speaking, it is not likely to continue indefinitely' (Graham and Dodd, 1934). However, critically, they add: 'While this is orthodox economic theory, and undoubtedly valid in a broad sense, we doubt if it applies with sufficient certainty and celerity to make it useful as a governing factor in common-stock selection'.

Our own work, done with infinitely greater processing power than could have been used in the early 1930s, shows that Graham and Dodd were right in their very insightful observation; it is almost impossible to observe company returns fading in a straight line to the cost of capital under the sole driver of competitive pressure. If the theory were observable at the stock level, it would be possible to detect companies with a clearly identifiable downward trend in returns, regardless of how their own capital moves. In this instance, their high returns would attract competing capital, which, outside the group, would be busy competing the excess return away. Some examples do exist, but are complex to analyse. Figure 6.6 shows the case of General Motors.

In Figure 6.6, which plots the CROCI of GM, we can clearly identify the business cycle of the early 1990s. Since the peak of 1994, however, a worrying trend has emerged: the almost continuous erosion of returns. This could be the sign of competitive pressures from other car manufacturers, especially since some of GM's competitors are showing a much healthier cash return profile. Figure 6.7 shows the CROCI chart of Toyota.

However, the balance sheet of a car manufacturer is so complex to analyse (because of the integration of intricate finance operations) that even such an

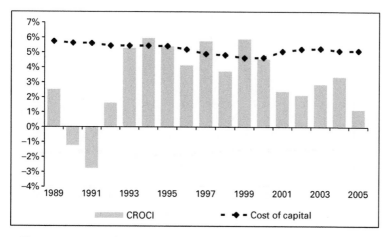

Figure 6.6 General Motors: CROCI and cost of capital, 1989–2005.

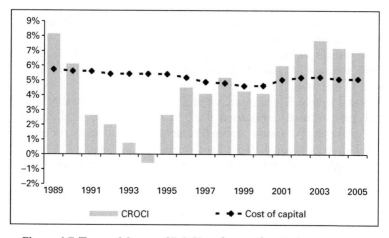

Figure 6.7 Toyota Motors: CROCI and cost of capital, 1989–2005.

ostensibly clear-cut case might be inconclusive. In Graham and Dodd's own words, there is just not enough certainty and celerity in the application of the above economic principles, at least at a single-company level. Capital is supposed to 'attack' super-returns. In the case of GM, the peak return of 1994 was far from spectacular, barely breaking the cost of capital. What was the economic incentive to compete this meagre excess return away?

The day-to-day use of the CROCI model suggests that, at the company level, returns are much more likely to respond to the company's *own* capital cycle. This does not invalidate in any way the economic principles of the capital cycle. Excess capital kills returns, and capital is put off by low returns. But we are dealing here with the company's own capital allocation process, rather than its competitors. Between 1994 and 1999, Carrefour, the French-based global retailer, invested heavily in new markets such as Spain, as well as in Latin America and Asia. The growth in capital

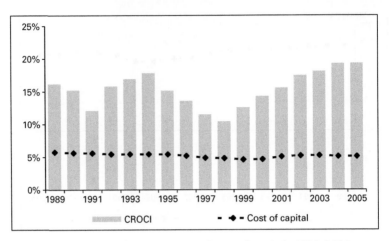

Figure 6.8 Carrefour: CROCI and cost of capital, 1989–2005.

invested averaged 30 per cent per annum during this period. The historical CROCI profile is shown in Figure 6.8.

The dent in returns, which started in 1994 and ended in 1998, is perfectly syn-chronised with the capital cycle of the company, which ended in style in 1999 with the takeover of Promodes, a competitor. There followed six years of below average growth in capital invested (economic capital actually shrank in 2001 and 2002), during which cash returns normalised back to their original level. In the case of B Sky B, the British pay television channel, returns collapsed while the company was 'acquiring' subscribers through the subsidisation of decoders and the acquisition of programme rights, and recovered as soon as it eased off its investment spree (Figure 6.9).

There is strong anecdotal evidence to support the assertion that the cash return cycle is more likely to be the result of the company's own rate of accumulation of

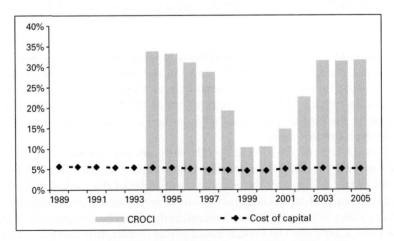

Figure 6.9 B Sky B: CROCI and cost of capital, 1989–2005.

assets rather than the strict consequence of competition theory. If this sounds like an abstruse point of debate, it isn't, and has important consequences on the analysis and interpretation of economic data. In practice, it suggests that *the capital cycle may be as behavioural as it is structural*. The cost of capital is sometimes described as exerting a gravitational force on returns. This is an excellent analogy, which can be used to make the behavioural point as well. In order to feel the attraction, an object will need to be close enough to a mass; if it does not get close, it will carry on drifting through space. However, space is largely made of nothingness, and matter only occupies a fraction of the volume – which means that the object/return could carry on travelling for a very long time before, eventually, getting attracted to a planet/cost of capital. So what gets it there, apart from randomness? In the behavioural theory of the capital cycle that we propose, it is the company's *own actions* (accumulation of capital at too high a rate, or in the wrong area, for instance) that precipitate the reversion of returns to the cost of capital – a bit like a space vessel using its booster rockets to break away from its geo-stationary orbit to come down to earth.

In practice, it will always be possible to argue that a company used its booster rockets – started to accumulate capital at a lower marginal return on capital – in response to competitive pressures. There are undeniably some instances where this is the case, as in the example of the telecom industry in the late 1990s. The new mobile licences were then auctioned to the highest bidder, a government-inspired competitive situation which forced companies into uneconomic behaviour. Strikingly, but not surprisingly, the CROCI of Vodafone collapsed from 16 per cent to almost the cost of capital (7.5 per cent) after these auctions. However, these are exceptional circumstances, rather than the norm. In most cases, and on the basis of the previous observations, it is tempting to argue that fades are self-inflicted. The 'behavioural aspect' of a fading return implies that its analysis always has to be done *in conjunction with the analysis of the firm's own capital allocation*.

Note that the metaphor of gravity does apply all the way. If the company is strong enough to pull away and recover its previous level of CROCI, as was shown for Carrefour or B Sky B, this is all benefit for shareholders, in application of the residual income formula:

$$E = NCI + \frac{(CROCI - CoC) \times NCI}{CoC}.$$

The case of a higher net capital invested on *unchanged or recovered CROCI* clearly warrants a higher price tag. The danger only comes when the company is losing too much CROCI because it is adding too much capital, and the gravitational pull of the cost of capital becomes too powerful. There were numerous such instances in the aftermath of the technology bubble. Remember that the level of cash return dictates the maximum level at which the company can grow organically. The cutting-edge innovators of the technology area, like Juniper Networks or Ciena Systems, were able to grow their economic capital (which includes R&D) at very high rates only because their cash return was correspondingly high. Once these technology companies started to accept a lower marginal return, and were eventually caught by the downturn, they simply could not grow fast enough to keep up with this innovation rate. They needed to retrench, cut down their ambitions, or sell assets to larger competitors. We have already seen the case of Alcatel as an illustration of the importance of the level of cash return in the pursuit of the corporate strategy.

Although it is always a good idea to check the self-inflicted fade theory, it does not apply to all companies and all situations. What if there is no identifiable pattern in the company's own rate of accumulation of assets? Many analysts who want to model cash flows explicitly for a reasonably long period, say two business cycles (fifteen years), feel compelled to make returns fade to the cost of capital during a standard 'fade period', at a concomitant 'fade rate'. This practice can be misleading, because the analyst will tend either to overestimate or underestimate the fade rate! For a company with a strong competitive advantage, and in the absence of a misjudgement in capital allocation on its part, the fade a few years forward is likely to be negligible. This is the case of Colgate, for example. By forcing a fade onto the return profile, the analyst will overestimate the future attrition of returns, resulting in an undervaluation of the company's assets. Conversely, if a real loss of competitive advantage should occur, then the company is more likely to fail completely than to fade. We have already approached this issue in Chapter 4, when addressing the cost of capital. We could fill the rest of this book with examples of abrupt falls in the level of CROCI, but it would take some doing to find more than ten companies where the CROCI does fade gently and predictably towards the cost of capital. As we have remarked before, sectors fade, but companies, in general, tend to fail. Just consider the example of Schering Plough, which saw its cash return going from 20 per cent to zero (Figure 6.10), or Sun Microsystems, which swung from more than 25 per cent CROCI to minus 15 per cent in just two years (Figure 6.11).

In these cases, forecasting a gentle fade to the cost of capital would have been of no use, and would have resulted here in overestimating the value of the company's assets. We will detail in Chapter 9 how to deal with fades in a forward-looking model. For now, let us conclude that forecasting fades in return brings more subjectivity and less clarity to modelling, and that a fading return should always trigger questions on the management's own capital allocation policy, before blaming competitors'.

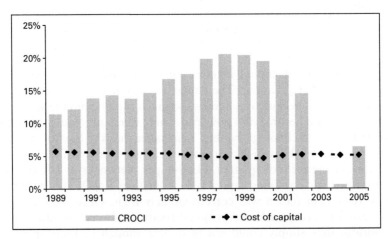

Figure 6.10 Schering Plough: CROCI and cost of capital, 1989–2005.

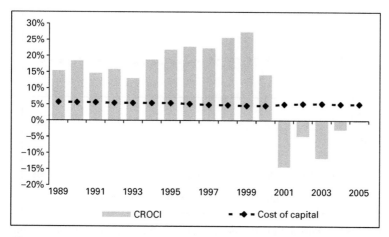

Figure 6.11 Sun Microsystems: CROCI and cost of capital, 1989–2005.

Pattern three: cyclicality of cash returns

The abrupt drop in the level of CROCI for structural reasons, *alias* 'failing returns', will not look different from the result of a cyclical downturn, 'falling returns'. Yet the analyst must be able to distinguish between the two. A cyclical company has a cyclical cash flow but can be a stable company, whereas a failing company never is. Equally, the analyst will need to distinguish a seemingly cyclical pattern coming from the capital cycle, as described above, and a conventional cyclical pattern coming from margin contraction and expansion, following the vagaries of top-line growth. Given enough history, and with a strong hint from the sector in which the company competes, identifying cycles should be relatively easy. Cyclical cash returns tend to be remarkably stable from one cycle to the next. The example of Texas Instruments (see Figure 6.12) shows that the company seems to live through a very stable five

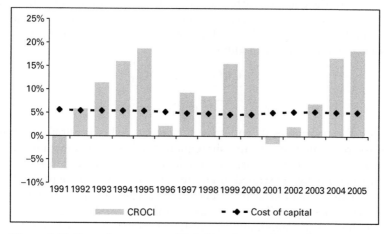

Figure 6.12 Texas Instruments: CROCI and cost of capital, 1991–2005.

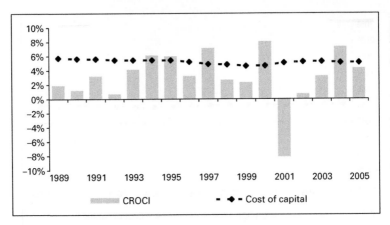

Figure 6.13 A European consumer business with an erratic CROCI pattern.

year cash-flow cycle, with 1991–1995, 1996–2000 and 2001–2005 looking quite similar. Trough returns are always well below the cost of capital, and often negative, which suggests a very vicious competitive situation. Peak returns invariably occur on the fifth year at 18 per cent, perhaps slightly below for 2005. Strikingly, the acquisition in 2000 of Burr-Brown, a semiconductor business, does not seem to have altered this pattern in the slightest.

This clock-like regularity is quite rare. However, some regularity needs to be observed in order to qualify as a cyclical company. Erratic patterns are not signalling a cycle but, more likely, erratic management. Figure 6.13 provides an example of a return pattern carrying hardly any information on the shape of the cycle.

What matters is to identify that peaks and troughs occur at more or less regular intervals. This will allow the analyst to calculate the amplitude of the cyclical swings, necessary on two counts. First, it will help in predicting the amount of debt that is accumulated in the downturn, which will indicate the extent to which this might threaten the company. Second, peak and trough returns will indicate the likely mid-cycle point for the company. Although the daily fluctuations of the market will follow the ups and downs of the cyclical swings, long-term valuation measures will tend to rely on the mid-cycle level of cash return. In other words, for cyclical stocks, the Equivalence will be slightly modified to

$$\frac{E}{NA} = \frac{\dfrac{CROCI_P + CROCI_T}{2}}{CoC}$$

where P and T represent peak and trough readings. This is surely a source of frustration for the management (and shareholders) of cyclical companies, but it is hard to blame the market in this instance. Look at International Paper, the US-based pulp and paper company, illustrated in Figure 6.14. The share price probably never benefits from a full valuation at the cyclical peak, which tends to occur every six years, as shown in the figure. This is because, for the rest of the time, its cash return is well below the cost of capital, and the average CROCI comes out at 3.3 per cent between 1989 and 2005.

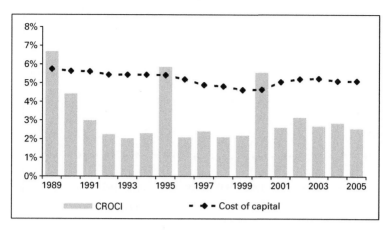

Figure 6.14 International Paper: CROCI and cost of capital, 1989–2005.

However, investors are not always harsh on cyclical companies. Even in the previous case, the average asset multiple comes out at 98 per cent over the period, implying a cost of capital business – hardly a severe assessment, given an actual average CROCI of almost *half* the cost of capital. On average, the market is willing to assume that mid-cycle returns will not fall below half the cost of capital, by seldom putting low-returning cyclical companies on an asset multiple of less than $0.5\times$. In practice, most cyclical businesses will see their CROCI average between 40 per cent and 100 per cent of the cost of capital over a cycle. In application of the Equivalence principle, so should their market value as a percentage of the replacement cost of assets. These low CROCIs are especially noticeable in mature industries, and in regions of low capital productivity, such as Japan or Continental Europe. Remember the case of the two chemical companies at the beginning of this chapter, a mature industry *par excellence*, which averaged 4.8 per cent CROCI over two cycles, or approximately 80 per cent of the global cost of capital. However, some cyclical companies will do better, especially in new sectors such as technology; Taiwan Semiconductor averaged 17 per cent CROCI between 1995 and 2005 (Figure 6.15), and at the lowest ebb of its cycle, in 2001, returned above the cost of capital (just).

However, some will do worse, with cash returns unable to exceed 2.5 per cent over a cycle. Yet it is very rare to observe a company trading at less than 50 per cent of replacement cost, which is equivalent to a mid-cycle CROCI of about 3 per cent. This explains why very low CROCI companies are hardly ever attractive on a systematic EP-based stock selection process. On the other hand, those that do trade below this threshold do so presumably because of extreme distrust on the part of investors. Management would be well advised to take some notice, before a corporate raider does.

One final point on cyclical companies. If the market prices these assets off their mid-cycle returns, which rarely change from one cycle to the next, this implies that their market value does not change much either – a conclusion at odds with the common belief (and observation) that cyclical shares are hugely volatile. This demands two comments. First, high volatility does not mean that the *average* valuation changes much, say over a month or a quarter. It could simply be that the

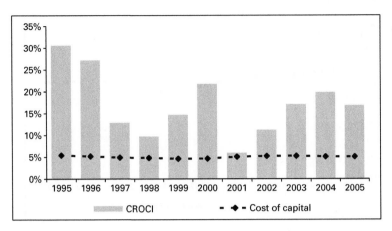

Figure 6.15 Taiwan Semiconductors: CROCI and cost of capital, 1995–2005.

dispersion around the mean value is high, perhaps because of the pollution of accounting information, or random assessments of the business cycle. Second, and more importantly, an economic profit model deals with the value of the whole enterprise. Even if this overall value does not change, the equity value within it can vary quite a lot, by the amount of debt accumulated or paid down through the cycle, since the enterprise value is largely made of the market value of equity plus financial liabilities. In practice, the EP model suggests that, within a cycle, the value of cyclical shares should vary by the change in net debt, and be similar from mid-cycle to mid-cycle, unless of course the cost of capital changes. Whilst this assertion needs to be verified historically company by company, this is what we notice by and large, which makes net debt an extremely important variable for cyclical shares, but sadly not always one that is easy to forecast.

In this non-exhaustive typology, we have focused on the tails of the distribution curve, the extraordinary cases, the good-looking and the ugly guys. Yet many companies live their lives without much of a cycle, without fades and without the opportunity to invest at a higher marginal return than their core business. They deserve a quick mention. In pictures, calm, competitive waters provide a return profile like the one of Coca-Cola shown in Figure 6.16.

Note that flat profiles are more likely to occur with returns significantly above the cost of capital. Value-destroying companies will eventually incur the wrath of their shareholders, and be either sold or forced to restructure. As a result, there are very few examples of flat returns below the cost of capital. Far from being uninteresting, a flat high-return profile signals a very strong competitive advantage, a truly defensive business. Usually, these companies do not need to add much net capital invested to consolidate their competitive position either. As such, they are not 'growth' businesses but simply extremely profitable ones, and usually core holdings for a diversified investor. Analytically, there is very little to do in such cases, other than check that the rate of accumulation of assets is not about to get out of hand. Yet this does not mean that this type of company should be bought at any price. With no expansion of CROCI and limited growth in net capital invested, we are in a situation where the Equivalence should be applied in its strictest sense, and the asset multiple

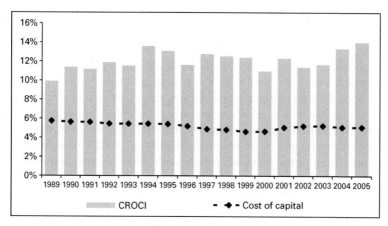

Figure 6.16 Coca-Cola: CROCI and cost of capital, 1989–2005.

should track the relative return very closely. This is a good illustration of systematic investing clashing with 'emotional' investing. In the latter framework, investors may be tempted to apply a super-rating to these (unquestionably) super-companies. In the former framework, investors should observe that a flat CROCI and almost no net expansion in net capital invested is the exact definition of equilibrium. And, as we have seen in Chapter 2, *if they expect this profile to continue*, investors will have a rare case of PE ratio at equilibrium, which should be exactly the inverse of the cost of capital. At all times. There is no economic reason to acquire the shares of these super-companies above that limit.

Asset growth – another insight into corporate behaviour

Asset growth and returns are largely interrelated, and separating the two for the sake of clarity in this chapter must not suggest otherwise. Indirectly, we have already said as much in the previous section, by attributing fading returns *a priori* to too aggressive an accumulation of capital, not from competitors, but from the company's own doing. In the case of Enron, already mentioned in Chapter 5, it was only the joint analysis of its cash return rate (5 per cent) and its growth rate in assets (21 per cent) that could give a hint of the catastrophe lying ahead: a yearly 16 per cent (of assets) funding deficit.

The rate of accumulation of assets defines growth and risk

The prime information released by the study of net capital invested – net economic assets – is the economic growth rate of the company. In the EP framework, where

$$EP = (CROCI - CoC) \times NCI,$$

a company which grows earnings by expanding its cash margin is not a growth company. On the contrary, one could argue pedantically that a company which does not grow its earnings because its capital expansion is exactly cancelled by cash margin contraction *is* nevertheless a growth company, for the reason that it is adding to its Net Capital Invested (NCI). The fact that it is growing its assets unprofitably is another matter altogether. We have already detailed in Chapter 5, from a theoretical point of view, why the source of earnings growth (expansion of cash return or asset growth) matters. Let us take here a more practical angle. Investing in asset expansion is a bet on the future, on the ability of management to extract, from this additional capital, a cash return at least as much as that which the existing capital is producing. In other words, the marginal CROCI must not fall, or at least not more than in the proportion seen with the Walgreen example, or

$$\frac{NCI_1 - NCI_0}{NCI_0} > \frac{CROCI_1 - CROCI_0}{CROCI_1 - CoC}.$$

As a result, investors treat such companies, which we will call 'asset growers', in a very binary manner, as shown in the following example. We have analysed the performance of all the asset growers among the top 700 global non-financial groups between October 2001 and March 2005. For the purpose of this study (conducted by Janet Lear in April 2005), asset growers were those companies that grew EP *predominantly* by asset growth, not cash margin expansion, at the beginning of the period. The universe was then segregated in clusters according to the economic characteristics at the end of the period. *Status quo* (the asset grower remained an asset grower) was 'rewarded' by an unchanged value: this cluster's median value fell by 2 per cent during the period (the world index increased by 5.5 per cent in local currency during the same period). On the other hand, the group of asset growers that subsequently saw their level of CROCI falling was severely punished, with a 40 per cent drop in the median value. And, conversely, the group that managed to become 'CROCI growers' at the end of the period, in other words which switched the source of EP growth from asset growth to cash margin expansion, enjoyed a median uplift in valuation of more than 50 per cent. Interestingly, those companies that grew EP predominantly by expanding cash margins rather than assets at the beginning of the period did not offer a symmetrical pay-off. *Status quo* (CROCI was still growing at the end of the period) was rewarded by an 18 per cent increase in value for the median stock. However, for those companies that morphed into asset growers, there was a median drop in value of 11 per cent.

As such, these results do not have statistical value, since they were measured over one discrete period only. Furthermore, this period includes two atypical market moves; the 2002 collapse of equity markets, followed by the sharp rebound of 2003. However, they are striking enough to warrant this digression. Cash margin expansion does not carry a binary outcome for investors, because it can never go wrong from their point of view. But capital expansion *is* binary. It can either produce a higher marginal return on capital, or a lower one.

A typology of asset growth

A typology of asset growth can be built broadly along the same principles as the study of the CROCI profiles. Some historical depth is necessary, to capture at least one or two capital cycles; 1980 or 1989 are good starting points for the same reasons as previously outlined. A true growth profile will show a regular, rather than lumpy, rate of accumulation of assets. See, for instance, the beautiful profile of Apache, the US oil company, shown in Figure 6.17.

Japan provides an interesting special case. It is possible to find genuine growth stocks in Japan, even among the large companies. Canon provides a good illustration, with a regular increase in net capital invested since 1989, at an average rate of approximately 4 per cent per annum (Figure 6.18).

However, because Japan has been, at various levels of intensity, in a deflationary environment for most of the past decade, the yen deflator can also be negative. For mature industries where assets are barely replaced, and no new capital is added, this produces the profile shown in Figure 6.19.

In real terms, the replacement value of assets of East Japan Railway is *declining*, simply because inflation is negative, and the cost of an asset will be less tomorrow than today. This achieves a similar result to a high rate of technological progress,

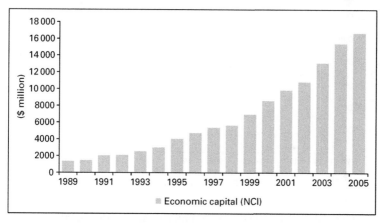

Figure 6.17 Apache: economic capital, 1989–2005.

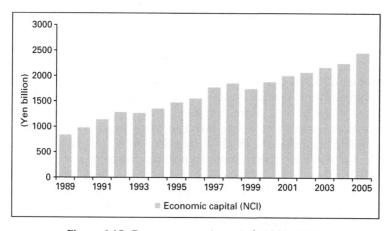

Figure 6.18 Canon: economic capital, 1989–2005.

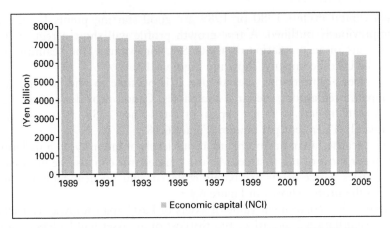

Figure 6.19 East Japan Railway: economic capital, 1989–2005.

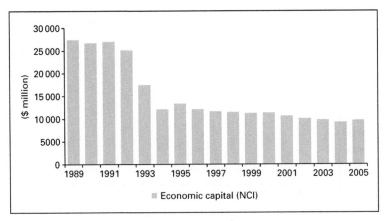

Figure 6.20 Eastman Kodak: economic capital, 1989–2005.

which reduces the cost of replacement through higher productivity. Such profiles are unique to Japan and are different from active retrenchment (disposals or closures), which produces a lumpy profile, such as the one shown in Figure 6.20, plotting the net economic capital of Eastman Kodak. In the early 1990s, the emergence of digital photography and aggressive Asian competition forced this company into heavy retrenchment from the other businesses that it held (Pharmaceutical, Chemical and Household products, etc.), more than halving the level of economic capital.

The *rate* of accumulation of assets can also carry important information. Its average (excluding acquisitions, which distort the series) will provide an idea of trend growth, and will enable the analyst to position the company on a theoretical lifecycle similar to the one at the beginning of Chapter 3. Because these assets are measured in real terms, the average rate of growth is directly comparable to GDP. Steel and other mature businesses tend to grow at a rate no higher than 1 to 2 per cent, or 'half GDP'. Food, beverage and other staple businesses will tend to grow at 4 to 5 per cent, or 'GDP',[4] and so on. Outliers can easily be spotted.

The *speed* of growth is also a very useful indicator, as it will signal a steady company, one with increasing growth opportunities, or one that is slowly going ex-growth. Home Depot is one of these successful US retailers which has grown from East to West with tremendous growth rates and profitability. In Figure 6.21, it can be seen that the accumulation of assets has been relentless since the late 1980s.

At the same time, the cash return has increased. It averaged 10 per cent in the first half of the 1990s, and moved steadily towards 15 per cent in the late 1990s, presumably thanks to the consumer and real estate booms. The combination of higher CROCI and increasing capital had a predictable effect on economic profits, which have exploded in the past fifteen years, going from less than $100 million in 1989 to more than $3 billion in 2004. But what happened to the economic PE ratio of Home Depot? *It de-rated massively.* The company was on an economic PE of 27.6× in 1989. It spent the first half of the 1990s between 30× and 50×, a phenomenal rating for a phenomenal company. The second half saw a range of 30–40×, except for 1999 and 2000, at the peak of the equity bubble. By 2005, its economic PE ratio was less than 17×. Of course, all equities de-rated in 2001 and 2002, as investors reasserted their required risk premium; however, Home Depot's de-rating was much more severe than the average equity. In the period 1989 to 2000, Home Depot traded on an economic PE relative to the US market of between 108 per cent and 152 per cent. By 2001 its rating had fallen below 100 per cent, and it was 75 per cent in 2005. What happened?

Let us look again at Figure 6.21, the chart of economic capital, complemented this time by the yearly rate of change (Figure 6.22).

It jumps out of Figure 6.22 that the company is finding it impossible to sustain its growth rate of the earlier years, and that it is gently normalising towards a low multiple of GDP (say twice GDP, or 8 per cent) – still a very enviable speed limit. Management could quite possibly accelerate the rate of accumulation of assets again, but in all likelihood this would exert some pressure on the firm's cash return, which it is apparently not willing to see. This is a clear illustration of the assertion that, according to an EP framework, it is the expectation of growth in assets, not in earnings, which drives the multiple. It is also a good and rare example of a high

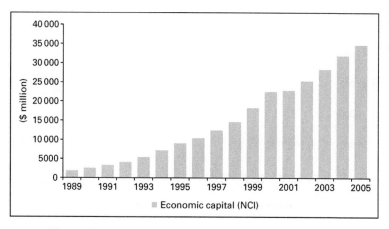

Figure 6.21 Home Depot: economic capital, 1989–2005.

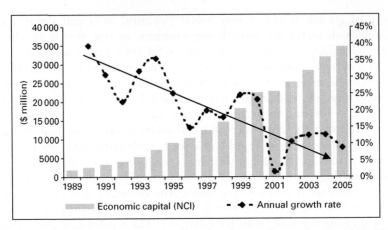

Figure 6.22 Home Depot: economic capital and annual growth rate, 1989–2005.

return business for which both the level of cash return and the growth rate in assets matter for the asset multiple.

Finally, the study of net capital invested will enable the segregation of acquisitive companies from those which grow organically. For example, the acquisitive nature of LVMH, the luxury goods business, is clearly shown by the steady accumulation of goodwill on top of its economic capital (Figure 6.23). By definition, an EP model is agnostic about the choice between acquisitive and organic growth at the right price, since it is based on the premise of an equivalence between market value (existing assets) and replacement value (new assets). But this does not prevent the analyst from checking that the company does not overpay for its acquisitions. Other factors, such as execution risks, need to be taken into consideration as well. In particular, a distinction must be made between an acquisition's marginal return on operating capital and its overall financial impact. In this case, the level of cash return has remained fairly stable (at around 15 per cent), indicating that the acquisitions

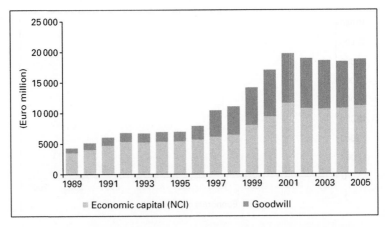

Figure 6.23 LVMH: economic capital and goodwill, 1989–2005.

did not dilute the operating (i.e. pre-financing) profitability of the firm. However, LVMH had to take a large impairment of goodwill on some acquisitions, suggesting that some of them were in fact done at an inflated price.

Everything and nothing

Arguing that the analysis of cash returns and economic capital is the all-encompassing answer to the daily puzzle of equity markets would take a pretty naïve observer of financial markets. It is not. The price of an asset is the result of an immensely complex process, which includes a good dose of randomness, and behavioural patterns impossible to model. If investing were painting (after all, many argue that it is more of an art than a science), this analysis would merely be the background, the very first layer of paint applied to the canvas. But who can imagine a painting without a background?

There is, on top of the 'Does your thing work?' of Chapter 1, another taboo question to ask any CROCI analyst. It tends to arise after investors have listened politely to a full CROCI pitch, where the shape, level and direction of cash returns, how they compare to the sector, the market and competitors, the rate of accumulation of assets, the funding gap, and the acquisition policy are discussed for a company. And here it comes: 'But how does it look . . . *on fundamental analysis?*' After a second of disbelief, a mental scream answers: 'But this *is* fundamental analysis!' – and indeed it is. Fundamental means 'at the basis of'. Cash return and economic assets are precisely that: the basis on which the company can grow, produce profits and pay dividends, sustain (or not) its competitive advantage, acquire other companies or be acquired, etc. It is everything. And yet, altogether, it is still not quite enough for investment analysis. Investments based solely on these variables would achieve catastrophic results, because investors need at least two other major inputs. Unless the company is totally monolithic, which is rare for large international groups, they need to understand the *dynamic* of the various assets (in organisational speak, *divisions*) that make up net capital invested. Which assets or regions are viewed as promising by management, and will benefit from further investments? Which ones have a high profitability, even if not particularly high profile? Which ones are essential for the profitability of the others, even if they themselves are not very profitable? And, of course, investors need to draw the appropriate conclusions from these investigations for expected future cash flows. The Chief Executive of a successful European department store once explained to me why so many of his US competitors failed. 'They analyse profitability department by department', he said. 'If the carpet department is unprofitable, they close it down. Without realising that people who buy carpets will also buy lamps, and curtains, and picture frames. You need to analyse the dynamic of cross-departmental selling'. A good financial analyst will attempt the same analysis on the assets that make up his company – a task impossible to perform by simply observing the change in net capital invested.

The second major input required is, simply, the price tag. There is a world between fundamental analysis (CROCI-based or otherwise), which measures how good a company is, and investment analysis, which measures how expensive it is, with respect to an investor's risk appetite, cost of funding and expected return. This is an entirely different subject indeed, which deserves an entirely different chapter.

Notes

1. For those interested in the subject, I would recommend *The New Financial Order* (Shiller, 2003). Shiller frames these latest innovations in a vast historical perspective, and argues that the increasing use of complex derivative instruments is simply the continuation of a historical trend that started 300 years ago with the discovery of probabilities. This discovery enabled the statistical computation of risk, and its consequence was the ability to lay off small quantities of risk onto a great number of investors willing to bear it against remuneration.
2. Consumer goods companies also give large year-end rebates to their distributors, which they usually book as 'accruals' in net working capital. This practice increases the imbalance between 'payables' and 'receivables', and optically decreases NWC requirements further.
3. Retailers operate with negative working capital because they have no receivables – all their clients paying cash at the tills – but pay their suppliers up to ninety days or more after they have received the goods. Very large payables accounts are able to finance, and more, their inventories as a result.
4. World GDP trend growth is currently slightly lower than 4 per cent per annum. The 700 global companies that constitute the CROCI universe tend to grow at a higher pace, 4 to 5 per cent. This is because GDP includes less dynamic sectors than the non-financial competitive part of the economy. This is also due to a certain survival bias in our sample.

References

Chancellor, E. (2004). *Capital Account: A Money Manager's Reports on a Turbulent Decade 1993–2002*. Texere.

Gilovich, T. (1991). *How We Know What Isn't So: The Fallibility of Human Reason in Everyday Life*. The Free Press.

Graham, B. and Dodd, D. (1934). *Security Analysis*. The McGraw-Hill Companies.

Lowenstein, R. (2002). *When Genius Failed*. Fourth Estate.

Shiller, R. (2003). *The New Financial Order*. Princeton University Press.

7 Investment analysis

Corporate anatomy: is a super-company always a super-investment?

Fundamental analysis is a health check, the end result of which produces a rough judgement, a guideline, on the level of fitness of the company. A company that over-invests will risk obesity. Its arteries will become clogged up with fatty assets for which there is no use, and which will prevent it from being fleet-footed in its reactions. If, for some reason, the supply level of blood (cash flow) drops, it will risk death. A company that under-invests will risk anaemia. It will become too weak to respond to an increase in demand, and will lose out to its fitter competitors. A company with too low a CROCI will become the corporate equivalent of an asthmatic; as soon as the pace of competition picks up speed, it will get out of breath. It will not have enough cash flow to fund this higher tempo. A company able to grow its net economic capital and its CROCI will be the corporate equivalent of a young, top-level athlete, with everything firing on all cylinders. A few years later, this corporate body will probably still have a superior level of CROCI, but may have lost some spark with respect to the growth rate of economic capital; it will have become the body of a 'well looked-after' forty-something.

However, the shape of your body does not determine the size of your wallet. There are some extremely wealthy tall and skinny people, and some very poor ones, too. Asthma does not strike a certain level of wealth, to spare the others, at least within a socially homogeneous group. In the same way, a good, healthy company does not necessarily make a good investment. There is a surprisingly large number of investment professionals who cannot see this distinction, and equate 'good company' with 'good investment'. Similarly, all Financial Directors and CEOs assume that if an investment professional has a negative opinion on the shares of their company (i.e. it is an investment which, in his opinion, has the wrong risk/reward characteristics), it means that their company is a bad company. Things are changing slowly. Part of the problem stemmed from the arrogance of certain analysts, who passed peremptory judgements on companies based on approximate analysis in the heyday of the bull market. Certain managements had an equally immature attitude towards financial analysts as well, and considered that a daily praise of their company should be part of the job description too, for reasons that are all too obvious. The new regulatory framework of research, coupled with a more sanguine view of analysts' opinions on shares, has of late quietened down this storm in a teacup.

We often read of legendary investors advising us to ignore the market moods and volatility. This must not be the source of a misunderstanding. When Warren Buffet says: 'As far as you are concerned, the stock market does not exist. Ignore it', this does not mean 'ignore the market price of the business that you are considering buying'. On the contrary, Warrant Buffet, to carry on with this emblematic example, is always meticulous about the price that he pays. Of his own admission, this has even caused his company, Berkshire Hathaway, to miss out on some opportunities, such as a sizeable and lucrative investment in Wal-Mart, which he never pursued because 'the price did not come back a bit' (Berkshire Hathaway 2003 Annual Meeting, May 2004). In his own words, 'the critical investment factor is determining the intrinsic value of a business and paying a fair or bargain price', only *then* can you safely ignore the market's opinion. Or, in splendid 'Warren and Charlie' style, 'you are neither right nor wrong because the crowd disagrees with you. You are right because your data and reasoning are right'. Thus, in our framework, *fundamental* analysis is about the economic characteristics of a company, the profile of its return on capital and growth in capital invested. *Investment* analysis is about the price that the market is putting on this profile. These are two separate issues that must be conducted separately.

The following example is about a superstar, the young, top-level athlete of a few paragraphs ago. This company is not only returning way above the cost of capital, but it is also increasing its competitive advantage; its CROCI has gone up from 7.4 per cent in 1992 to more than 13 per cent in 2004/2005 (Figure 7.1).

In addition, its economic growth rate is relentless (Figure 7.2). It is able to add, on average, more than 20 per cent per annum to its economic capital. Such a combination of increasing levels of cash return and superior growth in capital invested is quite rare. We could only count a handful of such companies worldwide.

This company is Starbucks. It is typical of a young US retail business expanding briskly from coast to coast in the US, and using domestic cash flows to fund international expansion as well. McDonald's would probably have looked very similar twenty years ago. Judged by its economic parameters, Starbucks is a good, indeed a very good, company. But is this 'best of breed' a good *investment* as well? Are we paying 'fair or bargain price for it'? This is a different question altogether, which brings in a host of exogenous variables – including the current risk appetite

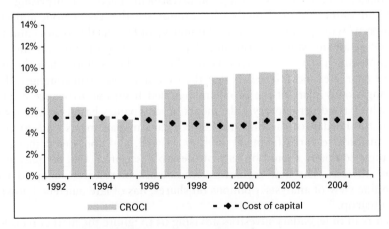

Figure 7.1 A strong competitive advantage . . . .

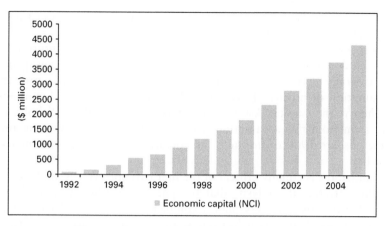

Figure 7.2 ... coupled with relentless growth.

of investors for this type of investment, their current market and company-specific expectations, as well as the legacy valuation (i.e. the price that was put on these assets yesterday, at the close of business). Note, incidentally, that companies have very little control over these variables and therefore, ultimately, very little control over their share price. From the point of view of investors, without a thorough investigation of these issues, there is no way of knowing if this super-company is a super-investment.

I want to fly – the madness of crowds[1]

Human beings have always wanted to fly and to know about the future; by now, they have pretty much mastered the technique to fulfil this first desire, but the second is slightly more tricky. Pascal, the French philosopher who formalised the basic rules of probabilities, gave them just enough of a tool to reassure themselves: it is probable that the sun will rise tomorrow, and it is probable that the sky will not fall on our heads. If this sounds lame, remember that this was not obvious to men who lived less than a thousand years ago, and who were, for the past 30 000 years at least, physiologically exactly like us. Investors are in the business of predicting the future as well. In their language, they call it 'risk'. Benoit Mandelbrot, the self-proclaimed maverick mathematician we met in Chapter 1, distinguishes three ways to handle risk, in chronological order; fundamental analysis, technical analysis and modern finance theory (Mandelbrot and Hudson, 2004). In this framework, fundamental analysis is the study of causality. As Mandelbrot describes it, 'if one knows the cause, one can forecast the event and manage the risk'. It is what financial analysts do for a living, at brokers' and fund management firms. It implies a definitely deterministic approach to world events, by suggesting that the future is predictable for a much wider field of events than general prophecies about the sun and the sky. It is a curious remnant of eighteenth century thinking, which Mandelbrot sources back to the mathematician Laplace, who once said that he could predict the future if he knew the present position and velocity of every particle in the cosmos. In the financial world, it translates into 'if I know enough about what causes cash flow to rise or fall, I can predict its future profile'.

At the opposite end, modern finance theory proclaims that the future is unpredictable (which does not mean of course that future events have no cause), and that future risks can only be comprehended mathematically with the help of probabilities and an assumption of normal distribution. The Efficient Market Hypothesis, the Portfolio Theory, the Capital Asset Pricing Model and the Black–Scholes option formula all stem from this assumption, which, as we have already seen, finds its origin in the obscure 1900 doctorate of an equally obscure French mathematician Louis Bachelier.

Benoit Mandelbrot is equally critical of the first two approaches, and so scathing about the third (technical analysis) that he spares us further, disparaging, comments on it. He proposes no less than a complete reform of the mathematics of the 'modern' finance theory, which are now more than a century old. These are based on the assumptions of independence and normal (Gaussian) distribution of returns. He refutes these hypotheses with great flair and some success, even though the argument against the normal distribution of returns is based largely on the observation of the 1990s, which saw a number of 'six sigma events' falling outside of the normal distribution curve. Mandelbrot's alternative solution is based on fractals, a branch of mathematics which he developed, and that is used, amongst many other applications, by students of 'chaos theory'. By his own admission, the maths is 'frankly, so forbidding' that it is unclear if this work will find broader sympathy in finance any time soon, irrespective of its relevance to the understanding of markets. Mandelbrot is not alone in his criticism. Andrew Lo and Craig MacKinlay, two Professors of Finance at the MIT and Wharton, respectively, have spent the last decade testing the EMH and its associate, the Random Walk Theory. Their conclusion is that 'the Efficient Market Hypothesis is an idealisation that is economically unrealisable, but which serves as a useful benchmark for measuring relative efficiency' (Lo and McKinlay, 1999). Like Mandelbrot, who believes that share prices have 'memories', they find that stock-market prices are predictable to some degree.

Likewise, our approach to *investment* analysis is equally sceptical of both the causal approach and the Bachelier legacy. For the latter, enough daggers have been driven into the heart of the CAPM model that it can be proclaimed dead. This is literally what Eugene Fama, the very same man who invented the Efficient Market Hypothesis, wrote in 1992 (French and Fama, 1992). In this famous paper, previously mentioned in Chapter 4, he showed that the difference in performance between two stocks could partly be accounted for by the difference in valuation, using price-to-book and accounting PE! In the CAPM framework, only volatility, 'beta', is supposed to explain performance . . . One cannot help pointing out a slight irony in the whole debate, in that it is Professor Fama who was able seriously to unhinge the CAPM model. The foundations of both CAPM and EMH depend in fact on the same Bachelier-inspired tenets. The criticism of one leads, albeit indirectly, to the criticism of the other.

As for the causal route, that is, the explicit forecast of cash flows, twenty years of market experience can convince pretty much anybody that this leads to a dead-end. Each effect has its cause; this is plainly undisputable, and with hindsight the cause is always obvious. But the consistent *ex ante* identification of causes is impossible, and forecasting is just a random game at which some are luckier than others.

One cannot help admiring the bravado with which Benoit Mandelbrot wants to take down an edifice of nearly a century of age, modern finance theory. If he is right about fractals applied to finance, there can be no doubt that, soon enough, a Sharpe, a Markowitz or a Merton will emerge from a reputable (or even obscure) university, rework and rewrite the intuitions of his mentor into an elegant formula, and obtain a Nobel Prize for it. It is possible that this new model would revolutionise the finance industry. However, the breach that behavioural finance has created in 'model-based' finance may well already be too large to be ignored, let alone fixed. The practitioners who deal daily with equity markets know that asset prices are more than occasionally driven by irrational behaviour. When this is not the case, any of the models mentioned above does just fine. But in their day-to-day practice, investors need a simple, practical and reliable tool that flags 'the madness of crowds'.

In the decade that spanned 1989 and 1998, Coca-Cola, another quintessential US flagship briefly met in Chapter 6 as a model of stability, displayed all the right economic characteristics – world dominance, which translated into a superior cash return of 11.9 per cent on average. This cash return was not expanding as fast as Starbucks' is today, but it stood at more than twice the cost of capital, a formidable excess return. Furthermore, this cash return was very stable, with less than 1 per cent of difference from one year to the next (Figure 7.3).

As a result of, among other factors, a systematic policy of outsourcing their bottling activities, capital invested had ceased to grow quickly, but still managed to keep up with GDP, with an average real growth rate in economic capital of about 3 per cent per annum during the period (Figure 7.4).

Altogether, a very enviable set of economic characteristics; an entrenched competitive position (there are not many companies that can come and dislodge Coca-Cola from its markets) yielding a formidable excess return (as you would expect in a *de facto* duopoly), and a real growth rate in sync with world GDP. It was a good (even a very good) company, with strong defensive characteristics. But was it a good *investment*? In 1998, Coke's share price reached $90. In the following four

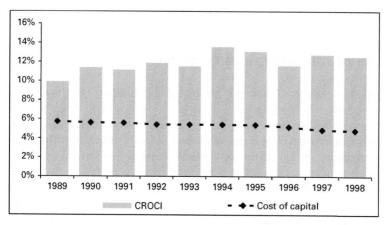

Figure 7.3 Coca-Cola: CROCI and cost of capital, 1989–1998.

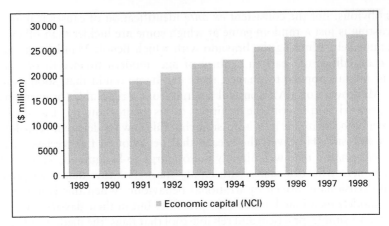

Figure 7.4 Coca-Cola: economic capital, 1989–1998.

or five years, the share price halved. Think about it: *it halved*. It halved despite the fact that the market went up strongly in 1999 and at the beginning of 2000, and it halved despite the fact that the technology bubble exploded soon after that, which meant that defensive investments (such as utilities, or indeed food and beverage shares) were eagerly sought. In fact, a typical defensive investment in the US went up 10 per cent in 2001 and down about 12 per cent in 2002 (the market went down 22 per cent that year). From the end of 1998 to the end of 2002, investors could have expected defensive shares to go up by about 35 per cent[2] – and Coca-Cola's shares went from $90 to $45 ... This excellent company turned out to be a nightmare investment. Can there be a better example of the disconnect between fundamental and investment analysis? But there is more important to come. Whilst its share price halved, Coca-Cola's economic characteristics suffered no change. The CROCI remained roughly at between 11 and 13 per cent, and the company carried on accumulating economic assets at a rate of 3 per cent per annum. Quite clearly, it is the behaviour of investors towards the stock that was modified. One of the two prices, either $90 or $45, was a 'mad' price. Finding out which one is what investment analysis is all about.

A suspicion of rational causality: beacon in the dark

The fundamental analysis that we proposed in Chapter 6 does not escape Mandelbrot's criticism; it is, in essence, deterministic. But at least it is not *randomly* deterministic. It argues that a share price will rise or fall largely, if not solely, because of certain economic features, the level of cash return and the real rate of capital accumulation, not because of interest rates, the weather, or the price of fish. And to the question of what causes these patterns to occur, we can answer: the economic cycle and the competitive advantage of the firm. We know that we can relate CROCI and Net Capital Invested to them, because they are calculated with only one objective – tracking the economic reality of the firm. However, how well can this framework *predict* what cash flow will look like in the future? As well as it is possible to predict what the economy will do, assuming that the link between the two, as defined in the EP model, is reasonably predictable. We have given enough examples in the previous chapter to assert with confidence that there is *some* predictability in economic patterns. But, it would be foolish to give them too much credibility. *Ex ante*, the future is an abyss full of emptiness, where the causality between events will always appear random, until it is, *ex post*, justified. At which point, of course it is too late, and fortunes are already made or lost. Let us say that an economic profit model may arm investors with a *suspicion of rational causality*. This is probably in itself a far superior source of accuracy of forecasts than any other model. Still, using this insight to make explicit forecasts would be falling again into the same behavioural trap identified at the beginning of Chapter 6 of believing that 'we know something that *they* don't'.

This conundrum (how can I know if the price is right if I don't know what the future holds?) is as old as the markets themselves. The pricing of an option creates a similar problem. You need to price the right to buy or sell a share at a certain price, for a certain period, but you don't know how much the shares will be worth in the end or at any point during this period (certain options give you the right to buy at expiry only, others whenever you want to during the life of the option). How can you then determine the price of the premium which gives you this right? The genius of Black, Scholes and Merton was to understand that it was possible to price the premium without knowing the price of the underlying share in the future. All you needed to know was the structure of the option (maturity and strike price), the *volatility* of the underlying share, plus a few bits and pieces to make the maths work – such as expected dividend payment and the level of short-term interest rates. Similarly, there is no way of knowing exactly what the future cash flow of a firm will be. But you don't necessarily need to know, because its current market value is equal to either FCF/d, or NA + (EP/d).

This gives you a pretty good idea of what is expected, on average, by investors. There is a beacon in the dark. The combination of a suspicion of rational causality, provided by the fundamental analysis of economic data, and that beacon, the average expected level of EP or FCF, is in essence how we suggest to perform investment analysis.

Practicalities of the asset multiple range

In practice, investors can carry out two types of investigation. The first will sound familiar, as it is a derivative of the Equivalence, which compares the asset multiple and the relative return. Given the volatility of equity markets, the strict comparison of these two ratios would trigger all sorts of buy and sell signals, not to mention the fact that the Equivalence does not take growth in assets into consideration, as we have repeatedly pointed out. It is therefore more insightful to frame the relative return within a *valuation range*. In practice, the lower valuation boundary is the asset multiple calculated with the lowest share price for the year, and the upper boundary is the asset multiple calculated with the highest one. As in the case of fundamental analysis, investment analysis must be put into the historical context of at least one, if not two, cycles. History and current valuation will provide three important insights. First, as already seen in Chapter 2, the relative return is often the 'bedrock' of a firm's value over time. In other words, the relative return should be an indication of the lower boundary of the valuation range. There is no theoretical justification for it; in practice, market volatility often brings a share price to the level of perfect equivalence between relative return and asset multiple. Because most companies manage to grow their assets somehow, this no-growth valuation level ends up representing the low-water mark of the valuation range. Second, the *spread* between high and low valuation will give at worst an indication of the volatility of valuation and, in the best cases, a trading range with which short-term investors can potentially make some money. Finally and most importantly, the current asset multiple will give a hint of what investors are expecting, today, for the future.

It is not always possible to analyse the Equivalence principle in these terms. Some shares trade at inexplicably (to us) low discounts to the relative return. Others enjoy an equally unexplainable premium. For instance, after its acquisition of Duracell in 1996, investors decided to put Gillette on such a premium, despite the fact that this purchase objectively slowed down the rate of growth of Gillette's economic capital (Figure 7.5). Nevertheless, the group looked attractive enough to Procter & Gamble for a takeover bid to be launched eventually.

These discrepancies find their origin mainly in a different level of risk premium; higher than ours when the shares appear at a discount, and *vice versa*. But, in most cases, the analysis of the Equivalence *will* yield a result, even if the conclusion is that the shares are fairly priced, which is a common (if frustrating) outcome. This is, for instance, the case for Sony, whose share price at the end of 2005 was indicating *status quo*. First, a quick glance at Figure 7.6 ensures that the relative return has, historically, been a reasonable proxy for the lower boundary of the valuation band. This is indeed the case, especially over the past eight years when the relative return ceased to be extremely cyclical, as shown in Figure 7.6. As for the *current* asset multiple, represented by the dot, it is right in the middle of the recent valuation range, and slightly above the relative return. This indicates that investors are discounting a similar range of asset multiples going forward, and, by extension, a similar profile of cash returns. Trading in the middle of the valuation range does not offer any

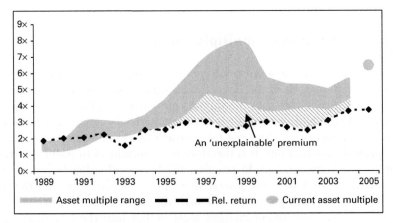

Figure 7.5 Gillette: an 'unexplainable' premium.

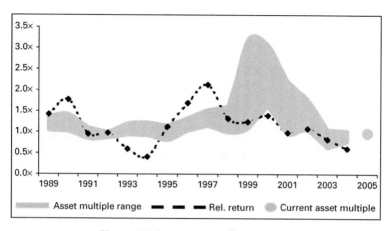

Figure 7.6 Sony: a case of *status quo*.

particular short-term trading opportunity either. Conclusion: *status quo*. Unless you have a good reason to believe that things will change radically in one way or another, Sony's expected return is falling nicely into a typical distribution; there is no valuation anomaly.

Fortunately, shares are not always priced in this indifferent fashion. In May 2004 we spotted Apollo, a fast-growing US education firm, priced as shown in Figure 7.7. We remarked:

> Apollo is a classic asset compounder, an operational star – growing assets aggressively, at the same time as managing to improve its returns. But the market is pricing significantly more than what it has managed to achieve. At $93, the market is expecting 2004 returns to be sustainable, and annual growth equal to the historic maximum.

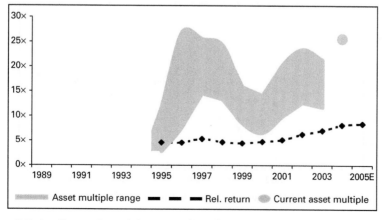

Figure 7.7 Apollo: market pricing more than the company has managed to achieve.

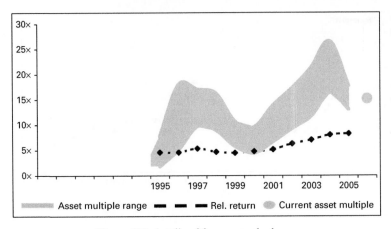

Figure 7.8 Apollo, fifteen months later.

Fifteen months later, the shares had lost exactly $20, or 21 per cent *in a rising market*, producing the chart shown in Figure 7.8.

Two months later, in July 2004, we spotted Sungard Data Systems, an IT service company in the US, priced at $24.5 (see Figure 7.9).

This time, the current asset multiple (the dot, in Figure 7.9) was towards the bottom end of the valuation band and, more significantly, well below the relative return. We remarked: 'We are mindful of the risks from a heavy exposure to financial services [Sungard has a large proportion of its clients in financial services]. Still, applying a worst case scenario relating to this exposure, we find the stock on the cheap side'. Apparently, we were not the only ones. A few months later the company was subject to a management buy-out – unusually, triggered by outside investors. This corporate activity prompted a major re-rating of the shares, of about $12, or more than 45 per cent. Figure 7.10 shows the valuation band at $36 one year later.

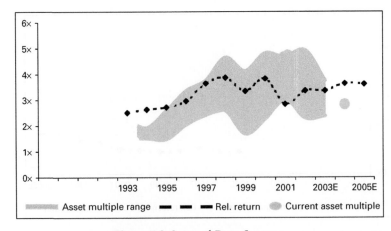

Figure 7.9 Sungard Data Systems.

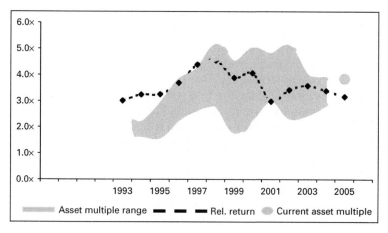

Figure 7.10 Sungard Data Systems, one year later.

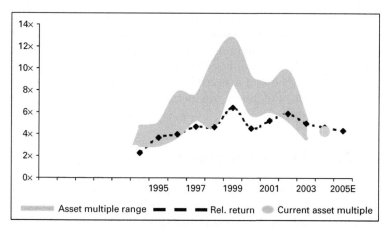

Figure 7.11 Securitas, September 2004.

Yet another two months passed before we could see the Swedish security company Securitas looking like Figure 7.11, in September 2004.

We argued that 'the market [was] overly bearish with regards to Securitas' prospects'. This was again predicated on the observation that the current asset multiple was towards the bottom end of the valuation band, and below the relative return. In the following months, the share price gained SEK 40 on top of the SEK 97 share price from September 2004, an increase of 41 per cent.

Sadly, such clear-cut examples do not occur very often. In a fair amount of cases the analysis will be inconclusive, as in the Sony example. Even when investors are able to spot such outliers, some further analysis has to be performed and some risk has to be taken. In the Sungard case, for instance, we took the view that the firm's exposure to the financial services industry was not such a big risk after all. This view could obviously have been wrong, and the relative return could have started to go down (because the cash return was going down), perhaps to a point where there would have been no discount left between it and the asset multiple. In other words, the study of the valuation band is not a constantly reliable device. But it *is* an instrument, signalling potential anomalies in the normal relationship between asset multiple and relative return, which we know is the lynchpin of asset pricing. There are worse investment techniques.

It is possible to increase slightly the level of sophistication of this analysis by combining it with derivative instruments. Quoted options will give some idea of the *expected* valuation range, since they imbed a view on volatility. Let us say that, at year zero, the high and low asset multiple of a company is observed at 1.3× and 1.1×, respectively. The current share price is $40 at the beginning of year one, there are 100 million shares outstanding, no debt, and the economic asset base is $3.33bn. What is the option-implied trading range expected for year one? The answer will be given by the cost of buying a twelve-month call and put option at the money, i.e. with a strike price of $40. Let us say that the total cost of buying these two options is $6. For an investor, this straddle will be neutral (it won't cost or earn anything) in the coming year for a share price at $34 or $46, and positive for a share price beyond these limits. Therefore, the option market does *not* expect this particular share price to move beyond these borders. It is then easy to express this expected volatility in terms of asset multiple. Assuming that economic assets grow to $3.5bn, the lower option-implied asset multiple will come out at ($34 × 100 m)/3.33, or 1.02×, and the higher boundary will be calculated as ($46 × 100 m)/3.33, or 1.38×. Analysts will then need to pursue a detailed investigation of where they see the level of cash return in year one, and assess whether the implied boundaries of the asset multiple are reasonable or not.

Actual and implied economic profits

The second analysis of market pricing is centred on the generation of economic profits. A series of actual economic profits is easy to generate for any company, since it is calculated simply as the excess return spread (the level of cash return less the cost of capital) times net economic assets. Figure 7.12 shows economic profits for Coca-Cola since 1989.

Using the market value formula based on EP, it is possible to derive an *implicit* level of EP discounted by the market with this simple transformation:

$$E = NCI + \frac{E(EP)}{d}$$

$$E(EP) = (E - NCI) \times d$$

where E(EP) denotes the level of EP *expected* (by the market) going forward, not an explicit forecast. E(EP) is the 'beacon'. To see this, we can now complete the story of Coca-Cola. Figure 7.13 shows again the actual amount of economic profits generated by the firm, complemented this time by a line plotting the *expected* level of EP. Let us stress again that the latter is not an explicit forecast but an implicit amount derived from Coca-Cola's market value, according to the formula above.

The line can be thought of as the 'normalised price of the bars'. By 1998, Coca-Cola was generating an excess return of approximately 7.7 per cent, on about

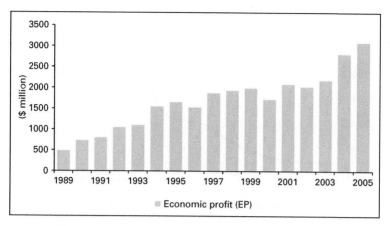

Figure 7.12 Coca-Cola: economic profit, 1989–2005.

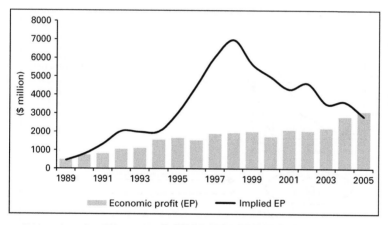

Figure 7.13 Coca-Cola: economic profit and implied economic profit.

$24.5bn of economic assets, resulting in $1.9bn of economic profit. As Figure 7.13 shows, the market was willing to 'pay' (discount to perpetuity) about $7.2bn for it, 3.5 times more! This is what explains the halving of the share price. Intuitively, not many people would be willing to buy an annuity of $100 for $350, and, *circa* 1999, investors in aggregate decided that such a price was wrong. But the laws of compounded interests can be deceiving: 100 compounding interest at 10 per cent per annum will give 350 in slightly more than 13 years, or in 9 years at 15 per cent, or in 18.5 years at 7 per cent . . . How do we know that 'paying' 3.5, or 2 or 1.5 times current EP is too much?

The importance of lamp posts: General Electric

To answer the above question, let us take the example of EP and implicit EP for a random sector shown in Figure 7.14.

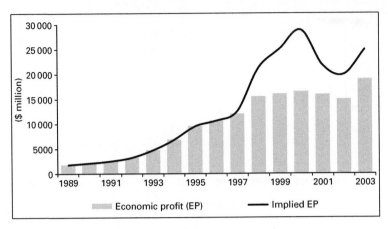

Figure 7.14 EP and implicit EP for a random sector.

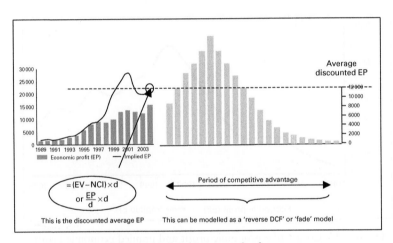

Figure 7.15 Looking into the future.

If investors could look into the next few decades with perfect foresight, Figure 7.15 is the likely profile that they would see.

We have chosen here a sector rather than a firm in order to be able to model a nice, orderly fade towards the cost of capital, at which point economic profits disappear, and the sector has become 'a cost of capital business'. Implied economic profits, as defined above, can be thought of as representing the average of these future economic profits, in theory to infinity, but in practice to as far as it matters – which is a few decades. In other words, because 'fades' are complex to model and extremely subjective (there is an infinity of likely paths from the current level of EP to its eventual extinction), we replace them by an equivalent (by definition) constant stream of EP, as Figure 7.16 shows.

In this simplification, which transforms the future reality into a constant flow, it looks as though investors are losing a lot of information. However, this is putative information that they do not really have: they do not know what is the most likely

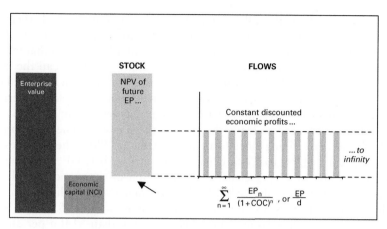

STOCK

FLOWS

Enterprise value

NPV of future EP...

Constant discounted economic profits...

... to infinity

Economic capital (NCI)

$$\sum_{n=1}^{\infty} \frac{EP_n}{(1+COC)^n} \text{ , or } \frac{EP}{d}$$

Figure 7.16 Turning a stock into a flow.

future EP profile, the net present value of which gives the difference between market value and replacement value. On the other hand, they *gain* a lot of information: the knowledge of the *constant flow* (EP) whose net present value gives that same result. Imagine that you have lost your keys in a very dark back street. Your only chance to find them is to look under the lamp posts . . . (a Polish saying). With current EP, investors know their starting point and, somehow, have to travel to the beacon, the (constant) implied EP. For the market value to make sense, the path of that travel *has* to make sense.

In the case of Coca-Cola in 1998, it simply did not. In order to generate an average constant flow at more than 3.5 times the 1998 level, the firm would have needed, for instance, to grow EP by 10 per cent per annum for more than twenty-five years, without fail. With flat returns and a 3 per cent rate of accumulation of assets, it is obvious that the best Coca-Cola could achieve was a 3 per cent growth in EP, unless something dramatic was about to happen to its economic characteristics. Had he had a clear idea of the type of odds he was taking on, perhaps the last investor who bought the last share of Coca-Cola at $90 may have thought twice about it. Before leaving this example to history, it is worth making two further points. Figure 7.13 shows that it took *seven years* to weed out 'the madness' from Coca-Cola's share price. Seven years of pain for those who could not see why the market value was wrong, despite the fact that the company was in superb economic shape, and seven years of outperformance for those who could. Equity investing is not a short-term game. Besides, it is worth pointing out that the market value did not normalise randomly, to any target. It normalised *precisely* to the level of EP that the firm generates today, as if it had learnt a lesson and was coming back onto a path that it should never have left. Charts like this go a long way towards proving that economic data *are* relevant to market values. Finally, let us make a point of *not* trying to explain why these shares got so highly valued in the first place. This belongs to a popular hobby in financial markets: *ex post* rationalising. With hindsight, there are *always* causes to events – but they are irrelevant, especially to those who lost half of their investment in the process.

Readers unfamiliar with the EP framework may be tempted to ask themselves whether this does not represent an extreme, therefore unrepresentative, example. In a sense, it is true; the valuation was certainly extreme, and it is not often that investors have the chance to spot such a situation. On the other hand, how can the market value of Coca-Cola, one of the best-known firms in the world, publicly quoted in the largest equity market in the world, ever represent 'an extreme example'? Experienced investors know that such 'extreme valuations' are in fact extremely common in the market. We don't even need to leave the club of the bluest of blue chips on Wall Street to find another striking one: General Electric. In 2000, these shares were priced in a copycat fashion to Coca-Cola's two years earlier. GE was generating an excess return close to 12 per cent on about $30bn of economic capital, or an economic profit in the region of $3.5bn. With an average market value of more than $350bn that year, there was $320bn worth of EP expectations ($350bn–$30bn) to explain. In 'constant flow equivalent', this was more than $14bn per annum – exactly four times the 2000 EP. We know from the Coca-Cola example that this is an absurd multiple. However, it was also possible to use fundamental analysis to achieve the same conclusion. Suppose that market expectations were right, and that GE was going to reach, from $3.5bn – that's 'A' – a level of economic profit of $14bn – that's 'B'. How do we get there? If the excess return stays constant at 12 per cent, it will need $116bn of economic capital to produce the expected level of EP. Over ten years, that's a rate of accumulation of assets of almost 15 per cent per annum. If, on the other hand, it is assumed that most of the increase in EP is to come from margin expansion, then the excess return will have to reach somewhere in the vicinity of 35 per cent, assuming that net assets grow gently to $40bn. In reality, the market was pricing a bit of both; combining the two would have given the picture of expected EP illustrated in Figure 7.17.

Such investment analysis does not always lead to a definite conclusion; but it more often than not gives a very vivid picture of what is expected (or discounted) by the market, which can be compared to the fundamental analysis. Combined, these two analyses give a risk/reward profile. In the case of GE in 2000, the risk/reward was not attractive unless you were willing to expect extraordinary things, which is

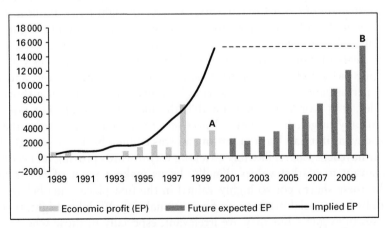

Figure 7.17 A potential path of EP from current to expected.

not usually a good idea for an investment. In fact, this risk/reward analysis would easily have turned any investor away from the GE at $60 a share – which, as it turned out, would not have been such a bad thing, since the shares bottomed out only slightly above $20 a few years later.

Man, the eternal optimist . . .

When implied EP overshoots widely, as in the examples above, it is almost always certain that investors are too optimistic. Strangely, the reverse demands a more cautious assessment, and the relationship between actual and implied EP may not be exactly symmetrical. Witness the following example. Electronic Data Systems (EDS) is a global provider of IT services, business process services and technology solutions. Around the end of 2002, the share price of this company was slightly lower than $40, and its economic profit chart was looking like Figure 7.18 on the CROCI model.

From 1989 to 2001, EDS' profile of economic profits had been generally trending upwards. The firm was obviously benefiting from the general IT boom of the second half of the 1990s, and had apparently not been affected by the slowdown in the technology sector following the explosion of the 2000 bubble. Nevertheless, the market had been putting the value of this EP at a slight discount since 1997 – that year the line, which represents the implied level of EP, fell below the bar, which represents the actual level of EP. By 2000 the discount was more noticeable and, at the time the picture below was taken, the market was not willing to pay for more than 50 per cent of what the 2002 EP was expected to be (2002 EP was still a forecast, but usually forecasts for the current year are relatively accurate by the fourth quarter). This could plausibly have been explained by an understandable caution to invest in an IT-related company. Potential investors could easily have further reasoned that the market was already pricing a halving of economic profits, something that never happened in the thirteen years of history available for analysis.

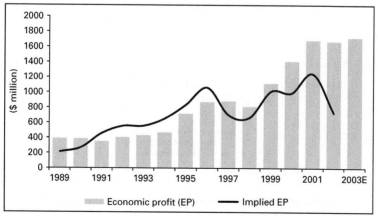

Figure 7.18 Electronic Data Systems: EP and implied EP.

And, if it did happen, this would have taken the company back to its 1998 level of EP generation (roughly), safely before the frenzy of the technology bubble. In short, for a rational investor, albeit one with a slight taste for contrarian investment, this could easily have appeared to be a bargain.

However, this rationale was wrong. The level of EP did far worse than halve; it fell by 100 per cent and hit zero – EDS' share price fell to below $10, a fourth of what it was worth during that last quarter of 2002. This sharp fall in the level of CROCI was the result of the cyclical downturn, which eventually took its toll on EDS' business and caused the loss of a few very large contracts, notably with General Motors (its original parent) but also with companies such as WorldCom and US Airways, which both filed for bankruptcy. Furthermore, legal difficulties with respect to the firm's accounting policy, notably with respect to revenue recognition, and a subsequent SEC investigation, probably limited the ability of the firm to capture any new business for a while.

Did the market 'know'? Yes and no. The market obviously did not know three years in advance of the precise level of profits in 2005. Neither did the market know in advance that the company was going to be investigated by the SEC; between 2000 and 2003, many technology companies were. Yet it is very clear in Figure 7.19 that, between 2001 and 2002, the low boundary of the asset multiple range was in free fall, well below the relative return. This is in contravention of both the history of the company and the principle of the Equivalence. Observe further how the market had, by the end of 2002, put the asset multiple at $1.1\times$, implying almost no value creation – a 'prediction' that turned out to be remarkably accurate in the end.

Everything else being equal, the market had no reason to put the shares of this company under such pressure, and to break the Equivalence principle in such a way. Although the market 'did not know' as such, the collective knowledge of investors about the company and its general business context prompted them to break the Equivalence principle *well before* the new pricing level was justified by the facts. In this respect, the market 'knew'. . .

This apparent prescience can be reformulated with the help of some DIY behavioural psychology. Naturally, investors will, for a going concern, be inclined to

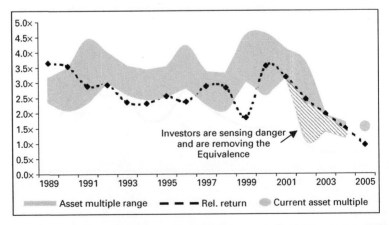

Figure 7.19 Electronic Data Systems: asset multiple range and relative return, 1989–2005.

assume 'business as usual', or the continuation of historical trends. In other words, the natural proclivity of man is to be optimistic. If this appears not to be the case any more, questions have to be asked. Note that we are not arguing here that all companies trading at a discount to their fair value are suspect. Investors anticipate the fluctuations of the business cycle in this way, and it is to be expected that cyclical shares are priced at a discount to their current EP regularly, as it is thought that they are reaching the peak of their profitability. What *is* suspect is an abrupt change of mind (by the market) on companies that have not obviously changed, are not cyclical, or have a steady historical profile of cash return and capital invested.

This chapter ends the third part of this book, the description of both the fundamental and economic analyses of economic data. We now have all the tools ready for the fourth and final part, the real implementation of an EP model in the market.

Notes

1. This expression comes from the title of a classic book written by Charles MacKay, *Extraordinary Popular Delusions and The Madness of Crowds*, first published in 1841. A behaviourist ahead of his time, Charles MacKay tells the stories of various schemes and scams, the bankruptcy of John Law and the South-Sea Bubble of the early eighteenth century, the 'Tulipomania' of the sixteenth century in Holland, etc . . . A great read!
2. Based on the performance of the US CROCI index, a defensive index made of the forty cheapest stocks selected monthly by their trailing economic PE.

References

French, K. R. and Fama, E. F. (1992). The cross-section of expected stock return. *Journal of Finance*, 47(2).

Lo, A. W. and MacKinlay, A. C. (1999). *A Non-Random Walk Down Wall Street*. Princeton University Press.

MacKay, C. (1980, first published 1841). *Extraordinary Popular Delusions and The Madness of Crowds*. Three Rivers Press.

Mandelbrot, B. B. and Hudson, R. L. (2004). *The (Mis)behaviour of Markets: A Fractal View of Risk, Ruin and Reward*. Basic Books.

Building the House: Implementation of an Economic Profit Model

8 Stock-picking with an economic model

The inescapable question – investing and stock-picking

Two hundred and twenty days of research and development for the CROCI model; two thousand two hundred days of parent-like nurturing of the economic data; one thousand lines of model per year per company; gigabytes and gigabytes of testing, processing, analysing – all to answer, finally, the dreaded but inescapable question: 'does this thing work?' The 'thing', or indeed any economic profit model, can 'work' in two ways. It can first provide the scaffolding for portfolio construction; this is what we refer to as 'investing', which is the subject of the ninth and final chapter of this book. But it can also support stock-picking, the present topic. If investing is only an art, then stock-picking is even less formalised than that – maybe more than Sunday DIY, but perhaps not quite handicraft, which implies too much application and not enough inspiration. Money managers are often referred to as good stock-pickers, more rarely as good investors. Being 'a good stock-picker' is closer to having a good nose for wine, which suggests an innate ability, than to having an immaculate backhand at tennis, which suggests hours of practice against the wall. How then can CROCI, which we have painstakingly described as providing an unemotional picture of the economic reality, support what seems to be more instinct than labour? By steering the stock-picker towards what really matters for the share price; real cash return, real growth rate of economic assets, expected level of economic profits, etc. However, the end result, the success or failure of the investment, is still largely in the hands of the stock-picker himself.

This preamble is important, because to claim that an EP model 'works' for stock selection can only be done on the basis of a *systematic* investment strategy, where human judgement is totally excluded. What we show here is more ambiguous. Although the decision (to buy or sell) is based almost exclusively on economic information, it is the *interpretation* of the charts by an investor, together with an assessment of the risks involved, which triggers the investment decision. Here, the economic information is no more than a crutch. There is only one way to illustrate how CROCI information can be used to take investment decisions, and this is to select previously published research reports. This is necessarily a subjective exercise. First, we had to select our examples from among reams of published material,[1] and such a selection is unavoidably arbitrary. Other issues needed to be tackled as well. For instance, should we present successful examples only? Or a mixture of good stock-picks, slightly less good ones, and perhaps a disastrous recommendation? Yet the purpose of presenting unsuccessful calls is far from clear, false humility apart. If this simply reflects the inability of one of us to analyse our own data correctly, it does not do much more than reinforce an earlier point – namely that the human brain is ill-suited to make investment decisions. Incidentally, what was going to be the definition of a successful stock-pick? Evidently, the stock performance, but over what period?

In the end, we settled on the following. We would present ten published successful recommendations, because we wanted to illustrate primarily how the CROCI charts (figures) discussed in Chapters 6 and 7 can be used, not how they can be misinterpreted. However, everybody knows that investors sometimes simply get it wrong, with or without CROCI charts. For this reason we added an eleventh one which did not 'work' to make the point that using economic data unfortunately does not always ensure success. We took most examples from the recent past, mainly from the period 2001–2004. Thus, we would still be relevant to current investors, who may not care about what happened fifteen years ago, but would not run the risk of interfering with our current business and recommendations. Since stock-picking is predominantly concerned with absolute returns, success would be measured by the absolute performance over the three, six, nine and twelve months following the recommendation, with a focus on the nine-month result. We would occasionally keep an eye on the relative performance as well, so as to avoid gloating too much over a recommendation which simply followed the market. We would present the relevant charts as published at the time, with a faithful reproduction of the comments made then, as well as current charts and comments where necessary.

The growth/return interplay: Takeda at ¥6080, 9 February 2001

This first recommendation on Takeda Chemical, as it was then called, illustrates how to analyse the growth/return interplay discussed in Chapter 5. As a quick reminder, we saw then that (1) growth in assets is the only relevant economic measure of growth to take into consideration when assessing the fair level of the asset multiple, and (2) growth in assets only really matters for high CROCI businesses. Recall that growth matters fifteen times more for the asset multiple of a 20 per cent return business than for the asset multiple of a 6 per cent return business. Takeda is a Japanese pharmaceutical business (which, incidentally, explains its change of name to the more appropriate Takeda *Pharmaceutical*). Historically, the company had a very low level of CROCI for the health-care sector, only slightly above the cost of capital in the mid-1990s. In 1999, the cash return was starting to move towards a level more appropriate to this kind of business, eventually reaching about 22 per cent by 2003–2004 – an acceptable, if slightly low, level for a health-care business, but a very honourable level for any business in Japan. In early 2001, we published a lukewarm comment on the shares of this company with the following opening remark: 'Takeda Chemical has a solid management plan which it hopes will turn it into a world-class pharmaceutical company. The share price seems to have anticipated this already.'

With hindsight, that management plan was indeed so solid that the level of CROCI more than quadrupled. Commenting on the rise in CROCI, we wrote: 'Return improvement in 99/00 credited (in part) to the strong US market', but could not help adding 'how long can that last?' – a touch of scepticism that turned out to be inappropriate, since it *did* last. Far longer, in fact, than probably anybody had anticipated. However, our case was not based on the inability of Takeda to raise and sustain its level of cash return; scepticism is simply standard form for us. Rather, what was bothersome was the chart shown in Figure 8.1, plotting the level of invested capital in the business.

We annotated this chart with the following remark: 'but the organic growth of the business is very low'. Indeed it was – three per cent on average! At best a third of what similar businesses elsewhere could achieve. We further pointed out that Takeda invested, according to us, about 8 per cent of sales in R&D, 'a low investment rate', we remarked, 'compared to J&J [Johnson & Johnson]'. A low real growth rate in economic capital was not just an attribute of Takeda; all Japanese pharmaceutical companies grow, in real terms, substantially less fast than, say, their US competitors. The trouble was that Takeda shares were priced, then, as if this growth rate was far higher. The market was swept along by the fact that the company was morphing into a world-class pharmaceutical business, with a level of cash return to match its new status, and investors were putting the shares on the same premium as a company with a comparable level of CROCI, but with a much higher growth rate. There were therefore two problems with the valuation. One, investors were pricing this company's shares with a far higher growth rate than was actually being delivered, and two, even if it *did* deliver a superior growth rate in assets, the level of CROCI was not yet high enough for a higher growth rate to impact the asset multiple materially. As so often, the chart of economic profit (Figure 8.2) was telling the story more eloquently than words could.

Whilst this chart did not look as 'crazy' as some others that we have seen, notably in the previous chapter, the market was nevertheless willing to pay about one dollar for fifty cents of economic profits. Our conclusion was a laconic 'an economic PE of 36.3× looks rich'. At such a low growth rate, the market should have applied the Equivalence principle in its strictest form, only possibly slightly relaxed by the expectation of some further cash margin expansion. Incidentally, we also commented on the cost of capital in this report. 'Arguments in favour of a lower cost of capital should not apply to a company in this global sector, we think.'

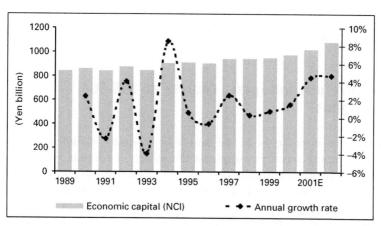

Figure 8.1 Takeda: economic capital and annual growth rate, 1989–2001.

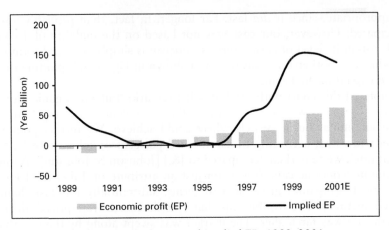

Figure 8.2 Takeda: EP and implied EP, 1989–2001.

This is echoing the point that we made in Chapter 4 on the use of a global cost of capital.

In the nine months following these comments, the shares of Takeda fell by almost 10 per cent, and a further 4 per cent in the following quarter, to make it a 14.5 per cent drop at the twelve-month mark. Although the premium paid in February 2001 was totally unwarranted given the growth rate of the company, this was not, in truth, a great recommendation. The market was shaken by the implosion of the technology bubble at the time, and these shares, simply by being outside of the suspicious sectors, were seen as safer than many other options. They did in fact outperform the market for a while, but the economic analysis was right. Without a superior growth rate, a firm, whatever its level of cash return, should not command a premium, and its asset multiple should trade in line with its relative return. This is so true that the shares of Takeda did in fact linger for years after that, despite an objectively outstanding achievement with their cash return. Investors went from paying one dollar for fifty cents of economic profits in 2001 to exactly the reverse in 2003. Only then was it a truly great buying opportunity, and the value was eventually unlocked, as we could have guessed, as soon as its growth rate in economic capital increased (albeit temporarily) to 10 per cent, in 2003/2004.

The growth/return interplay: Colgate at $58.50, 24 October 2001

The growth/return interplay is at the source of so many misjudgements that we cannot resist including another example on the subject. To repeat our mantra, what matters in the study of the Equivalence is not growth in earnings, not even growth in economic profits. Rather, what allows a premium to be paid over the relative return, in other words to depart from the strict application of the Equivalence principle, is growth in *assets*. If assets do not grow and are not expected to grow, then the asset multiple of any company, however outstanding it is, should be in line with its relative return. Recall that this, in turn, implies that the level of cash return is constant over time. Depending on how believable this assumption is (not very, in the case of a cyclical company, for instance), the asset multiple may depart from strict equivalence to the relative return.

The chart of economic profits and implied economic profits (IEP) offers a very quick visual check on how much growth in assets is discounted in the valuation. If IEP equals EP, then the shares are priced with the assumption of constant CROCI and no real growth in assets. Let us say that a company has an excess return of 15 per cent over the cost of capital of 5 per cent (its CROCI is therefore 20 per cent). Its relative return is 4× (20 divided by 5) and, in application of the Equivalence, its asset multiple should also be 4×. If Net Capital Invested (NCI) is 1000, then the Enterprise Value is 4000. EP is 150 (1000 times 15 per cent) *and so is implied EP*, calculated as the price paid above the value of the assets, or 3000 (4000 − 1000) times the cost of capital. In other words, 3000 represents a constant flow of EP (150) discounted to infinity. The calculation above is simply the reverse of the standard discounting formula, *assuming no growth*.

We have already met with Colgate in Chapters 4 and 5, as a business with the rare ability to increase its competitive advantage over time, another way to describe an increase in its level of cash return. In Figure 8.3 we show what Colgate's CROCI profile looked like in 2001.

'Doubling in a decade!', we annotated. An impressive achievement, deserving this opening remark: 'we would love to buy this stock, but just can't bring ourselves to pay up for this valuation'. As with Takeda, the trouble was the EP/IEP chart, shown in Figure 8.4.

Was the premium of implied EP over EP justified? Not in the slightest. In order for such a premium to occur, assets need to grow and, at this level, grow fast. Admittedly, one could have tolerated a small premium over EP, representing the expectation of a further rise in cash returns (Colgate's historical CROCI profile had better to offer than *constant* returns, the assumption behind the Equivalence principle). But the stumbling block was that Colgate was able to produce such an expansion of cash margin at more or less *constant net economic capital*, which had

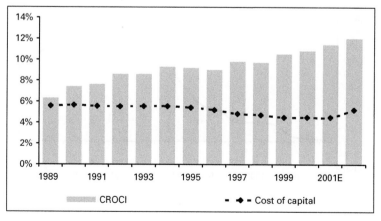

Figure 8.3 Colgate-Palmolive: CROCI and cost of capital, 1989–2001.

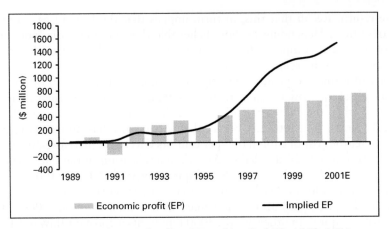

Figure 8.4 Colgate-Palmolive: EP and implied EP, 1989–2001.

stood at about $10bn since the mid-1990s. A low consumption of capital is nothing but a virtuous achievement for a firm. It could be that management is achieving high productivity on existing capital. It could also be that the company is particularly astute in its financial management (for instance, by securitising some receivables), or that the replacement cost of assets is falling fast (such that expansion is consuming less and less capital). However, whatever the reason for not consuming capital, if NCI does not grow then the asset multiple cannot be more than the relative return, and that meant that the shares of Colgate were expensive at the time.

The shares fell by about 14.5 per cent in the nine months following this recommendation. What is perhaps more interesting is to see what the chart of EP and IEP looks like four years later (Figure 8.5). The premium over EP has now been substantially reduced, such that Colgate's asset multiple is, as it should be in the absence of real growth in economic capital, better in line with its relative return,

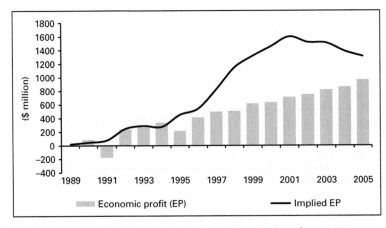

Figure 8.5 Colgate-Palmolive: change in EP and implied EP from 2001 onwards.

which has carried on expanding. Importantly, the share price is still about $6, or 10 per cent *below* that of October 2001 (adjusted for splits).

Unemotional investing: Carnival Corporation at $20.80, 24 October 2001

In the aftermath of the terrorist attacks in the US on 11 September 2001, equity markets became extremely volatile, with many emotions interfering with the valuation of equity assets – and understandably so. The share prices of businesses linked to travel and tourism were hit hard. Carnival Corporation is such a business, operating cruise ships in the Caribbean. The share price had already plummeted in 2000 following some concerns over additional capacity in the sector, and was taking another beating. In this instance, the help provided by the CROCI charts had very little to do with the maths of the Equivalence or the correct anticipation of the growth rate in economic capital. This investment was more a matter of common sense applied to the right data. The key question was to figure out whether 11 September had changed this business for ever, or just prompted a temporary downturn. The first clue could be gathered by the analysis of the historical series of cash returns, which had been remarkably stable between 1989 and 2001. We observed that 'the big difference between [the cruise operators] and hotels or airlines is that they do not appear to have a cyclical profile in returns, at least historically'. In fact, it even seemed that they might be countercyclical, as the returns of 1991 and 1992 (two recession years in the Anglo-Saxon world) were, at 13 per cent, higher than the very stable 10–11 per cent produced otherwise. We calculated that the average historical relative return came out at 2.15×, against an asset multiple that day of 1.8×. In other words, the market had already removed the assumption of constant return from the Equivalence, and was expecting the future return on assets to depart materially from its long-term average. But there was more. Unlike Takeda or Colgate, Carnival does grow its economic assets, at an average rate of 10 per cent per annum. Consequently, the market was anticipating both a structural fall in returns *and* a collapse in the growth rate of economic assets. Following the attack, the situation was bad, scary even; the future looked uncertain and forever changed ... and everybody knew it.

We produced the EP and IEP chart shown in Figure 8.6, incorporating the 2002 level of economic profits based on the consensus forecasts of earnings per share at the time. Unsurprisingly, analysts' expectations translated into a collapse in EP. If the magnitude was exaggerated, the direction was right; economic profits did fall, for two years in a row. But, as we mentioned above, it seemed as though everything was already in the price.

This turned out to be a particularly successful pick. The shares rebounded by almost 60 per cent in the following six months. Even those who did not sell after that short period did well, with a gain of 23 per cent at the nine-month stage, or 24 per cent at the twelve-month stage. A share price of $21 or so also proved to be a very good entry price for long-term asset holders; it was possible to double the original investment and sell the shares at above $45 a few years later. Fear, like greed, is usually a great ally of equity investors.

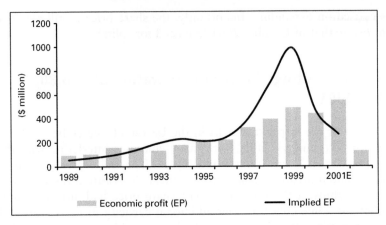

Figure 8.6 Carnival Corporation: EP and implied EP, 1989–2001.

How to assess growth: eBay and Wal-Mart, 9 February 2001

The idea of comparing the relative merits of eBay and Wal-Mart (for investment purposes, that is) came from a comment made by eBay in 2001 about the largest retailer in the world. 'eBay describes Wal-Mart as one of its biggest competitors', we recalled; 'that's a good reason to look at this pair'. Pair trades can be implemented in different ways, depending on the type of funds concerned; long and short positions for hedge funds, underweight and overweight positions for funds following a benchmark, or simply a position in one but not in the other for stock-pickers. However it is implemented, though, the trade carries the same message: for similar economic characteristics, one stock is more attractive than the other.

In this case, the economic characteristic standing out for both companies was growth. Wal-Mart had approximately 1500 stores in 1989 and 4000 in 2001, or an average growth in economic capital invested of almost 20 per cent per annum in twelve years. As for eBay, which had been on the market for only a few years, there was no history, but it was already clear in 2001 that this company's business model was very successful, and that growth would not be a rare commodity in the promising Internet sphere. We warned our readers right away: 'the result [of the pair analysis] is maybe not what you would expect. In short, we find eBay cheaper than its bigger "competitor"'. How could that be, with Wal-Mart on an economic PE ratio of 34×, against an apparently extravagant 84.6× for the Internet company?

The first point to note was that there was not much to expect from the cash return of either company; we remarked that both had 'a similar fade rate', or the rate of decline of the marginal return on capital invested. What was going to make a big difference was the rate of growth of economic capital, because in both cases the companies were high CROCI businesses; 13–15 per cent for Wal-Mart, and 35–40 per cent for eBay. At these levels, growth (in assets) *does* matter, and so do growth expectations. In the Wal-Mart case, we calculated that 'with stable returns, [the company] must double its asset base to justify this valuation. This looks too optimistic,' we added, 'when 60 to 70 per cent of the next five years' growth is expected to come from the US stores.' (This last piece of information was not an explicit assumption, but an expectation coming from either the company itself or the consensus of analysts.) The capital base of eBay presented more of a challenge. As we wrote, 'most of the capital base is invisible. The company spent $45m on advertising and $24m on development of the site in 1999 alone'. Small change for Wal-Mart, but enormous sums for eBay, which we capitalised to make them 'visible' using the principles explained in Chapter 3, over four years on average. This enabled us to calculate a growth rate in invested capital of about three times that of Wal-Mart, logically commensurate with eBay's CROCI, also three times higher. As it turned out, this estimate was too conservative. Between 2000 and 2005, net economic capital increased by 50 per cent per annum at eBay, against slightly more than 10 per cent for Wal-Mart. But even without the benefit of foresight, this comparative analysis allowed us to conclude that shares in eBay were probably a more attractive investment, with 'a valuation less than 2.5× that of Wal-Mart, despite returns and a growth rate being three times higher'.

In the short term, this turned out to be a lucrative call. After nine months, shares in eBay were up almost 28 per cent whilst shares in Wal-Mart were up only slightly more than 9 per cent. But long-term asset holders, once again, benefited the most; in four years, from October 2001 to October 2005, shares in eBay went up an astonishing 250 per cent, whilst shares in Wal-Mart went *down* 10 per cent.

Looking at the EP and IEP charts for both companies four years after this recommendation tells us a bit more about how the market takes growth into consideration. For Wal-Mart (Figure 8.7), the familiar shape of 'the line meeting the bar' emerges once again.

Note that in this case the market has not cancelled an undue historical premium, as for Coca-Cola in 1998; Wal-Mart has been and is still growing its capital invested. Rather, investors are unwilling to pay any growth premium anymore, following a slowdown in the rate of accumulation of assets, as well as, perhaps, a cyclical concern about the sustainability of cash returns (remember the all-important assumption of *constant* cash return in the Equivalence). It is clear from Figure 8.7 that this is not the first time that this has happened; a similar pattern occurred in 1997/1998. eBay, on the other hand, has kept a sizeable growth premium throughout its short

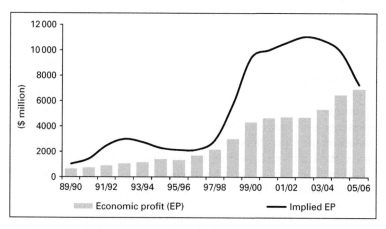

Figure 8.7 Wal-Mart: EP and implied EP, 1989/1990–2005/2006.

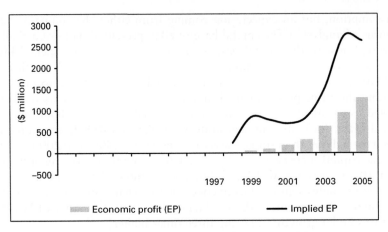

Figure 8.8 eBay: EP and implied IP, 1997–2005.

history, having produced a rate of growth in assets in line with (in fact *better* than) investors' expectations (Figure 8.8).

The madness of crowds: Colt Telecom at £21.30, 7 November 2000

It would have been easy to pick out many illustrations of a successful implementation of CROCI following the explosion of the technology bubble. CROCI, or indeed any model based on the careful analysis of economic value added, has a value slant, and therefore avoids shares valued with assumptions that simply do not make any economic sense. Easy, but unnecessary; common sense achieves the same result, and many investors managed to avoid these shares during the heyday of the bull market. However, this example is special on two counts. First, it is one of the rare examples where a market value was given in the absence of any return number, as we will see shortly. It is bad enough to give an inflated valuation to any economic number, but to no number at all ...! This alone deserved a mention, we thought. Second, my comments on the valuation of these shares (and *not* on the business itself) were judged so offensive that my boss at the time got various phone calls of complaint. I was never told of the precise content of these conversations, and still don't know whether these complaints came from the company's management or some institutional shareholders. Had this occurred in the early 1990s, perhaps I would have lost my job – like Terry Smith, then an analyst at UBS, when he exposed some dubious accounting practices in *Accounting for Growth* (Smith, 1992). For all these reasons, the Colt Telecom story is very close to my heart.

There was nothing contentious about the company itself, which was just a product of its time, an 'alternative carrier' ('altnet' in the jargon) specialising in corporate networks and Internet solutions. The very fact that it survived proves that its business model was valid. What *was* contentious, though, was the valuation that investors were willing to put on these freshly issued shares. And shares there were aplenty!

Due to its relentless growth rate, the company was a hungry beast to feed; it raised £204m of new capital in 1997, £626m in 1998, £1.3bn in 1999, £724m in 2000, £494m in 2001. However, what was extraordinary about the whole situation was the lack of any *gross* cash flow. It was not until the third quarter of 1999 that EBITDA became slightly positive. Nobody expects a company so early in its life-cycle to produce profits, or free cash flow. But *gross* cash flow! In the 'boring' world of capital intensive industries, such as steel, chemicals or cement, this is called 'running the business for cash'. At the trough of the economic cycle, when business is very, very bad, production is kept alive and sold unprofitably simply to cover the cash operating costs; automatically, EBITDA goes to zero. However, this is very different from the situation of Colt in 2000. To start with, no industrial stock in this situation would have the audacity even to try to raise close to £3.5bn – not to mention the fact that investors had no idea how soon this company would be able to produce some gross cash flow, or indeed how much, although it was certain that it would, some time in the future.

So, thinking nothing of it, we published an empty CROCI chart with the following comment: 'Hello? Anybody there? We can't calculate a return, despite the fact that CROCI is based on gross (pre-depreciation) cash flow'. It was presumably this mischievous (?) comment that annoyed some readers. The asset multiple at the time was almost 17×. We commented: '17 times price to book value is consistent with a growth rate of 30 per cent per annum and a return of 20 per cent for ten years. Colt has the growth rate, but no return to support this.' And, in order to make the point in another way, we concluded, using the 'beacon in the dark' technique: 'Starting from a base of zero, Colt must generate £750m of EP per annum indefinitely in order to justify the current share price'.

It is worth remembering that, at £21 or so, the share price had already halved in the space of six months. Alas, this was just the beginning. It halved again, and again, and again, all the way down to about 60 *pence*, where it eventually stabilised. The lesson to learn from this episode is not so much that an EP model is good at spotting overvalued stocks, although this *is* always true. What is worth remembering is that investors were quite willing to pay a market value of some £17bn (or £34bn at the peak) for a company with no gross cash flow. All that the behaviourists have written about the shortcomings of our human brain as far as investment is concerned is encapsulated in these figures.

How to spot a takeover target: AT&T at $15, 8 September 2004

Let us defuse this explosive statement right away: CROCI *cannot* spot takeover targets. What it *can* do is spot undervalued assets, which may or may not become takeover targets. In Chapter 6, we briefly mentioned that investors rarely put a market value on a company of less than half the replacement cost, regardless of the level of cash return. There is no particular theoretical reason for this; rather, investors assume that returns of half the cost of capital (the hidden assumption behind a 50 per cent asset multiple) are not sustainable, and that the company will be restructured, either by the existing management team or by a new one, after a takeover.

To be sure, things were not looking great at AT&T, the long-distance telecom business in the US. Between 2001 and 2004, cash returns had more than halved, going from 9.4 per cent to 4.5 per cent. The market was anticipating a level of cash return of about 2.2 per cent one year out, i.e. for 2005. However, management was taking some steps towards cost containment, which, for telecom businesses, mainly means controlling capital spending. We pointed out that 'the long-distance business is as tough as it has ever been, but capex has been cut to half the level of depreciation, putting AT&T on an EV/FCF ratio of 4.5×'. We have already seen why the ratio of capex to depreciation is a useful one to analyse – for instance, to assess whether assets are ageing or getting younger. This ratio is also very important to watch in the case of an atypical capital spending cycle. If a company has spent a large amount of capital on a project, its depreciation charge will be correspondingly large, and its EBIT (operating profit) to interest charge ratio (the classic 'interest cover' ratio) may be dangerously close to one. In reality, the firm will stop spending for a few years after its big lumpy investment, such that its capex will be below depreciation. Correspondingly, its FCF to interest charge ratio will be a more relevant ratio to consider, and will be higher than the EBIT version.

Debt was not an insignificant issue for AT&T; in 2004 the market capitalisation was a short $14bn, but the economic enterprise value was $10bn larger. Although this is a comfortable gearing ratio for a stable cash flow earner, the steep fade in cash returns might have suggested to investors that the stability of cash generation in this case was not something which they could count on with that much confidence. In any case, the very low FCF multiple, usually between 25× and 35× in the US, showed that the market was not at all taking into account the company's flexibility on capital spending. Nor did it consider, apparently, the value of some of AT&T's peripheral businesses, despite a good historical track record in spin-offs: Lucent in October 1996, and NCR in December 1996. We remarked, rather tautologically, that an asset multiple of 0.50× only implied that '50 per cent of the NCI is worthless and the rest a cost of capital business'. Long-distance being, roughly, a cost of capital business (maybe slightly less), sceptical investors were running the risk that AT&T could sell some of its other assets for more than nothing, triggering a re-rating of the stock. We added: 'AT&T's exit from the consumer business (i.e. the decision, taken in July 2004, no longer to compete for traditional residential local and long-distance customers) and its strong position vis-à-vis corporate customers make it an appealing target'. As it turned out, the market was not completely wrong; the firm eventually recognised an asset impairment of some $11.5bn in 2005, representing about one-third of its net economic capital. The difference (between 33 per cent and 50 per cent of assets) was the extent of the undervaluation of the company, or about $6bn in aggregate. At about the same time, SBC offered to take over AT&T for $16bn – $4bn, or 30 per cent, above the market value of September 2004.

This example deserves a small digression, as it takes us into a new field of application for the EP model: corporate finance. The purpose of this book being investment analysis exclusively, there is no room in it to develop this aspect. However, the AT&T case is a good opportunity for this brief acknowledgement. Chief Executive Officers think about their business *economically*; they know the genuine replacement cost of their assets, the true economic value of their competitors, the long-run real return on investment in their industry. How could they not? Because an EP model does the same, it sees what they see, talks their language and, occasionally, reaches the same conclusion on asset valuation.

Beacon in the dark: Forest Laboratories at $36.90, March 2005

The story of Forest Laboratories is probably best started with its Equivalence chart (Figure 8.9).

This chart is similar to those presented throughout the book; the area represents the yearly high and low of the asset multiple, and the dotted line the relative return. As we illustrated in Chapter 2, it is often the case that, each year, the lowest point of a company's valuation corresponds to an almost perfect equivalence between asset multiple and relative return, which means that the market is assuming constant CROCI and no growth in economic capital. Graphically, this phenomenon creates the pattern shown in Figure 8.9, where the relative return becomes the low bound of the asset multiple range. In this respect, the shares of Forest Laboratories were predictably valued in the past; the company looked like an excellent candidate for an EP stock-picker.

Yet things are never easy for very long in investment analysis. At the time of the report, it was obvious that something very disturbing was going on. The current asset multiple, represented by the dot in Figure 8.9, was clearly way below the relative return – a situation that had never occurred before. Recall that in the last paragraphs of Chapter 7, we pointed out an asymmetry in the interpretation of the Equivalence. Whilst an asset multiple way above the relative return is almost always a sign of irrational exuberance, to quote a famous commentator, the contrary is not necessarily a sign of unmitigated cheapness. Rather, it is often the sign of trouble ahead. For shareholders and potential investors in Forest Laboratories, this situation demanded careful investigation. In fact, the 'trouble ahead' was in all the financial

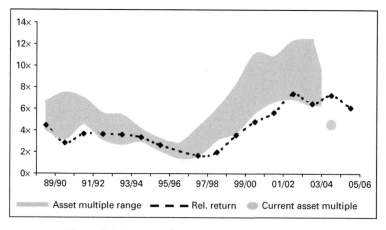

Figure 8.9 Forest Laboratories: Equivalence chart.

newspapers. Forest Laboratories, a pharmaceutical company, was having the patent of one of its drugs challenged in court. 'This puts,' we explained, 'some $1.6bn of sales at risk'.

Although no model can help investors to second-guess the actual outcome of a court case, or similar one-offs, investors don't necessarily need this information, in the same way as they don't need to know the level of the underlying share at the expiry date to assess the price of an option. What they need is the 'beacon in the dark'. We calculated that 'applying the group margin and a tax rate (higher than the group level) of 35 per cent ... some $440 m of cash flow would be lost, if all sales of the drug are lost'. All that was then needed was to use the EP and implied EP chart (Figure 8.10) to light the beacon, and measure how much loss of cash flow the market was already anticipating.

We read straight from the chart that 'the shares are pricing a sustainable EP of $400 m'. This is simply the level of the line, which is the amount of discounted annual value creation, or the difference between the enterprise value and economic capital annualised, i.e. multiplied by the cost of capital. 'This equates to a loss of cash flow from 2005/06 of $450 m,' we continued, 'unsurprisingly close to the loss of cash flow from Lexapro [the drug in question].' Readers unfamiliar with economic valuation models will be forgiven for thinking that the use of the word 'unsurprisingly' is verging on the condescending, and that we have looked long and hard to find such 'a coincidence'. But we have not, and it is not. Time and time again, these charts have given us the proof that the market has an uncanny ability to price, almost to the penny, the most likely scenario. And how could it *not* be the case? There are hundreds of experts in drugs, patents and valuation pricing the shares of Forest Laboratories every day. We were not the only ones who could work out that, should they lose their case, they would lose about $450m of cash flow. Is it *that* surprising that the market ended up pricing exactly this amount? What is *more* difficult is to ignore the daily comments from CNBC's guests or other such media, and to focus on what the market is actually pricing, *economically*.

In this case, it was straightforward to conclude that 'the current valuation is on the conservative side. If no new drugs are found to create growth AND the challenge

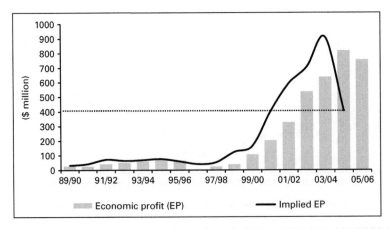

Figure 8.10 Forest Laboratories: EP and implied EP, 1989/1990–2005/2006.

to Lexapro is successful, meaning a loss of all those revenues, the shares are fair value. Any better news than that would have a big impact on the shares.' In other words, if the news was bad the shares would do nothing, and they would go up if the news was good. In the six months following the report, the shares increased by 16 per cent, and were up 6 per cent at the nine-month stage – not so bad in a flat market. Such an unstable environment is bound to produce volatile results anyway, especially since, in this case, the date of the trial had been postponed, casting further confusion on the whole situation. However, even in the absence of much visibility, the economic analysis was able to suggest a precise fair value level – therefore, by implication, a 'cheap value' level – together with an expected behaviour of the shares following the outcome of a binary event. Did investors need much more than this?

Distressed equity: Marks & Spencer at £1.98, 7 November 2000

Retailers spend their lives trying to steal customers away from each other. Those who let their customers go tend to suffer a vicious squeeze in profits, due to paper-thin operating margins which cannot protect the bottom line against operational gearing. In other words, retailers need volume. Those who can get this volume thrive and prosper. The extent to which retailers can suffer in a short period of time is illustrated by the chart of Marks & Spencer's CROCI as it looked in late 2000 (Figure 8.11). In the space of four years, the emblematic UK retailer had seen its cash return on capital go from 16 per cent to less than 5 per cent – only slightly above the cost of capital.

Such a loss of substance is serious for a retailer, not only for the reasons above. Retailers tend to run their business with a geared balance sheet, due to the heavy use of lease financing for their property investments. These financial commitments may well be off-balance sheet, but they still need to be honoured (they are in any case adjusted back into the economic value of the enterprise in an economic profit

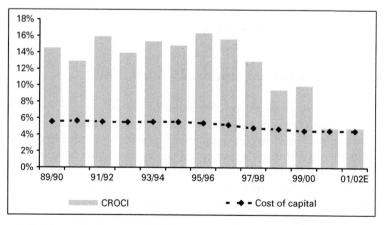

Figure 8.11 Marks & Spencer: CROCI and cost of capital, 1989/1990–2001/2002.

model). If too much turnover is lost, the company will struggle to keep a tolerable financial situation, and could simply end up insolvent – as Kmart did in the US. But there was no such risk for M&S; even at a depressed share price of less than 200 pence, the market capitalisation was a comfortable 70 per cent of the enterprise value. If bankers could still sleep well at night, shareholders were not amused, though. Historically, the Equivalence principle had applied rather tightly to this company. Therefore, since the relative return had been divided by three, so had the asset multiple, which meant that the share price had fallen by a commensurate amount – from roughly £6 to £2, a 77 per cent underperformance against the FT-SE index. We pointed out in the report that M&S was trading at less than one times assets for the first time in recent history.

The key in this situation was to understand that there was no insolvency risk for the company and that, if no improvement was forthcoming, M&S would simply remain at the cost of capital, not creating value for its shareholders any more, but unlikely to get into serious financial trouble. And, priced at less than one times assets, this is precisely what was discounted by the market. We remarked: 'M&S shares look like a possible investment opportunity (even if for the very brave). Broadly, the market believes that M&S' competitive advantage has gone for ever. This is now a "cost of capital" company, whose expected return is exactly in line with the IRR of the market.' Yet retailing is a value-creating business. In aggregate, the world's retailers earn an average economic spread (over the cost of capital) of some 450 basis points, with a low deviation (the worst year was 1996, with only 300 basis points of excess return). Retailing is, effectively, a 10 per cent CROCI business. Given the strength of the brand name, there was a good chance that M&S would be able to mean-revert to the industry average. And, indeed, this is precisely what happened. By the end of 2005, the cash return had crept back to exactly this amount. In the meantime, the share price had jumped back up to above 440 pence, more than twice the late 2000 level, although the bulk of the performance was achieved earlier on; at the nine-month stage, the shares were up 64 per cent.

With hindsight, this recommendation was not, as we had warned, 'for the very brave'. The assumption of mean-reversion was relatively safe for such a strong brand, although the speed at which Marks & Spencer was losing its economic substance in the late 1990s was scary, and could have suggested that something really wrong was going on at the company.

Debt and equity: Ahold at €6.10, 25 April 2005

The economic PE ratio is based on the value of the whole enterprise. Because it is necessary, in an economic framework, to take all associated liabilities into consideration (a subject broached in Chapter 3), the economic value of the enterprise gives an invaluable insight into the pricing of equity and financial debt, on and off balance sheet. This insight can be used profitably with heavily indebted companies, which will tend to look cheap on the basis of their market capitalisation, since most of the enterprise value is made up of financial liabilities.

Here is the case of another retailer, the Dutch company Ahold. In the late 1990s, Ahold pursued a rather aggressive corporate strategy of acquisitions, mainly in the

US. Its net economic capital went from €3.5bn in 1995 to €22.7bn in 2001, at which point the company was forced to pull back, under the weight of its debt. By 2005, economic capital employed was back to a more manageable €13bn, but this retrenchment had created some serious damage. As we pointed out in the previous analysis, retail is a 10 per cent CROCI business globally. Between 1992 and 2002, Ahold's average CROCI was ... 9.97 per cent.[2] However, in 2003 its CROCI level dropped to 6.8 per cent. The share price, close to €30 at the peak, had fallen to less than €5 within two years, as investors started to doubt the financial health of the business. In 2004, the company was still busy cutting back: '2004 net capital invested,' we observed, 'has been reduced beyond our expectations; in particular, lease commitments dropped 35 per cent with disposals. As a consequence, CROCI rebounded to 8.3 per cent from the trough.'

So was the company safe and its valuation attractive, then? This could have been the conclusion based on a superficial analysis of the economic profit chart (Figure 8.12).

Indeed, in 2004 and 2005 the level of implied EP (shown as the line in Figure 8.12) is well below the actual level of EP (shown as the bars). Whenever this configuration has emerged from the various examples that we have shown so far, we have tended to conclude that investors were expecting a fall in the level of CROCI. However, this is only one of three possibilities. Recall that EP is defined as CROCI minus Cost of Capital times Net Capital Invested. Therefore, a fall in EP can also stem from a rise in the cost of capital or a fall in net assets. In most cases, the CROCI explanation will be the most likely (as we saw in Chapter 5, the level of cash return is by far the most important driver of the asset multiple). For indebted companies, however, further scrutiny into the cost of capital is a compulsory investigation.

The Equivalence can obviously be solved for any of its four components, in this case the discount rate, provided that the others are identified. Two were directly observable: enterprise value and net capital invested. For the level of CROCI, investors had to determine which *sustainable* level the market would assume. Faced with turbulence, the market usually does not make many assumptions; what it sees

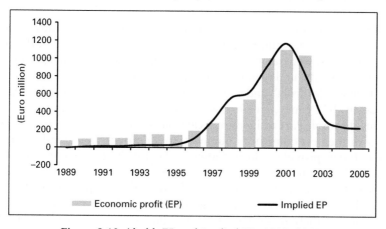

Figure 8.12 Ahold: EP and implied EP, 1989–2005.

is what it believes. In this case, we thought it reasonable to guess that the trend CROCI assumed by the market would probably be very close to the latest observable number, i.e. 8.5 per cent, especially since this number was not that far from the long-term return of the entire sector, 10 per cent. 'Assuming that investors approximate next trend CROCI on the basis of 2004, the implicit cost of capital that they currently apply to Ahold would be 100 basis points higher than the market cost of capital,' we wrote. The simplicity of the calculation must not put off the more sophisticated minded. Even a mere *approximation* of the risk premium that investors apply to an indebted company's equity still represents invaluable information. It can be compared to the CDS (Credit Default Swap) spread or, as we did in this case, to the corporate bond spread. 'This risk premium should be analysed in the light of the €9.4bn total net debt and assimilated financial liabilities that the group still bears, i.e. 100 per cent of the market capitalisation, and an interest cover of only 3.4× in 2004. This risk premium is in fact lower than the one observed for the MSCI Euro Credit Non-Financial Corporate Index BBB spread of 110 basis points (note that Ahold rating is BB), and lower than the one observed for Ahold May 2008 bond which averages 125 basis points'. Our conclusion was that investors interested in an investment in this company were probably better off with the bonds than with the shares.

At the end of 2005, this recommendation was looking spot on. The shares were trading at around €6, fractionally below the price at the time of the analysis. However, the volatility was still very high. The shares performed well initially, (more than 20 per cent after three months), only to collapse by 23 per cent in one month because of another profit warning. The bonds also suffered at the hands of this volatility but, as normal, to a lesser extent. Although space and time considerations have prevented us from including further research on the subject, this example illustrates that an EP model can equally serve equity and credit (corporate bonds) analyses, since its results concern the market value of the whole enterprise, regardless of the source of financing.

New kid on the block: Givaudan at CHF 457, 8 May 2001

We have observed on more than one occasion that the market finds it difficult to value new companies accurately. This may concern initial public offerings, or companies changing their asset mix dramatically. The spin-off of Lanxess from Bayer left 'new Bayer' largely undervalued. The disposal of Motorola's semiconductor business left 'new Motorola' undervalued. As did the sale of Eckerd Drugstores, a pharmacist, by JC Penney, which saw its share price doubling in the two years following this disposal. Part of investors' cautious stance may come from a lack of familiarity with the new company's numbers, trend growth and trend profitability in particular. Index providers do not always classify the new shares in the right sector, either, which blurs the picture some more.

In the case of Givaudan, the relatively small size of the company probably helped in keeping it hidden from too many large investors, who could not buy enough shares (additionally, there might have been a slight issue with its name; it is almost impossible to pronounce correctly for an English speaker!). Yet the company is a world leader in fragrances, which came to the market in 2000 via an initial public offering. It was wrongly classified at the onset as a chemical business, which probably put off some investors, who were unaware of the economic characteristics of the firm, and offered an opportunity to those who were. We wrote: 'Although classified as "chemicals", Givaudan is a defensive company and, what's more interesting, one that appears to offer some value'.

The 'defensive' comment came from the observation that the cash return was extremely stable, at more than 12 per cent. This value-creating level of return is not typical of a chemical company – remember the example in Chapter 6, where the average cash return on both sides of the Atlantic was 4.8 per cent in this business. The risk in this recommendation was that there was no history over a whole business cycle, with no data prior to 1997 – who knows what the cash return of Givaudan was like in 1991–1993? However, this was counterbalanced by the valuation. 'With a CROCI over 12 per cent,' we remarked, 'and valued at 1.8× NCI, a 30 per cent fade in return is expected by the market.' Considering their lack of prior knowledge of the company, investors' pricing was in fact sensible; they simply assumed that Givaudan was a cyclical business, and priced it at some putative mid-cycle (Figure 8.13). An economic profit of CHF 150 m was valued for around CHF 70 m.

This was sensible, but erroneous. The company simply continued to produce a cash return in the region of 12.5 per cent for another five years after its flotation, and the shares re-rated accordingly. Figure 8.14 shows the level of economic profits and implied economic profits between 2000 and 2005. See how the discount of 2000 progressively disappeared, to reach an appropriate level by 2005. Since the company does not grow its assets by much, the Equivalence should apply here, and implied EP should be close to EP, which it is.

This investment turned out to be a staple earner for early investors. The stock was up 9 per cent after 3 months, 10 per cent after six, 21.8 per cent after nine and 33.7 per cent after twelve months. Long-term asset holders doubled their money in four years.

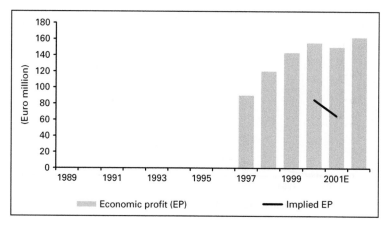

Figure 8.13 Givaudan: EP and implied EP, 1997–2001.

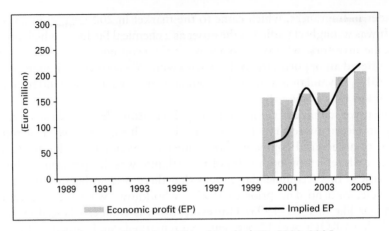

Figure 8.14 Givaudan: EP and implied EP, 2000–2005.

Painful memories: 'We'd rather own the bikes than the shares'

Where did we go wrong? A chart such as that in Figure 8.15 is a red rag to a bull for a CROCI analyst; no matter what, our analysis was going to be negative on these shares, because of this chart.

We even called this premium (of discounted EP over actual EP) 'indecent'. Of course, I was responsible for this particular comment; my colleagues being far too sensible to make such flippant remarks. Having already almost lost my job over Colt Telecom, I should have known better, and realised in any case that an investment analyst should always be humble in the face of the market. What agitated me so much in this case was that this chart belonged to Harley Davidson. Harley Davidson is a superb growth business. Its capital invested has grown at an

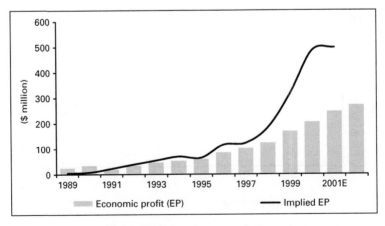

Figure 8.15 A red rag to a bull . . .

average of 10 per cent real per annum since the late 1980s. However, I observed that during the 1991 recession its cash return had gone from more than 16 per cent to 10.6 per cent in one year. Its expected 22 per cent cash return of 2001 (the report was written in February 2001) could have collapsed to anywhere between 14.5 per cent and 16.5 per cent (depending on how you measured the decline – in points or percentage) if the same slowdown were to occur. This would have put the shares on an economic PE ratio of between $51\times$ and $59\times$, since the average asset multiple was about $8.5\times$ at the time.

There was, strictly speaking, nothing wrong with this analysis. Perhaps I read too much into the 1991 drop in cash return. Other setbacks (1994 and 1998) had been much more muted, with cash returns dropping by twenty *basis points* only. On the other hand, none came from a consumer recession, and even the 1991 recession was fairly muted as far as the consumer was concerned – at least compared to the severe consumer recession of 1982–1983. Or perhaps Harley Davidson now sells its bikes, regardless of the economic cycle, to all those baby-boomers and ex-rebels of the 1960s and 1970s who could not afford them then, but are now lawyers, doctors, architects or even fund managers?

Mr Greenspan did not help either. His aggressive monetary policy saved the US consumer from a recession in the aftermath of the technology bubble, but did not save us from an embarrassing recommendation. The shares promptly went up another 10 per cent in the three months after the report, and were up 25 per cent twelve months later. Towards the end of 2005, they were still more than 22 per cent higher than when we wrote the report. The conclusion at the time, 'we'd rather own the bikes than the shares', was off the mark, at least in an investment context. EP models are not a panacea, and erroneous judgements can occur. All they can do is slightly shift the odds from total randomness to a few per cent above a 50 per cent rate of success. Compounded over time, this is enough to produce sizeable and consistent alpha, or outperformance, as the next chapter will reveal.

Notes

1. These documents took various names over time. We published originally under the name of *Apples and Pairs*, where we paired companies with similar economic characteristics but different valuations. *Apples and Pairs* was followed by *Global Eye-Catchers*, where we singled out a company or a pair trade. Other comments were published in our regular strategy documents, such as *Global Sector Strategy* or *CROCI Talk*. All had a similar format, namely a single six-chart page reproducing all CROCI information in a standardised format, and annotated to point out elements of our argument.
2. We will never cease to be amazed at the coherence of the economic picture that these numbers provide, considering how many different company-specific adjustments are made, on as many different accounting standards, to produce them.

Reference

Smith, T. (1992). *Accounting for Growth: Stripping the Camouflage from Company Accounts*. Century Limited.

9 Investing with an economic profit model

Prof. Markowitz's legacy: investing with style

By the end of the 1960s, research in finance had made giant strides following two decades of ebullient production of new theories and models – as Peter Bernstein reported in *Capital Ideas* (Bernstein, 2005). Somewhat fortuitously, the high inflation period of the 1970s forced some practitioners to try out some of these new theories, faced as they were with an unprecedented economic environment (price stability tends to be the norm and inflation the exception in economic history) for which the old recipes in money management did not appear to be suited anymore. As it turned out, these innovations truly revolutionised the way to manage money. Investors, especially institutional investors, became more sophisticated, and stock-picking, whilst still a useful skill, became less and less of an end in itself. Strange as it may sound, institutional investors do not always seek to buy the shares that will go up most (it is not possible to identify them consistently anyway). Long-term asset holders such as pension funds or insurance companies don't just pick stocks; they *invest*. In this context, 'investing' could be defined as stock-picking with a purpose other than exclusively seeking the maximum share price appreciation. The reason is that most of these institutions have to carry, against their assets, liabilities with a life of their own. And these assets and liabilities have to match. As a result, an institution could quite possibly decide to give up some returns in order to lower the volatility of its portfolio, if high volatility were an undesirable feature in the matching of liabilities (it almost always is undesirable for asset holders, but in various degrees). Typically, this would be the case for a mature pension fund, say a pension fund in the steel industry, with a large number of retired members and fewer active – contributing – members. Such an institution would almost certainly be looking for income and predictability in the value of its assets, because it would be faced with constant outlays (to pay for the pensions) and few inflows of new money. These considerations would have consequences on both asset allocation and style decisions. Such a fund is likely to prefer bonds, possibly even real estate (which provides steady income, but at the price of poor liquidity), to equities. If it were invested in equities, the fund would be likely to prefer a defensive strategy, favouring high dividend yield, low beta and low valuation. In this context, the knowledge that Nokia's shares could go up by 15 per cent in the next twelve months would not be terribly relevant.

In 2002, Boots, the UK chemist, shocked the London asset management scene by announcing that, between March 2000 and June 2001, it had switched its entire £2.3bn equity portfolio into bonds. With hindsight, the timing of this move was impressive, as the fund avoided most of the slide in equities which followed the explosion of the technology bubble. However, the decision was never based on a view of the market. The fund was sitting on a healthy surplus in 2000 (assets were covering liabilities by more than 100 per cent), and management decided to lock in this surplus to keep future contributions into the pension fund low.[1] In converse cases, investors could be willing to increase risk in order to increase the expected return. This could be the strategy that an underfunded pension fund might seek to pursue. If its equity strategy is too conservative, and the sponsor is unwilling to increase the contributions, the shortfall will need to be filled by taking additional risks which, in principle, yield additional return. Needless to say, the latter situation is infinitely less comfortable than the previous one; no pension scheme member wants to hear that the managers are taking more risks with their money.

These various examples show that investing institutionally is not necessarily the act of buying the shares that will go up most. Even for those investors who do not have specific liabilities to fund, such as the managers of conventional unit trusts, for instance, or hedge funds, there are many more considerations to contemplate than simply share price appreciation. Volatility is an important one: the net asset value of the fund cannot go up and down like a yoyo at high frequency. Turnover is another: the manager cannot change his mind every day about the stocks that he wants to hold, and turn over his portfolio once or twice a month. Buying and selling shares carries a cost of execution, which includes commission, stamp duty, bid and ask spread, and administrative costs. Too high a turnover is unlikely to generate a lot of alpha, unless it is managed in a very sophisticated way. Liquidity is a third consideration. Depending on the size of the fund, the manager will be able to buy more or less liquid stocks. It is a well-known case that small and mid-sized companies tend to have a higher expected return than blue chips. However, if the fund runs into billions of dollars, and needs to be kept relatively liquid for the benefit of its shareholders, the manager will need to keep an emphasis on large, liquid companies, no matter how much he would prefer to hold fast-moving, small start-ups. And, finally, diversification is a fourth and important consideration. An investor might conclude that pharmaceutical stocks offer good return prospects, with reasonable volatility and liquidity – but it would not occur to anybody, on that basis, to invest exclusively in this sector.

Harry Markowitz was the man who formalised portfolio theory and the mathematics of diversification, for which he won a Nobel Prize. In this context, diversification means that a portfolio made up of assets (shares) whose returns are uncorrelated will have an aggregated return equal to the weighted average return of the individual assets, but will have a lower volatility. In other words, it is not sufficient to assess the risk/reward of individual shares. Although a portfolio is obviously made up of these individual shares, once constituted it becomes alive and acquires characteristics of its own. The genius of Professor Markowitz was to understand this, and his theories spread with lightning speed. It soon became obvious to all that it was as important to get the right *combination* of shares into a portfolio as it was to pick the shares that would go up most. This theoretical breakthrough had deep organisational consequences. Asset management firms started to offer *style investment*, or portfolios each following a certain type of risk/return profile. Today, among the bigger firms, it is not uncommon to find a 'value', a 'growth' and a 'core' team within the same organisation. Each will have different universes, and their return profile should, in theory, be different and reasonably uncorrelated. Index providers have also jumped on the bandwagon, and now provide numerous benchmarks for various styles.

An alternative (and maybe more modern) approach to style management is to construct a portfolio following a clearly identifiable *investment process*, ideally following an equally well identifiable investment philosophy. 'Process' is an oft-heard buzzword in today's asset management circles, deriving from the belief that randomly picking shares which are expected to go up is not enough to control the risks of what can be extremely large pools of assets, covering correspondingly large liabilities. Hidden correlations with a market event, in particular, are an asset holder's worse nightmare. This point can be illustrated with two imaginary portfolio constructors, one particularly skilled at bottom-fishing cheap stocks at the trough of the business cycle, and the other at buying stocks with strong earnings growth. They will, on paper, buy very different portfolios. The value manager will have a portfolio full of airlines, chemical stocks, retailers, car companies, banks, etc. His growth counterpart will accumulate fast growers largely unaffected by the business cycle, which might include mobile telephone networks, pharmaceuticals and biotechnology companies, some software and fast-growing technology hardware manufacturers etc. A long-term asset holder might decide that it is a good idea to invest in both portfolios, as the two managers have such an obviously different style that the two portfolios are largely uncorrelated, and thus overall risk is lower (as per the Markowitz principle that uncorrelated assets held together keep their expected return with lower volatility). However, there may be a spanner in the works. Both portfolios will, in all probability, be more correlated to one another than assumed at first sight. The growth manager will naturally be exposed to strong 'year-two' (two years out) earnings growth expectations, because such is the nature of his stock selection: he is looking for fast earnings growers. The value manager has selected recovery candidates at the bottom of the business cycle. Although his selection process will be radically different from his growth colleague, and will almost certainly include such typical value criteria as a low asset multiple, he too (we assume he is skilful at his trade) will be largely exposed to strong year-two earnings growth at this stage of the cycle; in two years time, his recovery candidates will be in full swing and will have the same economic characteristics as the fast growers, as far as earnings growth is concerned. If an exogenous (to the business cycle) event affects the factor 'strong year-two earnings growth' in one way or another, both portfolios will be affected by their exposure to this particular factor. These assets will turn out to be more correlated than one would have expected, due to their fortuitous exposure to the same factor.

This is not just a hypothetical example. The debacle of Long-Term Capital Management, the hedge-fund which created 'a trillion-dollar hole' is a potent reminder of what damage hidden or unexpected correlation to a market event can create. Although the fund was involved in the entire spectrum of financial instruments and spread strategies, from credit spreads to risk arbitrage, and therefore appeared well diversified, most of these trades were a bet on the mean-reversion of spreads between safe and slightly more risky assets. Explains Roger Lowenstein:

> Long-Term had bet on risk all over the world [in the same way].
> In every arbitrage, it owned the riskier asset; in every country,

the least safe bond. It had made that one same bet hundreds of times, and now that bet was losing ... The correlations [among the trades] had gone to one. Every bet was losing simultaneously. The dice were not being thrown at random, or at least they seemed as if tossed by the same malevolent hand.

(Lowenstein, 2002)

Well before deciding on which stocks to select, investors are therefore faced with two decisions. Like the Boots pension fund, they need to come to a decision over whether the equity market is the appropriate asset class. Once this decision is made, they need to decide on the performance characteristics of their equity portfolios. This includes style choice, as well as more sophisticated decisions on factor exposure. In all these instances, the discipline of an economic profit model allows the creation of extremely powerful tools to support decision-making.

The price of risk: the equity risk premium

The equity risk premium is a crucial variable for anybody who needs to work on the basis of actuarial assumptions, and therefore with an expected return. This is especially the case for those who have to match assets with liabilities – for instance, pension fund managers – and also for those involved in planning, capital spending and acquisitions. Yet this is a surprisingly vague research area, with no apparent attention to the fundamental distinction between *realised excess return* (of equities over bonds) and risk premium. As we pointed out in Chapter 4, the realised performance of equities is just that, and includes all sorts of biases, ranging from the survival bias of equity indices (which is very substantial) to the actual deviation of outcome from expectations. Realised performance simply cannot be a good measure of *ex ante* expectations, in the same way as actual reported profits are not a good measure of earnings estimates. By definition, only the expected return of equities, which we define as the IRR of the market, contains the *ex ante* risk premium that investors are demanding from their investment at the time of measuring. We have already described the technique for extracting the risk premium from the overall expected return. The focus here is on the application of this measure to an investment process.

Figure 9.1 shows our measure of the risk premium for a global universe of the largest market capitalisations (approximately 700 stocks).

This risk premium will probably appear strikingly low, especially to those who have the Ibbotson Associates data in mind, which show that equities have outpaced bonds by about 5 per cent per annum over the past eighty years. In reality, both sets of data are correct, but don't relate to the same thing; one measures an *ex post* achievement, the other one an *ex ante* expectation. They are not interchangeable, as a very simple test can demonstrate. We have seen in Chapter 2 that the inverse of the PE ratio represents an approximation of the *real* expected return, at zero growth. Let us assume that the market is pricing a 5 per cent risk premium, in line with the historical observation of excess return of equities over bonds. We also know that the real risk-free rate is between 2.5 and 3 per cent, thus putting the expected

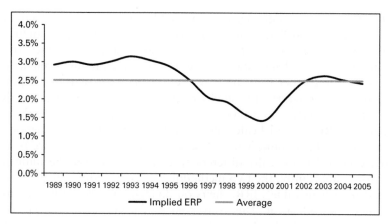

Figure 9.1 Global equity risk premium.

real return on equity investment in a range of 7.5 to 8 per cent, or an economic PE ratio range of 12× to 13.5× (the inverse of the previous numbers). This does not stack up with actual observations. Based on the *lowest* market value for each year, the average economic PE ratio comes out at more than 23× for the world, with the lowest historical reading being 18.5×, in 1995. True, the two measures are not exactly comparable, because it can be assumed that the market rating does include growth expectations, whereas our synthetic PE ratio of 12× to 13.5× does not. However, the difference is so large that it simply cannot be accounted for by growth expectations alone. This is especially so because the lowest asset multiple, which we have used to calculate the lowest PE for the year, will tend to be very close to the relative return, as we have seen in the study of the Equivalence. When that is the case, there is no growth assumption priced into the market.

The way to reconcile the two PEs is to assume that the forward-looking, *ex ante* equity premium observed in the market is significantly lower than the realised, historical excess return of equities over bonds. Arnott and Bernstein, whom we have already met in Chapter 4, say no different:

> ... a 5 per cent excess return on stocks over bonds compounds so mightily over long spans that most serious fiduciaries, if they believed stocks were going to earn a 5 per cent risk premium, would not ever consider including bonds in a portfolio with a horizon of more than a few years. The probabilities of stocks outperforming bonds would be too high to resist.
>
> (Arnott and Bernstein, 2002)

This subtle, but nevertheless fairly obvious, distinction between realised and expected risk premium is clearly under-researched, and many investors, companies and strategists are still persuaded that a 5 per cent risk premium is about the right number. For companies in particular, this must have serious consequences for their measure of value creation, which needs a cost of capital and therefore an assumption of risk premium. Equally, most acquisitions must appear very expensive to their

Finance Directors. So few studies have actually addressed this issue in detail that we have to quote Arnott and Bernstein again. These authors, through a sophisticated process of reconstruction of expectations, find a historical figure of ERP 'of about 2.4 per cent' for the US. They add that the 'normal risk premium might well be a notch lower than 2.4 per cent, because the 2.4 per cent objective expectation preceded actual excess returns for stocks relative to bonds that were nearly 100 bps higher, at 3.3 per cent'. So maybe 2.2 per cent? This happens to be the precise number that the CROCI model calculates as well for the 1989–2005 period in the US. This could well be a coincidence. However, some coincidences are troubling. Our reference period is radically different from theirs, and yet the numbers are identical. More importantly, the two methodologies could not be more different – ours is based on a firm value's IRR, theirs on dividend and real dividend growth. Yet the numbers are identical. This convergence of results may well be confirming a methodological and a fundamental point. As Chapters 1 and 2 painstakingly demonstrated, there is only one answer to the question of the value of an asset: the 'Net Present Value of . . . etc'. Whether calculated with dividend or cash flow, through an IRR or a perpetual constant annuity, the expected return cannot be different, and the answer *should* be the same. In the case of Arnott and Bernstein's work, and ours, it is. Fundamentally, this exercise also confirms that investors are not, apparently, using the realised excess return of equities over bonds as a proxy for their forward-looking risk premium. Rather, they are using a figure in the 2–3 per cent range.

The figures make sense for a global universe of stocks as well. If the average US equity risk premium is 2.2 per cent, what could a global one be, once other markets are added? Intuitively, the answer should be: 'higher'. The US market is the most liquid, the most advanced, the most regulated equity market in the world, although this did not prevent an unfortunate string of scandals in the early 2000s. In general, the level of disclosure is excellent, and the Security and Exchange Commission a vigilant watchdog. US companies are followed all over the world by battalions of analysts. Moving away from this environment to Europe, Japan and then emerging markets offers less disclosure, less English language, less liquidity, less frequent reporting and so on. It would make sense if investors, as a result, demanded a higher remuneration for their capital. They do. The same methodology as the one applied to a US universe gives an average *ex ante* risk premium of 2.5 per cent, 30 basis points higher than in the US case. The historical results are displayed in Figure 9.1. Of note is the fact that, pre-1995, the average comes out at 3 per cent exactly.[2] With these results, this empirical picture is now complete, and the 2–3 per cent range looks quite defensible. Markets with good liquidity and good disclosure would mean-revert towards the lower end of this range, whilst more illiquid and opaque markets would be priced with a risk premium towards the upper end.

Another way to test the 2–3 per cent risk premium hypothesis is to relate it to the overall expected return numbers. The real return of equities averages around 5.5 per cent, according to most sources (see, for instance, Dimson *et al.*, 2002), including our own research. Equally, the real government bond yield tends to oscillate around a mean of 2.5–3 per cent. Simply deducting the real risk-free yield from the real return on equity would suggest an equity excess return of between 2.5 and 3 per cent. It is difficult to be much more rigorous about these numbers, because global data can evidently only be expressed in a single currency, usually the dollar. The rise and fall of other currencies against it will create noise. However, the data are sufficiently clear to conclude that *there is no evidence of the risk premium being higher than 3 per cent*, and that the average number coming out of various, unrelated research efforts (using different methodologies) converges towards 2.5 per cent.

The risk premium is not a variable that changes very often, and it is certainly not a trading tool. Over the long run, however, its level still varies greatly with a seemingly strong mean-reversion characteristic, which is what makes it an interesting variable to watch. As a rule of thumb, a 10 per cent change in the value of equity triggers a 10 basis points change in the risk premium, although this relationship can vary a lot, depending on the level of valuation. As a result, the *ex ante* risk premium can be a tool for asset allocation, to support such macro-decisions as the view that the Boots pension fund management took on equities in 2000. Between 1989 and 1996 the global equity risk premium was above its long-term average (2.5 per cent) by about 40 basis points, indicating that equities were priced cheaply. In 1997 it dropped to a *discount* of about 40 basis points, which became 60 basis points in 1998 and 90 basis points in 1999, to culminate at more than 110 basis points in 2000. Decisions are easy with hindsight, but there can be no doubt that an asset allocator watching this indicator would have become increasingly wary of equities. The model clearly indicated that value was being lost fast in this asset class, if anything perhaps flagging it a little too early. Equally interesting is the fact that the implied risk premium again crossed its long-term average between 2002 and 2003. On average, the 2002 risk premium was two basis points below the long-term measure, and fourteen basis points above in 2003. Equity markets bottomed in the fourth quarter of 2002, and again in March 2003.

It is far too easy to conclude that the model gave a 'buy signal' on equities at the trough. I know full well the difficulties of correctly interpreting the signals of quantitative models. Based largely on the analysis of the risk premium, I wrote a strategy review in September 2002 entitled 'It is so bad, it could be the bottom'. Little did I know that, indeed, it was! I remarked: 'Structurally, we contend that an ERP [Equity Risk Premium] of 2.4 per cent is appropriate in a low inflation environment. [...] So the market might not fall much more, and indeed, Q4 could see the bottom'. However, after three years of bear market I did not *really* believe it, and promptly added: 'But it [the market] can't go up either. Discounting mid-cycle is not good enough for multiple expansion, and earnings expectations are too high' (Costantini, 2002). However, this example says more about my own inadequacies than about the model. Undeniably, an unemotional follower of this indicator would have concluded, as I did, that the risks (of an equity investment) were now even, as opposed to firmly tilted to the downside – and would have proceeded, as I did *not*, to increase its weighting towards this asset class.

The pricing of the norm: this time, it's different

'This time, it's different'; this motto is a staple among analysts, strategists and fund managers, and it is easy to see why, if related to a small amount of market psychology. We have seen at various points in the previous chapters how it can safely be assumed that a high percentage of the price of an asset is efficient – i.e. reflects all known information, especially past and present information. Therefore, in the absence of a change in the economic characteristics of the firm, its assets should be fairly priced, which means that the expected return ought to be close to the expected return of the entire market. In order to argue a case outside of this expected return, an investor willing to buy or to sell the shares has to be convinced that past and current information is no longer relevant to the pricing of the asset in question, and that indeed this time it will be different.

Of course, it rarely *is* different. Companies do have ups and downs, but a radical change in their economic characteristics is the exception rather than the rule. A cyclical firm remains a cyclical firm, and its cash-flow cycle can be predicted. A young company enjoys a higher cash margin than average, and competitive forces drag it down in a fairly predictable pattern, again, on average. Stable companies are just that. As for regulated businesses, they are given a return to earn on their investment, which by and large determines their growth rate.

Of course, if fundamental analysis was that easy, financial analysts would not exist. But these patterns are nevertheless recognisable, especially at an aggregated, sub-sector, economic sector or market sector. As a result, there is a clear benefit in assuming that the trend, or average cash return and asset growth – two key drivers of economic profits – are representative of the future. The more the valuation deviates from this trend, the more suspicious or interested investors ought to become, depending on the direction of the variation. Applied to individual companies, this model will have to cope with stock-specific situations, and a more careful analysis of the recent deviations from the norm, or trend, is necessary. Imagine, for instance, how expensive the Reckitt-Benckiser of Chapter 6 would look if an investor were to apply the old Reckitt trend to the new Reckitt-Benckiser valuation. However, such a framework becomes quite reliable at the aggregated level, as an indication of the level of attractiveness of the equity asset class. It is worth pointing out that *trend* and *perpetual* rates (growth or return) are two different concepts. By application of Michael Porter's theories, the perpetual cash return can only be the cost of capital, except perhaps in rare cases of monopolies, although even such special situations end up being dismantled or regulated. As for the perpetual growth rate, this can only be GDP or less, and, in any case, strictly smaller than the cost of capital. Conversely, trend growth and CROCI could be defined as the mid-cycle level likely to be observable in the past and coming few business cycles. Perpetual rates are there to make the maths work, but trend rates are what the market is *really* pricing, because they are what it sees and expects.

The following example is an illustration of how to work with trend values. There are many ways in which trends can be assessed and applied. The advantage of the following methodology is its simplicity. Say that a stock has an average CROCI of 12.5 per cent between 1989 and 2005, and 13.7 per cent between 2000 and 2005. The historical high is 15.1 per cent and the historical low is 9.5 per cent. It is very hard not to conclude that its trend CROCI is around 13 per cent. Let us say that a similar reasoning leads us to conclude that trend growth in net capital invested is 7 per cent. The firm has NCI of $55bn, and an economic market value of $155bn. The difference between the two numbers, or $100bn, is the net present value of all expected future economic profits, or the sum of all future value creation, in application of this by now well-known identity:

$$E = NA + \frac{EP}{d}.$$

It is immediately apparent that it is not possible to use 13 and 7 per cent to calculate a *perpetual* value, because such a high real growth rate in assets is likely to outstrip the real discount rate, which is in most cases between 5 and 6 per cent (as discussed in Chapter 4 and the previous section on the risk premium). Therefore, the growth-adjusted discount rate, or $d - g$, would be negative. The model has to be modified such that trend growth is applied for a limited period only. We usually use five years, as it is impossible to forecast beyond this horizon anyway. It will be necessary to do the same for the cash return, especially if the trend is significantly above the cost of capital. Thirteen per cent represents a limit case. However, if we chose in this case to assume a perpetual CROCI of 13 per cent and a growth rate of 7 per cent for five years, trend value would break down as \$88bn for trend CROCI to perpetuity, and \$32bn for five years of trend growth.

Value from trend CROCI is calculated as 8 per cent excess return – (13% CROCI – 5% cost of capital) × NCI (\$55bn), or \$4.4bn – discounted at 5 per cent to perpetuity. Value from five years of trend growth is slightly different. It is made of the excess return on additional capital, or 8% × NCI per year for five years, plus the constant contribution of the total additional capital (after five years) to perpetuity. In practice, where R is CROCI, g is growth and d is the discount rate, value from growth is:

$$(R - d) \times NCI_0 \times \left(\sum_{t=1}^{5} \frac{(1+g)^t - 1}{(1+d)^t} + \frac{(1+g)^5 - 1}{d \times (1+d)^5} \right).$$

In this example, the total value 'at trend' is \$120bn, 20 per cent higher than the expected value of \$100bn. This would be equivalent to saying that the shares discount a lower level of future trend than the observed 13 and 7 per cent for CROCI and growth, respectively. The more investors are ready to believe that the trend numbers are accurate, the more they will believe that these shares are cheap.

This model is necessarily simplistic. Five years of growth is an arbitrary number – it could equally be four, six or ten. Discounting a level of trend CROCI to perpetuity is equally amendable, and a shorter period could be chosen instead, after which the cash return could be deemed to revert to the cost of capital. Investors can choose these parameters as they see fit. As we have seen earlier, the benefits of this normalised value analysis are not necessarily found in stock selection. Rather, based on the ratio of 'value to trend' (how much five years of trend is worth) to expected (i.e. market) value, it is possible to ascribe a score of between one and five to each company, from deep value (value to trend is significantly above market value, most likely meaning that trend is expected to deteriorate significantly) to expensive (the reverse), and to aggregate them into sectors and regions.

Perhaps unsurprisingly, global equities strongly mean-revert around the mean category (aggregated score of 3), where market value and value to trend are not significantly different. And the monitoring of this rating can be used as an investment tool for the equity asset class, on the basis that trend is unlikely to change at the most aggregated level. We have tested this tool in the post-bubble years, i.e. from 2003, and it has proved quite a reliable indicator of relative performance. The US market's score, consistently above 3 during this period, shows that investors are willing to discount a higher than current trend value going forward. This is an optimistic outlook. Unsurprisingly, despite a roaring economy, this already highly valued stock market has not done much in this period. Europe, on the other hand, has shown scores that were significantly below 3 in early 2003 (2.60 in March 2003) and again in early 2004, with a low of 2.74 in January, another low aggregated score on this scale. Despite a poor economic climate in the region, the fact that investors were expecting a deterioration of the trend CROCI and growth going forward ensured that European markets had a strong performance in local currency. The bad news (the poor economic climate) came, but everybody knew about it, and assets were already priced accordingly. Since things could only get better, from March 2003 to August 2005 the EuroSTOXX 50 went up by more than 52 per cent, against 45 per cent for the S&P 500, in local currency. A macroeconomic analysis seeking to avoid the low growth of continental Europe to favour the buoyant US economy would have resulted in the wrong equity selection, which would have become catastrophic with unhedged currencies, given that the dollar fell by almost 15 per cent against the euro over this period. Incidentally, macroeconomic analysis often tends to mislead equity investors, because what *really* drives equity values is the legacy market price of assets and expected cash flows, not GDP growth. And the link between the two is not a straightforward relationship.

Implied risk premium and value to trend are two examples of how an economic profit model can be implemented to provide information on the attractiveness of the equity asset class. Such applications are largely ignored by money managers, who prefer to use top-down, or macroeconomic, analyses to decide on such matters. It is probably to their detriment. EP models are as relevant in this context as they are in the context of stock selection – their more natural habitat.

Do you trust your brain? Paper models

Throughout the previous chapters, the human brain has not been given much credit for any ability in the investment business. Mr Paulos called it 'inadequate'. Mr Gilovich accused it of a tendency of making something out of nothing, inferring too much from too little. And the early behaviourists founded a totally new approach to finance with the simple observation that humans did not know how to respond adequately to simple probabilistic choices. Asking the following question already gives the answer: can we trust the human brain to make stock selection decisions? This does *not* mean that there are no good active equity managers; I know many who are doing a very good job for their clients. However, these successful managers tend to be stock-pickers, as we discussed right at the beginning of this book. They have a very good feeling for which corporate strategies can and cannot work, and tend to be good judges of business models as a result. As such, they think as businessmen rather than as investors. Investing, defined as the optimisation of the risk/return ratio, requires another skill set, and I have only met one professional investor whose brain seems to be able to think consistently in this manner. Although he is a good friend, he is obviously a mutant.

The only way to cut out human emotion from investment decisions is to apply a systematic process to stock selection. Because of the ease with which an EP model can generically convey the results of complex analysis (economic value added) through the basic tool of the PE ratio, it is particularly suited to such a process. Yet systematic processes are not a panacea. Fund managers can be interviewed, their CVs checked, and it can be assumed that a degree in Industrial Economics will help more than a degree in Religious Studies, although there are exceptions. But what of a model . . .?

Before they are implemented with real money, models are assessed through 'back-testing' – in other words, by running them on paper, historically, without human intervention. Testing the validity of quantitative and systematic investment strategies is essential but controversial. Those responsible for these tests in research departments tend to be incredibly proud of their achievements, which sometimes involve some sophisticated maths, and always an enormous amount of data processing. However, those giving away the money always seem to be incredibly cautious about the results.[3] And yet it is, in principle, easy to back-test a generic investment process, such as the efficiency in the market pricing of value added, i.e. an EP model such as the CROCI model. All that is required is a good database, a stock selection process and a trading frequency.

Nevertheless, even armed with the best faith, it is difficult to avoid survival biases, a temptation for data mining and other subjective treatments of data. It is imperative that the tests are carried out on *actual historical data*, not data reconstructed *ex post*. But even this is not enough. The tests must be done on the numbers that the market knew about at the time, not numbers that eventually came through. This implies that the data with which tests are done be estimates, not finals. Once the quality of the data source is assured, a second difficulty comes in choosing the frequency of changes in the portfolio. Of course it is possible to decide to change the portfolio every day, but daily trading is not without its own issues. Quite apart from the costs associated with daily trading, small changes that are no more than market noise may trigger unnecessary transactions. Conversely, if there is too long a rebalancing period, then too much information will be lost. Trading frequencies have to be seasonally adjusted as well. Other issues add to the care with which these back-tests have to be conducted – such as, for instance, the choice of the selection pool. If the selection pool is not stable, companies will come in and out, creating unnecessary turnover on the tested strategy itself.

Designing a systematic investment strategy

The three systematic CROCI-based investment strategies that we are about to discuss cannot avoid all of the pitfalls mentioned previously, although the biggest pitfall of all, the use of *ex post* data, is almost completely eliminated. We have in our database actual historical CROCI data from the year the model was created, i.e. 1995, and calculate the results from 1996 only. Between 1996 and 2003 the performance of the three investment strategies is reconstructed, and is then run 'live' from January 2004. At about the same period, some structured products, using two of these investment strategies as underlying, were designed and sold to investors, such that the investment results from that date are not 'paper results' only, but 'real' results with real money.

The easiest way to design trading strategies is to build indices made of a constant number of stocks and rebalanced at a certain frequency, like the main market indices. First, this requires an answer to the following four questions:

1. How many stocks?
2. How frequently rebalanced?
3. At what weighting?
4. Out of what selection pool?

The number of stocks in each index is largely a function of the selection pool. In the case of the CROCI model, we cover the largest stocks only. In practice, this means that the selection pool in the US would represent about half of the S&P 500. As a result, our indices will necessarily contain a small number of stocks – typically thirty, occasionally forty. These are aggressive portfolios, where diversification is not the prime objective. The frequency of rebalancing obeys a simple enough rule: the longer the period, the less return available. This can easily be explained by the theory of market efficiency. Each day, some new information is captured in the share price of a stock. The longer investors let this information accumulate without adjusting their positions, the more out of date the portfolio becomes, making good performance less likely. In practice, all the examples given below are based on a monthly rebalancing of the index constituents. Of course, revisiting the index constituents does not mean changing all the stocks every month. On an unchanged selection pool, the average churn rate comes out at 4.8 per cent per month, or 1.44 stocks in a thirty-name portfolio.

It is a badly kept secret that capitalisation-weighting is not the way to optimise performance. Equally-weighted indices regularly beat their capitalisation-weighted brethren. Between 1989 and 2004, the S&P 500 equal-weight index has beaten the regular S&P 500 index by 169 basis points per annum. Comparisons in other markets give similar results, suggesting an uplift in performance of between 150 and 200 basis points. In a comprehensive study on indexation, Robert Arnott (the same from the risk premium paper), Jason Hsu and Philip Moore find that indices constructed with weights based on fundamental factors such as book equity, sales, dividends or earnings outperform capitalisation-weighted indices by an average of 213 basis points over long periods (Arnott et al., 2005). Although Arnott and colleagues do not test equally-weighted portfolios, but rather fundamentally-weighted ones, the magnitude of the improvement is similar. These results are in fact hardly surprising. A capitalisation-weighted portfolio captures, among other things, a size factor; the larger the capitalisation of a company, the more likely it is to be in the portfolio. Since alpha is inversely correlated to market size (small stocks tend to do better than big ones), these results are to be expected. This can be viewed as the price of liquidity, or the flipside of indexation. Index trackers are leaving alpha on the table because their job is to replicate the performance of an index, for which there can only be one criterion, liquidity.

Finally, the selection pool does have an effect on the performance of an investment strategy as well, especially if some parts of the market are systematically excluded. In the CROCI framework, we exclude two types of stocks; financials, for reasons that we have already explained in Chapter 6, and stocks with suspicious accounting practices. Both exclusions enhance the return of our indices. In the case of financials, the performance uplift coming from their exclusion will vary region to region – very large in Japan throughout the 1990s and up to 2003, it is more modest in the US and in Europe. On average, we estimate that the absence of financial stocks in a portfolio, *over an interest rate cycle*, will bring about 50 to 100 basis points of outperformance relative to a fully diversified benchmark.

The case of corporate governance is even more interesting. Systematically avoiding accounts which 'do not make sense' also brings additional excess return, even though this lack of understanding could, *a priori*, equally come from the murkiness of the accounts or of the CROCI analyst's mind. In this respect, the example of Asia-Pacific is striking. Although they are on the mend, reporting standards in this region are not among the highest. There are still many companies that neither report consolidated accounts nor accounts without detailed notes or in English. Not to mention certain instances of complex accounting practices – for instance, where a very large percentage of employees' remuneration is paid in shares or options. Systematically avoiding investment in these companies will, in the absence of any other selection criterion, generate substantial alpha, approximately 1000 basis points per annum, as shown in Figure 9.2. Perhaps these companies do have something to hide from investors, or perhaps investors don't like to invest in situations that they cannot fully appreciate and have next to no interest in the shares of these companies, which trade at an increasing discount to the rest of the market as a result. Either way, it pays not to invest in firms with accounting standards that are other than crystal clear.

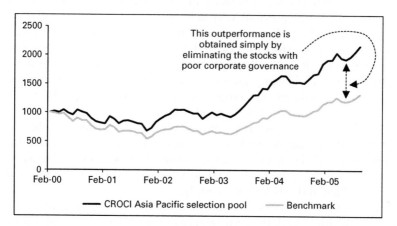

Figure 9.2 CROCI Asia Pacific Index: the filtering process is a major source of alpha in emerging markets.

Three EP strategies on the test bench

The answers to these four initial questions do not really make life easy for the CROCI model. By implementing an investment strategy in the way described, the model must deliver an average excess return of at least 300 basis points over the benchmark, since equal weighting brings about 200 basis points of alpha in itself, and the exclusion of financials and companies with opaque accounting standards at least another 100 basis points. We examine in the following sections the results of a value strategy in the US, a global sector rotation strategy and a thematic strategy in Europe, all based on the outcome of an EP analysis.

Investment strategy one: the value indices

In many respects, a value strategy should feel like home for an economic profit model such as CROCI. These models naturally lean towards the 'Warren Buffet Way' by comparing the market value of an asset to its replacement value, for a given level of return and cost of capital. In practice, this is where the advantage of the economic approach over what we have labelled the actuarial approach (i.e. DCF models) is at its best, because it is possible to use a simple PE ratio (albeit calculated with economic, not accounting data) to select stocks. But even the PE ratio does not solve the problem of forecasting errors. In January of any year, nobody knows what will happen to the market or the economy in the coming twelve months (although plenty of people will have an opinion about it). On this date, it makes sense to attach little importance to the forecasts. In order to dilute the effect of forecasting errors, we recommend using a twelve-month *trailing* economic PE ratio. In this framework, in January of any year, eleven-twelfths of all fundamental data necessary to calculate the economic PE ratio, debt, net assets and cash return will belong to the previous year, and only one-twelfth will be a forecast, i.e. the consensus estimate for the current year. As the year progresses, the weight towards current estimates increases mechanically. At the half-year point it is obviously 50 per cent (six months of estimates, six months of the previous year's result), and towards the end of the year the importance of the previous year fades away to 16.7 per cent, 8.3 per cent and, finally, zero. Trailing PE ratios do not simply limit the impact of forecasting errors; they also allow investors to stick to the change of the economic environment as the year progresses. It is equally important to avoid too much exuberance from the forecasters and to avoid being ignorant of a change in profitability in the current year, which analysts will, by and large, get right at the aggregated level. In this respect, a trailing PE seems to strike a good balance.

Once the selection pool, the frequency of portfolio adjustments, the size and weight of the portfolio and the stock selection tool have all been defined, testing the strategy is a matter of gigabytes and some statistical know-how. In Figure 9.3, we show the result of picking the forty cheapest US stocks based on trailing economic PE, equally-weighted and rebalanced monthly.

We can distinguish four periods over these ten years. The first spans 1996 to mid-1999. During this period, the performance of the CROCI value index is broadly comparable to that of the S&P 500, slightly ahead in 1996 and 1997, slightly behind in 1998. The second period is a brief nine-month span starting in mid-1999, during

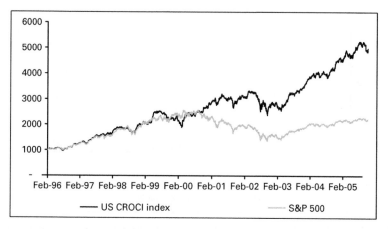

Figure 9.3 US CROCI index and S&P 500 (dividends reinvested).

which CROCI lags the S&P 500 by about 1000 basis points. The years 2000, 2001 and 2002 constitute the third identifiable period, during which the market collapses by nearly 40 per cent, and CROCI not only outperforms but also goes up, in absolute terms, by about 22 per cent. Finally, the fourth stage is the 2003–2005 period, the market recovery. Its pace is significantly slower than during the 1996–1999 bull market, with an average advance of approximately 12 per cent per annum – less than half the annual progression of the previous bull run. In this context, the CROCI index manages to outperform the S&P 500 by about 900 basis points per annum.

Those familiar with style indices will recognise the typical shape of a value index in the 1996–2005 decade, especially during the 2000–2002 bear market, where value outperformed massively, and during the last phase of the bull market (1999 and early 2000), where value underperformed on an equally large scale. Whilst the broad shape is similar, there is one big difference: *the CROCI value index did not lose any meaningful ground during the bull years.* In 1999, for instance, it was not unusual for a value index to be down in absolute terms; by way of example, the S&P/Citigroup Pure Value index (TR) would have been down by about 3 per cent that year (www.standardandpoors.com). The US CROCI value index, on the other hand, went up by more than 11 per cent, thereby losing significantly less performance relative to the main benchmark, itself up 21 per cent. Overall, the performance pattern of CROCI is characteristic of a value index in bear markets and in gently rising markets (e.g. 2003–2005 in the US), but loses this attribute in strongly rising markets, by being able to 'track' the main indices more accurately. In Figure 9.4, we show the performance by region of the CROCI value selection model during any ninety-day period of rising or falling markets between 1996 and 2003. The results are strikingly similar: there is no significant outperformance or underperformance during rising markets.

Finally, Table 9.1 details the average yearly performance and volatility of the CROCI value indices relative to a market benchmark for the decade 1996–2005, together with the 'live' performance of 2004 and 2005. In each of the three regions considered here, the CROCI value methodology easily clears the 3 per cent excess

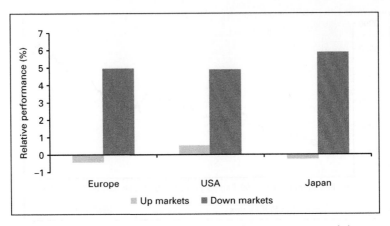

Figure 9.4 Ninety-day rolling relative performance of CROCI in up and down markets.

Table 9.1 Relative performance and volatility: the CROCI indices relative to a market benchmark, 1996–2005

	Annual relative performance and volatility	Euro CROCI relative to Euro STOXX 50 (%)	US CROCI relative to S&P 500 (%)	Japan CROCI relative to TOPIX 100 (%)
1996–2005	Excess return	+8.5	+9.3	+10.9
average	Relative volatility	−4.5	−2.2	−2.8
2004	Excess return	+8.1	+11.3	+1.7
	Relative volatility	+2.2	−0.2	−1.9
2005	Excess return	+0.5	+6.8	−8.1
	Relative volatility	−0.6	+1.3	−0.9

return hurdle which is due to the index structure. The average excess returns for the US and Europe (euro markets only) are very close. Japan is ahead, but in this region the exclusion of financials has had a much bigger positive impact on performance historically. Yet there is no reason to believe that the excess return in Japan should be materially different from the average observed in the US and Europe. As Japanese banks and insurance companies recover from the brink of bankruptcy, their exclusion will probably cease to bring additional excess return in the 2006–2015 decade.

Structuring factors excluded, the systematic use of an economic profit model for a value investment strategy translated into an average 600 basis points annual excess return in the 1996–2005 decade. How, then, can these 600 basis points of alpha be explained? In the first instance, by the fact that the index is built on the sound principle of buying the cheapest stocks. Buying cheap stocks is equivalent to buying assets below their replacement value, adjusted for their current level of return. This is simply sound economic behaviour, which replicates a broader aggregated economic pattern, as the early twentieth century economists have taught us and James, the cheap spectacles manufacturer of Chapter 1, has actually implemented. Leaving this aside, there can be little doubt that the use of economic data is also of paramount importance. Value strategies, for example, are often based on price-to-book, either directly or via the accounting PE ratio. Between 1996 and 2005, Kimberly-Clark, the US consumer goods company, has traded on an average price-to-book ratio of 5.2×. By definition, such a high number rules this stock out of any value universe. Value managers are typically looking for stocks with a price to book either close to one, or at least less than the market average (which was 4.2× over this period). In fact, the correct average *economic* asset multiple of Kimberly-Clark was as low as 2.6× over the period, against 2.4× for the market. These numbers are based on an adjusted asset multiple constructed as explained in Chapter 3, the ratio of the enterprise value to economic capital. The discrepancy between the two sets of ratios comes in the main from the fact that book values ignore capitalised brand values. For a company in the consumer goods industry, it is not unusual to spend up to 15 per cent of sales per year in advertising. Furthermore, strong consumer brands can have an asset life of eight to nine years, which means that this annual cost has to be capitalised for the whole of this period. The replacement value of such investments runs to billions, and actually represents more than the total accounting book value – which explains why, once advertising is capitalised, the asset multiple exactly halves in this particular case, and may consequently allow this high-quality company into a value index. As it turned out, it was a rather good idea to have Kimberly-Clark occasionally showing up in a US portfolio over this period. This company appeared twenty-four times in the CROCI US index, producing an average 4.6 per cent return per monthly appearance. This is far in excess of the 1.4 per cent average monthly return of the index itself.

Quite apart from the fact that an asset multiple calculated in this way simply gives a more accurate economic picture, there is a more subtle tactical aspect explaining the better performance of the CROCI indices over traditional value funds *in a rising market*. In these periods, the market tends to be driven by those companies with the fastest-growing and safest free cash flow. Whilst an accounting-based value strategy may be able to capture the cyclical shares as their cash flow accelerates, it will fail to identify the others. Our own work shows that the level of cash return (CROCI) is best correlated with free cash flow (unsurprisingly) and the percentage of intangible assets in total economic assets (*CROCI Talk*, 20 June 2005, Global Equity Research, Deutsche Bank). In other words, high-CROCI companies will generate the strongest free cash flow, and companies with a high intangible content will tend to be high-CROCI companies. Thus, a stock selection strategy based on accounting data (which ignore any capitalised intangible content) will have no method of selecting the very companies which perform best in a bull run – i.e. the high-return, high intangible-content businesses. Worse still, it will tend positively to *avoid* them, because they will trade on a high book value ratio almost by definition. The denominator of the ratio will systematically be too small, since book value misses out half (or more) of the economic value of a high intangible-content business, as the Kimberly-Clark example illustrates. This is why value strategies based on accounting data fail to follow, let alone beat, strongly rising markets. Any economic model that does capitalise advertising and R&D will avoid this pitfall and perform better. Over the long run, not losing ground in bull markets makes a big difference to the average performance of a value strategy.

Investment strategy two: sector rotation

The second illustration of a systematic investment with an EP model is still based on a value approach, but this time with the objective of capturing sector rotation ahead of individual stock value. The principles of index building are similar to the CROCI value indices: equal weight, a thirty-stocks index rebalanced monthly, and exclusion of financial stocks and stocks with unclear accounting standards. The structural advantage is therefore comparable: a 300 basis points head start against the benchmark. This time, however, the selection pool is global, and the CROCI sector index is measured against MSCI World, in euros. The stock selection is carried out in a two-stage process. The first stage is identification of the three most attractive global sectors (on the basis of a twelve-month trailing economic PE, as before), followed by the selection of ten stocks in each of these three sectors, provided that none is more expensive than the median stock in its sector. The profile of this stock selection is worth detailing. To start with, the index is obviously invested in three sectors only at all times. Furthermore, there is no geographical cap of any sort. If Health Care is one of the three cheapest global sectors and all the cheapest health-care stocks are in Japan, then one-third of the index will be invested in Japan. Finally, there is no currency hedging. The return profile of such a portfolio is shown in Figure 9.5, together with its closest benchmark, the world index provided by MSCI, expressed in Euros.

This translates into an average excess return of close to 15 per cent per annum, a staggering outperformance, with an average volatility approximately 200 basis points under that of the benchmark. Recall that some currency gains will be embedded in this performance. Any rise in the dollar or the yen versus the euro adds basis points of performance. In aggregate, though, these currency gains tend to cancel

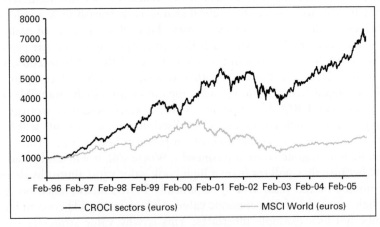

Figure 9.5 CROCI Sectors and MSCI World (euros) (dividends reinvested).

each other out in the long run. Faced with such a result, it could be easy to conclude that an EP model, or perhaps CROCI in particular, is better at picking sectors
than stocks. There is some statistical evidence (which would be too long to deliver
in detail here) that suggests that indeed this might be the case. A cross-sectional
regression analysis shows that 80 per cent of the performance comes from sector
selection, and only 20 per cent from stock selection. But the alpha seems to come,
again, from the ability of an EP model to pick the true economic characteristics
of an industry. It is a noticeable result that *all nine* economic sectors have made
an appearance into the CROCI sector index at some point in the past decade, as
Table 9.2 shows.

What other investment process could have achieved that? 'Growth' would never
have picked Utilities, or Energy. Although these two sectors have appeared only
twice, it was at key strategic moments. Utilities stayed in the index from 2000 for
about eighteen months, during the worst of the technology bubble. Energy entered
the index in early 2004, *prior* to the trebling of the oil price, and the doubling
of oil equities. 'Value' might have done OK with these two sectors, but would
have avoided Health Care, the single most frequent contributor to the index, or
Technology, which appeared five times. Of course, active managers do not need to
follow strict style guidelines. It is possible to imagine that a fund manager might
have been able and willing to pick any three sectors every month, just as the CROCI
sector index does – possible, but unlikely, because the bets involved are probably
too big for a human brain. It must feel *very* lonely to have one-third of a portfolio
in Utilities in February 2000, at the peak of the biggest bubble in market history.
In fact, it feels very lonely to have only three sectors in a portfolio at any time – all
the more so because the sector risks are also replicated at the geographical level. In
the index, Japan went from a zero weighting in 1996 to more than 30 per cent in
2005. This represents extreme deviation from its weight in the benchmark, which
is around 15 per cent on average. The US market, which is around 50 per cent of
the world index, was only at half that weight in early 2003, where more value was
found in Europe and Japan.

Table 9.2 Number of appearances of sectors in the
CROCI sector index

Sector	No. of appearances in the CROCI sectors index
Consumer Discretionary	7
Consumer Staples	9
Health Care	12
Industrials	5
Information Technology	5
Materials	7
Telecommunication Services	6
Utilities	2
Energy	2

Let us finish this review of the CROCI sector index with a puzzle and an open remark. It is clear that the performance of this investment strategy is commensurate with the risks taken. The benefits of diversification are intentionally ignored here, and a strong concentration on sectors and, indirectly, regions, is sought. The puzzle is not that this investment strategy is producing a large excess return; it is the contrary that would be surprising, since risks and rewards are supposed to move in the same direction. Rather, what is puzzling is the relatively low volatility of the index, on average lower than that of the benchmark. How is it that a high-risk strategy produces a low volatility? We are not very far here from the problematic that Professor Fama unearthed in his 1992 paper on the Capital Asset Pricing Model (French and Fama, 1992). Volatility is certainly *a* measure of risk, but it is not *the* measure of risk, as the quotation at the front of this book is here to remind us. The fundamental view that volatility-based models take, essentially via a stance of the dividend, seems far too narrow to embrace more complex risks, such as economic sector exposure. In this example, it is clear that the volatility of the investment strategy does not adequately convey the fundamental risks taken in its process.

Investment strategy three: innovation

We have seen in Chapter 8, notably with the eBay/Wal-Mart pair, that an economic profit model such as CROCI is not confined to selecting 'just' value, taken in the traditional sense of 'boring conglomerates and other low-growth equities with no growth prospects'. As we pointed out right from the start, in Chapter 1, the value/growth divide is an offence to logic; there can be, and indeed there are, good value high-growth stocks, as there are expensive ones. Therefore, CROCI, or any other such model, can also be implemented to select high-flyers. And this third and last example of a systematic stock selection illustrates how.

We arrived in Chapter 5 at this straightforward conclusion: for the valuation of equities, growth only really matters for high-CROCI businesses. Since they produce the cash flow to fund that growth, only high-return businesses can grow without accumulating debt, and therefore without putting the balance sheet structure of the company in danger. Therefore it is likely that, in the fishing pond of growth equities, most targets will enjoy higher than average returns on assets – say at least twice the cost of capital. Only a minority would be accumulating assets fast without generating enough cash to clear the cost-of-capital hurdle, being at the early stage of their economic life. They would be funded by capital providers with a high tolerance for risk, perhaps private equity firms or high-yield bond investors. For the rest of them in the shoal, though, investors must make sure that the high return is sustainable, if they want growth to be as well. It will be easy enough to ignore those companies which appear high CROCI in a single year thanks to the peak of their business cycle; the value-to-trend technique presented earlier in this chapter finds here one of its few applications for single stocks. If value-to-trend is significantly above the market value, this may be the sign that the investment analyst is mistakenly taking a cyclical peak return as representative of trend, or average return.

Once all the obvious traps are identified, it is possible to go further and test statistically what other economic variables than growth are best correlated to high CROCI over time. Some will emerge for obvious technical reasons: nobody should be surprised to learn that high CROCI and free cash flow are very highly correlated. Others, however, will be more interesting – such as, for instance, the correlation between high CROCI and the percentage of intangible assets in economic capital. Although this correlation may not have a high statistical significance, due to the lack of long-term economic data series (we have only tested it for the past seventeen years), it tells a story which makes economic sense. Those companies that invest most in R&D and brands (let's call them the Innovators) have the best chances of sustaining their high CROCI. How can this not be so? By investing in these intangible assets they are protecting their competitive advantage, lowering their fade in returns, if not inversing it. We have seen many examples of such 'relution' of returns throughout this book, Colgate being our favourite and oft-quoted example.

The influence of innovation on returns deserves a small digression, an incursion back to the days of the technology bubble. In November 1999, at a time when the technology craze was raging, we published a report entitled 'Why do investors keep buying techno stocks?' Although our models were saying that the valuation of TMT (Telecom, Media and Technology, as it was then called) was insane, I was intrigued by a special profile of returns, typical of very innovative technology companies, which I promptly dubbed 'the double wedge'. Figure 9.6 shows what a double wedge looked like; the re-birth of a company mid-through its life.

This rejuvenating process, (the 'second wedge') is extremely unusual; once a company starts to accept a fade on its marginal return on investment, there is almost no coming back. However, in this particular case the rate of innovation was so high and the product cycle so short that the stronger, more innovative companies were able to reinvent themselves through their R&D effort. The double wedge has now

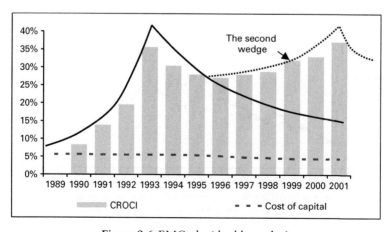

Figure 9.6 EMC: the 'double wedge'.

long gone, but I remain convinced that this once-in-a-century phenomenon started
the inflation of the technology bubble. Relative to a normally fading return profile,
the extra value given by the second wedge is very substantial and might, *rightly*
so, have triggered a multiple expansion. But what should have been limited to the
true innovators of the internet revolution (in other words, Cisco and a handful of
others) spread out of hand, and the rest is history. Yet the legacy of the double
wedge remains applicable to today's growth stocks: innovation in R&D and brands
is a boost, a prop, to returns.

Armed with this knowledge that innovation protects high returns, it is possible to
design a stock selection process that would identify the most innovative companies –
i.e. the ones with the highest percentage of capitalised intangible assets out of
their economic capital. They would be the companies most likely to enjoy a high
cash return going forward, and thus to deliver superior growth (in assets). Unlike
in the previous strategies, the stock selection needs here to be implemented in a
multi-factor framework where innovation is one factor and value (as always, twelve-
month trailing economic PE) another. Failing this, there might be plenty of *expensive*
innovators in this portfolio, which would not help the performance. We show
in Figure 9.7 the example of a thirty-European-names portfolio. Other technical
characteristics are as previously mentioned: equal weight, no financial stocks. Thus,
the 300 basis points head start remains.

It is immediately clear from Figure 9.7 that this investment strategy is able to
capture growth characteristics. See in particular how the index did outperform the
bull market during the period 1996 to 2000. Innovators went up fourfold from
February 1996 to August 2000, against slightly more than a threefold increase for
the DJ STOXX 50. Similarly, the period August 2000 to February 2003 was more
difficult for the Innovators, relative to the Euro value index, although there is no
marked underperformance. This investment strategy is effectively able to recreate a
'growth style' by identifying one of the economic reasons for growth, which is the
ability to innovate.

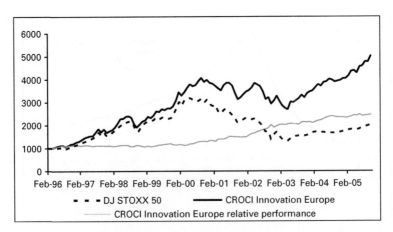

Figure 9.7 CROCI innovation Europe index and benchmark (euros) (dividends reinvested).

The thing 'works'!

We are at the end of our story. If we have been able to convince anybody of anything, we are hoping that it is the following: value creation analysis 'works'. Consultants demonstrated some time ago that the concept of economic value added can be a great management tool to align the interests of operating managers with those of shareholders. Capital is a rare commodity which has a cost and had better not be squandered. Some would say that managements have understood the lesson so well that they are pushing the logic of the system to its limits, thereby sacrificing some of the benefits of long-term planning. We are not insensitive to this argument, but we are not part of this squabble. Our goal was to demonstrate that it is possible to use an analysis of economic value creation and value creation *expectations* to invest more intelligently in equity markets. We hope that we have contributed to this debate, but are far from having exhausted the subject. There are many aspects that deserve further exploration, such as the application of an economic profit model to the credit market, for instance, or the extent to which such a model could provide an alternative fundamental opinion for the pricing of options. Perhaps even an adjusted measure of banks' risk weighted assets could serve as a good proxy for economic capital, post-Basel II, and could give birth to a 'bank CROCI'. Not to mention the very many improvements to the CROCI model itself, by refining further some of the transformations from accounting to economic data, or by applying risk adjustments to the universal cost of capital, or a growth factor to very high CROCI businesses.

Notes

1. There were other reasons as well; the move reduced the annual cost of running the portfolio from about £10 million to £250 000. Management fees, bid and ask spreads, commissions and stamp duties make equities an expensive business for investors!
2. 1995 is the point at which many things changed radically in the market and the global economy. 1995 represents some sort of gateway into the digital age, and it is always useful to measure a market-related variable pre- and post-1995, the former representing 'normal' conditions and the latter the 'super-productivity' period. No one knows yet if we will ever revert back to the pre-1995 conditions, but for the time being it is prudent to assume that we will, at least for investment purposes.
3. Note that we are not talking here about quantitative arbitrages. Although the techniques deployed in these arbitrages are quite advanced and heavily model-based, they do not represent an investment process. Furthermore, there is often limited scope for a comprehensive historical back-testing of the strategy.

References

Arnott, R. and Bernstein, P. (2002). What risk premium is 'normal'? *Financial Analysts Journal*, **March/April**.

Arnott, R. D., Hsu, J. C. and Moore, P. (2005). Fundamental indexation. *Financial Analysts Journal*, **61**(2), 83–99.

Bernstein, P. (2005). *Capital Ideas: The Improbable Origins of Modern Wall Street*. John Wiley & Sons Inc.

Costantini, P. (2002). It is so bad, it could be the bottom. *Sector Strategy*, Fourth Quarter 2002. Deutsche Bank.

Dimson, E., Marsh, P. and Staunton, M. (2002). *Triumph of the Optimists, 101 years of Global Investment Returns*. Princeton University Press.

French, K. R. and Fama, E. F. (1992). The cross section of expected stock return. *Journal of Finance*, 47(2).

Lowenstein, R. (2002). *When Genius Failed*. Fourth Estate.

By way of conclusion ...

The last straw for an old camel

The three-year collapse of equities, between 2000 and 2002, has left indelible marks on the way in which financial analysts perform their job. In a word, storytelling is out. Although markets have subsequently recovered some of the lost ground, the scars still linger. Professional investors are now demanding some guarantee that the analysis performed adheres to a minimum of intellectual standards, if not probity. After the shameful nonsense that we saw during what is likely to remain, for the foreseeable future, the biggest bubble in history, who can blame them? The 'sell-side', or the community of service providers to professional investors, was by no means the only to blame, though. I don't recall that investors were held at gunpoint to buy the latest, hottest, fastest IPO during the bubble. Remember my friend at the beginning who was 80 per cent weighted in TMT in February 2000 ... If sell-side analysis wants to survive, i.e. to receive a remuneration which at least covers the enormous costs of research departments, the least it can do is produce high-quality content and alpha-generating professional investment advice. In some quarters, this will require no less than a cultural revolution. When you have been led to believe that the crossing of some moving average by another *is* financial analysis, or that if a company is producing 20 per cent of earnings growth its share price has to go up by 20 per cent, regardless of valuation, proper financial analysis does not come naturally. Quite possibly, it never will. However, Wall Street and the City are nothing if not fleet-footed; a new generation of analysts is already fast emerging, more fluent in the disciplined valuation techniques such as those that this book advocates.

In many respects, traditional financial analysis was dying its own death anyway; the excess of the 1998–2001 period was merely the straw that broke the camel's back. The poor animal may never recover, but it had become an old and useless beast. Traditional financial analysis is incredibly mono-dimensional, and anybody given the task of building it from scratch would never think about organising it in the way it was set up. Company research is all about knowing everything there is to know about a particular company, from the name of the Chief Executive's PA to next year's earnings estimate. This model did have its *raison d'être* less than a couple of decades ago, when investors were progressively discovering overseas markets. Only ten or fifteen years ago, the Spanish equity market, say, was unknown to all but a few. The job of a financial analyst who specialised in such an 'exotic' market was primarily to educate investors about local companies, including how to spell and pronounce their names. However, faced since the early 1990s with an unprecedented wave of privatisations coming from all markets (except the US), large and sophisticated investors have diversified their holdings into virtually all equity markets on the planet. Japanese, French, German or Polish Chief Executives who did not know then that Fidelity is not just an admirable quality among friends, but also the name of a rather big asset management firm, have now built personal relationships with some of the largest and most influential money managers all over the world. They may well know Boston, the home of the US Mutual Fund industry, better than their own city. And, should they have to fight or defend a takeover bid, seek additional funding, or simply feel that their stock is undervalued, they will not think twice about embarking on a road show to tour the major asset management firms in the main financial centres. This was simply unthinkable only fifteen years ago. Of course, we are only talking about the same 700–800 of the largest firms in the world, which have been the reference universe of this book. However, given that they represent close to 90 per cent of the total market capitalisation of the world, they form the backbone of the global equity market.

Discrete and cluster knowledge: towards a new model of analysis?

So the times of handholding, spellchecking and storytelling are over, and now, even in 'emerging' markets, these skills are not in such demand anymore. It would be misguided, though, to conclude that financial analysis itself has become redundant. It could in fact be exactly the reverse, due to the major innovation of the past decade: the emergence of a radically new offering of financial products. At the forefront of this wave is of course the advent of hedge funds as mainstream asset management vehicles, but in many respects they represent just the tip of the iceberg. At the same time, investment banks have created increasingly sophisticated financial instruments: Collateral Debt Obligations (CDO), Credit Default Swaps (CDS), Exchange Traded Funds (ETF), Certificates, Constant Proportion Portfolio Insurance bonds (CPPI), Target Redemption Notes (TaRN), not to mention an innumerable amount of *ad hoc* derivative structures. These products are not for the sole benefit of high net-worth individuals or institutional managers. Most of them are in fact embedded in fairly ordinary mass-retail products, such as the popular capital guaranteed products, which ensure that capital is never lost, in exchange for a participation rate of less than 100 per cent in the performance of equities. All have fancy acronyms in common, as well as clever maths and reliance on option pricing. In addition, they share two characteristics that are likely to underpin the role of financial analysis as a pre-eminent content provider, and could revolutionise its implementation.

The first common feature in all of these financial instruments is the absence of *stories* about *companies*. Rather, they all require precise analysis and, as far as possible, prediction of the economic characteristics of the underlying *shares* – i.e. the expected return, of course, plus the volatility, the sensitivity to various factors, etc. So if two companies have approximately the same level and profile of cash return, the same level of growth in economic assets and the same financial risk, they are, for the proposal of building these financial products, the same investment. The fact that one might be called IBM and the other one Cadbury becomes less relevant than for traditional analysis. This *is*, in many respects, financial analysis much as we understand it today – more so, in fact, than a post-result note which explains that such and such a quarterly report has beaten expectations by one cent.

The second common denominator is that hardly any of these instruments depend on *a single share investment*. In their simplest form, they may offer some sort of payoff between the performance of one share against another, or perhaps a reward based on the divergence of returns between two sectors. In their most complex format, long and short structures are built around the entire market. Whilst traditional analysis is all about discrete knowledge, 'new' analysis could be said to be all about cluster knowledge. In this context, we define 'discrete' analysis as the knowledge of one company, or maybe one sector – as a financial analyst, you are the Oil and Gas analyst, or the Vodafone analyst. 'Cluster' knowledge is more about the investment characteristics of a group of *shares*. For instance, if the low-CROCI group is negatively correlated to expected earnings growth and the high-CROCI group positively correlated to it, then *any* low-CROCI company might become a 'hedge' for *any* high-CROCI one, everything else being equal.

This 'depersonalisation' of financial analysis (with the label, or name and sector, of the company becoming less relevant) does not, to repeat, sound the death knell for financial analysis – quite the contrary. Right now, 'cluster research' deals mainly with volatility and its associates, skews, correlations, etc. This is, and will remain, an important aspect of quantitative analysis, but it is not the only one. Quite apart from the role of luck pointed out by Nassim Taleb, the work of Professor Fama and his followers, the intuitions of Benoit Mandelbrot and the various findings of behavioural finance all point towards measures of risk beyond just volatility, frameworks other than the traditional Capital Asset Pricing Model. Recall the CROCI sector investment strategy of the previous chapter, able to deliver an average 15 per cent excess return per annum during a decade, with a lower volatility than the world index. This is not an easily explainable behaviour in the classic framework. It is our belief that share price movements can be explained (or at least analysed) by *behavioural* quantitative measures, in which we put volatility studies at large, together with *fundamental* quantitative measures, in which we put the analysis of economic characteristics (such as, for instance, those studied in this book). This in itself still requires resources dedicated to fundamental financial analysis, even though it would imply a number of changes in the organisation of research departments. Quantitative research, which by and large provides the content for systematic research, would become somewhat more prominent, and company-specific research somewhat less so. But the total amount of fundamental research need not shrink by much.

As this quantitative research develops, new products will, in turn, emerge. By way of example, ETFs look like a fertile ground that could continue to be ploughed. These products offer cheap and liquid exposure to various parts of the market by tracking an underlying index, or basket of shares. There are ETFs for the entire market, or for individual sectors. There are also 'style' ETFs, such as 'value' or 'growth'. There are, however, no or very few 'alpha ETFs' yet. These would be ETFs built in the same 'systematic' or passive way as the others, but based on investment strategies designed to *beat* this or that benchmark, not simply *replicate* it. Of course, this outperformance could not be guaranteed as a NASDAQ ETF is guaranteed to replicate the performance of the NASDAQ. Investors in such products would need to be very clear about the meaning of the words *expected return*, and understand that this is a statistical concept based on probabilities and normal distribution – in other words, an estimate only. But this is no different from the situation of any shareholder in a mutual fund today. If such products were to emerge, there can be no doubt that the asset management industry would need to adapt to a radically new situation.

A new asset management industry?

In this framework, the asset management business could be seen as being broken up into three building blocks: content provision, wrapping, and distribution. Content provision would cover the design of investment strategies. This could, as now, be sourced from active fund managers, or be the product of quantitative processes, such as the three that we presented in Chapter 9. Distribution would simply be the retailing of investment products by those who have the network, in an open architecture, i.e. without a systematic alignment between the brand of the network and the brand of the financial product (in an open architecture, bank XYZ distributes the funds of bank ABC). Finally, wrapping would include, as now, the fiduciary duties of those running classic funds, as well as the ability to transform content into an investable financial product such as a Certificate, a capital guaranteed instrument or an ETF.

If this business structure were to end up being widely implemented, a convergence between asset management and certain market activities of investment banking would necessarily occur. Both businesses can, in principle, provide content, but both cannot wrap. In order for some content to be structured into financial products, the wrapping firm needs to be able to hedge the risk efficiently in order to competitively price the option, which is *always* the basis of structured products. Only an investment bank with enough intellectual and financial capital and a sizeable flow can carry out this operation. Pushing the model further, it is possible to imagine that each of the three building blocks could be independent of each other. Perhaps a quantitative content provider could outsource the wrapping of its investment strategy to a bank with superior option know-how, and distribute the resulting product with another one.

This would transfigure the profitability, and thus the structure, of the entire industry. Each building block should of course expect fair remuneration for its contribution. The split between the three, however, is still work in progress. It can be expected that hedge funds would largely be unaffected by these changes. They would continue to appeal to investors who wish to 'speculate', be it high net-worth individuals or institutions. Conversely, traditional institutional asset managers would be put at a structural disadvantage, squeezed between those who can manufacture cheap 'trackers' and the investment banks who can hedge risks efficiently and therefore structure ('wrap') sophisticated financial products at an attractive price. As for those who cater mainly to the retail business, they will in all probability suffer from the competition of ETFs – although nothing prevents them from issuing such products themselves, except that a large part of their staff, analysts and investment managers, might become redundant in the process. This story is beyond the remit of this book, and remains to be written. Quite how the final outcome will look is still very unclear; in many respects, the most exciting period is still to come.

Further reading

Basu, S. (1977). Investment performance of common stocks in relation to their price-earnings ratios: a test of the efficient market hypothesis. *Journal of Finance*, **32**, 663–682.

Bernstein, P. L. (1996). *Against the Gods*. John Wiley & Sons Inc.

Bernstein, P. L. (2005). *Capital Ideas: The Improbable Origins of Modern Wall Street*. John Wiley & Sons Inc.

Carret, P. L. (1930, reprinted 1997). *The Art of Speculation*. John Wiley & Sons Inc.

Cornell, B. (1999). *The Equity Risk Premium: The Long-Run Future of the Stock Market*. John Wiley & Sons Inc.

Gladwell, M. (2000). *The Tipping Point*. BackBay Books.

Homer, S. and Sylla, R. (1996). *A History of Interest Rates*, 3rd edn. Rutgers University Press.

Madden, B. J. (1991). *CFROI Valuation: A Total System Approach to Valuing the Firm*. Butterworth Heinemann.

Malkiel, B. G. (1973). *A Random Walk Down Wall Street*. W.W. Norton & Co.

Thaler, R. H. (ed.) (2005). *Advances in Behavioral Finance*, Vol II. Princeton University Press.

Wilcox, J. W. (2004). The PB/ROE valuation model. *Financial Analysts Journal*, **Jan/Feb**.

Index

Printed and bound by CPI Group (UK) Ltd, Croydon, CR0 4YY

08/05/2025

01864778-0002